State of play

This book is due for return on or before the last date shown below.

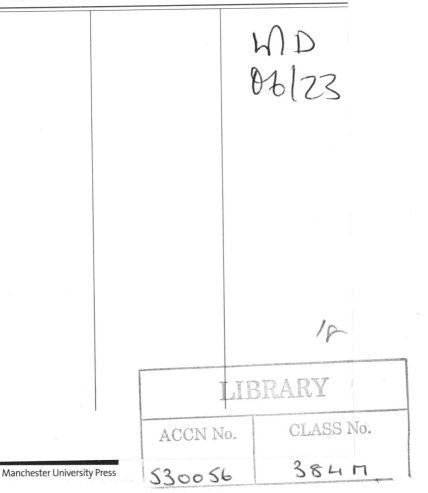

WD
06/23

Manchester University Press

For Avril and in memory of David

State of play
Contemporary "high-end" TV drama

Robin Nelson

Manchester University Press
Manchester and New York
distributed exclusively in the USA by Palgrave

The right of Robin Nelson to be identified as the author of this work has been asserted by him in accordance with the Copyright, Designs and Patents Act 1988.

Published by Manchester University Press
Oxford Road, Manchester M13 9NR, UK
and Room 400, 175 Fifth Avenue, New York, NY 10010, USA
www.manchesteruniversitypress.co.uk

Distributed exclusively in the USA by
Palgrave, 175 Fifth Avenue, New York,
NY 10010, USA

Distributed exclusively in Canada by
UBC Press, University of British Columbia, 2029 West Mall,
Vancouver, BC, Canada V6T 1Z2

British Library Cataloguing-in-Publication Data
A catalogue record for this book is available from the British Library

Library of Congress Cataloging-in-Publication Data applied for

ISBN   978 0 7190 7310 6 *hardback*
ISBN   978 0 7190 7311 3 *paperback*

First published 2007
16 15 14 13 12 11 10 09 08 07   10 9 8 7 6 5 4 3 2 1

Typeset
by Frances Hackeson Freelance Publishing Services, Brinscall, Lancs
Printed in Great Britain
by Biddles Ltd, King's Lynn

Contents

Illustrations

Acknowledgements

I should like to thank the AHRC and Manchester Metropolitan University which together funded a period of leave to research and write this book. In particular I thank Prof. Stephen Lacey for his friendship and support for my work, and Kim Akass and Janet McCabe, Sarah Cardwell, Lez Cooke and Matt Hills, who, through discussion and feedback, have helped my thinking develop. Because the book is wide-ranging, I draw heavily in parts on the research of others whom I acknowledge here generally, as well as specifically in the body of the text. I am indebted also to colleagues in the small, but growing, TV Drama Studies community for insights at conferences and in publications. I thank Matthew Frost of Manchester University Press whose positive attitude and genuine interest in TV drama has facilitated the process of publication. Finally, I thank those staff in the Department of Contemporary Arts at Manchester Metropolitan University who have graciously facilitated my new role focused primarily on research, and I thank generations of TV Drama Studies students for insights into their viewing modes and preferences.

Some of the material included in the book was developed for the TV Drama symposia at the Universities of Reading and Kent in 2006 and has been aired in different versions in those forums. The analysis of Poliakoff's place in the British TV drama tradition was developed in relation to a piece published in *Journal of British Cinema and Television*, 3:1. A version of my analysis of *Ally McBeal* features in Creeber (2001).

Abbreviations

C4	Channel 4
CGI	computer-generated imagery
DBS	Direct Broadcast Satellite
Desperates	*Desperate Housewives*
FCC	Federal Communications Commission
Fin Syn	Financial Interest and Syndication
HBO	Home Box Office
HDTV	High Definition/High Density Television
LOP	Least Objectionable Programming
Ofcom	Office of Communications
SatC	*Sex and the City*
Sopranos	*The Sopranos*
StP	*Shooting the Past*
PSB	Public Service Broadcasting
PSP	Public Service Publisher
Pov	point of view

Editorial note

Single inverted commas are used in the standard way for short, referenced quotations. Double inverted commas are used to mark well-worn but unavoidable phrases such as "quality TV" (when not part of a quotation), and for arguable, but much-used, concepts such as "cinematic". Where used with some irony, terms such as "reality" are also marked with double inverted commas like pairs of raised eyebrows to indicate a postmodern awareness of their questionability. I recognise that this is not an entirely established mode of punctuation but it does seem to me to make a useful distinction. To use single inverted commas throughout would leave some apparent quotations without references and thus cause another editorial problem.

Introduction: aims, scope, methods and standpoints

> I'm not saying all TV is good: the majority of it isn't. I'm arguing that the best of TV is very good indeed [and] that television should be taken seriously enough to be judged in context, without preconceptions, on its merits. (Bianculli, 1992: x)

The overall aim of this book is broadly to review the output of "quality" TV drama between the mid-1990s and 2006 (see Chapter 1) and to assess the "state of play" in television cultures at a time of significant technological and market change. Amidst frequent accusations of the "dumbing-down" of television, this book aims to offer a measured, self-reflexive, assessment of "high-end" drama on contemporary television. It seeks also to offer insights into TV drama as a cultural form, both noting how provision has changed and sketching the force-field of influences which has given rise to new product. Evidently, such a project is ambitious and thus one purpose of this Introduction is accordingly to acknowledge the practical constraints on both aims and scope. Furthermore, since the various dimensions which need to be addressed – aesthetics, economics, institutions, cultural trends, new technologies – are bound up in each other and thus not readily separable, it will be helpful at the outset to indicate the methods adopted to address TV drama cultures and how they play out in the structure of the book.

A key method is to ground the broader arguments by selecting for aesthetic and contextual analysis specific examples of "high-end" TV drama drawn primarily from American and British output. Thus a distinguishing feature of the book is the mix of cultural studies and arts approaches it takes in, setting analyses of compositional principles of specific TV dramas against a broader context of production and, to some extent, reception. The American and British contexts have been chosen because the USA remains the dominant producer in terms of volume of exports,[1] whilst Britain has a long-standing, distinctive television culture and continues to wrestle with its public service ethos in an increasingly commercial world context. Thus, the two cultures taken together mobilise key aspects of key current debates about "globalisation" and "quality" and they afford examples of a range of "high-end" products.

I take the primary definition of "high end" from the industry to indicate big budgets and the high production values associated with them, along with a "prime-time" position in the schedule of a major channel. But, as with all such definitions when placed under scrutiny, the concept is more elastic than it at first appears. The scheduling of the networks in subscription and cable channels varies considerably and the networks function differently in the UK from the USA, as Johnson's account of *The X-Files* (Fox TV) and *Buffy the Vampire Slayer* (WB) relates (see 2005: 95–123). Precisely because much "high-end" product is multilayered and generically hybrid as we shall see, partly in an attempt to appeal to audiences beyond its primary target market (see Nelson, 1996), it is perceived and placed differently in different markets. The industry term "high concept" partly informs my sense of "high end" but, where in the UK this might be inflected towards a social realist drama with a social purpose or an adaptation of a classic novel (Austen, Eliot, Dickens) with high-art connotations, in the USA it might indicate the philosophical dimensions of *Star Trek*. Hopefully, the idea of "high end" will become clearer by exemplification as the book progresses but an indication at the outset of some conscious exclusions might assist.

There are many important kinds of small-screen fictions which my selection of "high-end" American and British examples inevitably excludes. Thus I do not in this book directly discuss examples of regular TV fare, daytime television, the soaps or series and serials which elsewhere I have dubbed popular "flexi-narratives" (see Nelson, 1997). This is not because I do not find them significant or worthwhile. Indeed, I recognise that they afford a viewing experience of great importance, as testified by the fact that, worldwide, audiences are known to prefer programming which appears to resonate with, or reflect, their everyday lives. Besides Anglophone output, the *telenovela* in Spanish, for example, has become a worldwide phenomenon. TV movies – mainly the products of American media conglomerates, though often made outside the USA – are similarly transnational and watched by audiences in multi-millions. But they do not fit with the conception of this book. Though some of my examples (e.g. *Spooks* or *Life on Mars*) might fall under the "quality popular" tag (see Chapter 7), my focus is mainly on those TV dramas whose 'narrative image' (Ellis, 1994: 30 ff.) is constructed as "must-see" or appointment viewing, programmes which themselves make a claim to distinction or have such a claim made about them. There are fine lines to be drawn here also since so much television is currently constructed in these terms, both channels and individual programmes. When, for example, it was suggested that I might include the new *Dr Who* (BBC) in this book, I recognised that the much-vaunted makeover and success of the series' revival made it a contender. But, immediately, it seemed to me to fall outside my conception of "high end", given its history and relatively low budget status.[2] Another writer might have drawn the line elsewhere but, in any event, my selection is meant ultimately to be illustrative of a range of ideas and it could not possibly be exhaustive in a book of this scope.

Following this Introduction, Chapter 1 articulates in more detail the different aspects of the force-field impacting on current TV drama provision, Chapters 2, 4, 6 and 8 all focus on specific examples, grouped to illuminate one or other of my key lines of inquiry, through linking the specific to the general. Thus Chapter 2 opens up the quality debate by analysing aspects of the textual aesthetics and production and reception contexts of three distinctive dramas, each of which illustrates a different claim to "quality". Chapter 4 explores a risky, "edgy" television which flouts the historic tendency for small-screen fictions to be conservative, particularly in the USA where a Least Objectionable Programming (LOP) strategy dominated the "network era". Chapter 6 considers developments in television dramatic form and style in the context of 'cultural discount'. Hoskins and Mirus, who coined the term, argue that a 'particular programme rooted in one culture, and thus attractive in that environment, will have a diminished appeal elsewhere as viewers find it difficult to identify with the style, values, beliefs, institutions and behavioural patterns of the material in question' (1988: 500).

Indeed, countering the blazon of transnational blockbusters, Steemers concludes from her overview of current market conditions that, 'given a choice, most people prefer home-grown programming' (2004: 6). In reviewing quality, this book will take account in abstract of audiences and features of reception in the contemporary context, though it does not engage in ethnographic, or other, audience study. It considers rather the tensions between the local and the global in specific programme production and distribution. Indeed, this study seeks to locate itself in that 'middle range approach' to research which Cunningham and Jacka see as lying between the totalising explanations of political economy and a narrow ethnography (see 1996: 22). But it owes a debt, freely acknowledged, to research in these more specialist domains and it is good to see that TV drama, and television generally, is being taken seriously by a small, but increasing, number of academic researchers who are undertaking detailed studies on which a broad overview such as is offered in this book is able to draw. Though it is too risky confidently to predict the future of drama on television, the largely positive approach to the "state of play" in the book is based upon cultural and technological trends. A key objective of the study is to foster better understanding of the play between production circumstances, texts and locally situated viewers and to invite forethought about the direction of television culture and, specifically TV drama output within it.

A key tension, if not an apparent contradiction, needs to be addressed in this context. TV drama production aspires increasingly to transnational and multiplatform distribution and yet audiences, as noted, prefer home-grown product. Thus, the play between the global and the local is of increasing cultural importance. Interspersed between the chapters focusing on specific examples are more general chapters fleshing out the contextual aspects of the study. Chapter 3 addresses the macroeconomic and industry context, Chapter 5 deals with developments in aesthetic form and style, drawing on a range of illustrative examples, and Chapter 7 revisits questions of quality and the cultural implications of "quality TV". In the final chapter, some instances of a sustained singularity in British TV drama are discussed to reflect upon how traditions may successfully adapt to new circumstances without altogether abandoning cultural heritage.

"Quality", of course, is a highly contested term. Currently, very bold claims are being made in some quarters about "American Quality Television". With texts such as *The Sopranos* and *Buffy the Vampire Slayer* in mind, Peter Krämer has gone so far as to claim that American 'fictional television is now better than the movies' (cited in Jancovich and Lyons, 2003: 1). A debate about the cultural value of television as a medium and of types of programming within it has rumbled on since the medium's inception. But there are specificities about evaluations made at various moments in television history in terms of who adjudges the medium, or specific programmes, and on what terms. As Jeffrey Miller has documented, in the mid–1960s in contrast to the current trend, '*The Avengers* amplified the argument, increasing in loudness, that British television was better than American' (2000: 74).

Although in an age of relativism it is nigh on impossible to achieve a consensus on what is of value, it is possible to bring out the institutional forces at work promoting some kinds of programming over others. Moreover, it is possible to delineate the aesthetic characteristics of what people term "quality TV" as distinct from shows they really enjoy but would not categorise in this way. As Robert Thompson has noted, 'Serious novels, paintings and films have a distinct set of characteristics that distinguish themselves from bestsellers, K-Mart seascapes, and Hollywood blockbusters' (1996: 16).

But conceptions of "quality" change through time and shifting socio-economic circumstances have impacted on taste formations to complicate things. Ultimately, I aim to place the above kind of hierarchical evaluation in a broader context of the history of cultural and aesthetic worth. Precisely because values today are taken to be neither fixed nor absolute, no single set of criteria will suffice. However, Thompson's insight into an implicit (if not occasionally explicit) industrial and critical association of "quality television" with "high-art" values has particular resonance for renewed interest in the aesthetics of TV drama, as we shall see.

Since I take all evaluations to be to some extent coloured by the passions and interests of those making the judgements, it is important at the outset to be self-reflexive about my standpoint in writing this book.[3] In a wry essay, Alan McKee points not only to the selectivity of written accounts of television but also to the tendency for academics to 'comment as an expert without actually watching it' (in Jancovich and Lyons, 2003: 181). Today, commentators watch and write about television in very different ways. Following Hills (2002), I have referred recently, for example, to the categories of 'fan scholars' and 'industry scholars' alongside 'scholar fans' (see Nelson, 2005). That is to say that, besides academics who happen to get deeply caught up in the fandom of a particular series, there are fans who contribute to a fuller understanding of television culture by writing in knowledgeable and insightful ways about TV drama – on websites for example. Industry practitioners, engrossed from day to day in the business of making programmes, frequently offer scholarly insights into their subject when asked, even though they do not typically construct themselves as academics. All these perspectives enrich the study and understanding of television and I shall draw upon a range of sources in the book. However, to sound a note of caution at the outset, I shall not follow the drift of consumer individualism in reducing everything to "personal choice" but insist that, in Television Studies, criticism should be both historically aware and self-aware. In the absence of a consensus on signification let alone value, the negotiation of meanings and pleasures must be made all the more visible in the construction of a dialogue between various voices.

To out my own position, I am more of a scholar than a fan in the sense that, though I can become very involved, intellectually and emotionally, in watching some TV dramas, I am not as committed to any particular programme as some of my academic colleagues. Perhaps because of my age (beyond the desirable 18–49 demographic) my education (initially in philosophy and literary-dramatic frameworks and practices), I am personally disposed towards the "high end" of TV, some of which Raymond Williams would term 'serious' drama.[4] I might accordingly stand accused of indulging what John Hartley dubs 'the intelligentsia mode of television reception' (Hartley and McKee, 2000). But I enjoy watching a wide range of dramas on television and I am aware through my teaching and research that there are many ways of watching television no doubt more significant than my own. Indeed, fans who regularly watch, and (on video and DVD) repeatedly rewatch, their favoured programme have a mode of engagement different from my own and may know the specific programmes I discuss in this book in a more detailed and nuanced way than I do. Though, in writing, I try to take account of other modes of engagement, I apologise in advance to those whose viewing experience is not fully represented in this book or who read the examples I discuss very differently from me. The overall task of the academic study of television, as I understand it, is to take account of, but also significantly to extend, everyday discourses on the medium and its programmes. In particular, I use the optics of history throughout the book to throw the present into relief, but by no means to suggest that the past was always better than the present. In sketching the force-field of influences on television dramas, of which reception in my account is only one aspect, I am inevitably expounding and inviting the relatively critical detachment of a wide-angle view rather than the passion of an extreme close-up. The pleasures of watching television are, however, increasingly recognised to be of importance in the study of the medium, certainly alongside – and perhaps even in place of – meanings. Though pleasure has been theorised in various ways in the academy, concepts such as 'the Sublime' and 'jouissance' seem somewhat lofty for a primarily domestic medium. It may be, however, that new accounts of the pleasures of television are required and these will be considered in respect of the specificity of the medium in Chapter 1.

From a bullish, free-marketeer's perspective, Rupert Murdoch defies the scep-tics' cries in arguing, 'The television set of the future will be a global cornucopia of programming and nearly infinite libraries of data, education and entertainment. The arguments that have recently dominated British Broadcasting ... will soon sound as if they belong in the Stone Age' (Murdoch, 1989). As my narrative un-folds, it will become apparent that, though not uncritical of contemporary televi-sion culture, this book expounds the view that the current state of play in TV drama gives perhaps more ground for hope than for despair. Indeed, though my discursive position is very different from that of Rupert Murdoch, I concur that it is possible that new circumstances might afford a broader range of "quality" dra-mas than previously supposed "golden ages". What the term "quality" might mean, and to whom, remains an interrogative theme running throughout the book.

Notes

1   In 2002 the USA accounted for three-quarters of the global trade in television by value (ITC, 2002).
2   Ellis proposes that the 'narrative image created for (and from) a film is the deciding factor in its commercial success' (1994: 30) but the failure of Cold Feet (see Chapter 6) and other British dramas remade for the American market following success in Britain suggests 'nar-rative image' has limitations.
3   Kant famously argues for 'disinterestedness' in the making of aesthetic judgements, but contemporary cultural and linguistic theory has questioned its feasibility. For a discussion of Kantian aesthetics, see Kemal, 1992.
4   Williams defined 'serious television' in terms of 'programmes that looked as if someone had successfully meant something in making them, rather than simply slotted them into a market' (cited in Brunsdon, 1990: 87), but he applied his criteria to all kinds of program-ming. Thus Williams challenged entrenched canonical assumptions and instigated the idea that popular programmes with mass appeal might be adjudged 'good'.

1

Mapping the territory; blurring the boundaries

Conceptual map

This chapter maps out the conceptual framework of the book, introducing the key factors in the force-field of both the production of contemporary TV drama and the relevant core debates in critical analysis of the television medium and its dramatic forms. A key premise to be explored in this book is that a distinctive era of television practice has emerged in the 1996–2006 decade under consideration.

Historically, various optics have helpfully been used to assist in denoting and understanding changes in television culture across spaces and through time. Kaplan's *Rocking Around the Clock* (1987), for example, focused synchronically upon a worldwide textual phenomenon, MTV, whilst, in the specifically American context, Feuer's *Seeing Through the Eighties* (1995) followed a timeline of socio-cultural development diachronically. More recently, Ellis (2000), focusing upon the UK context but with an eye to global developments, has delineated three eras of television, Scarcity, Availability and Plenty, the last approximating to the period under discussion here which, in my judgement, has emerged further than Ellis allows. Taking an approach based on industry economic structures, Behrens (1986) coined the terms TVI and TVII as shorthand for the network era of television in the USA (roughly 1948–75) and post-network era (roughly 1975–95). Following Behrens, Rogers, Epstein and Reeves have proposed 'TVIII' to cover the post-1995, digital–global context. They prefer this means of distinction to the 'broadcast', 'cable' and 'digital' characterisations of eras, since, as they rightly point out, 'broadcast and cable television continue to exist in the "digital era"' (2002: 55). TV3 (the formulation I will borrow and adapt), whilst it appears to follow on from a periodisation in the USA, applies in fact to world television, since it marks a new era hailing the triumph of digital–satellite capacity to distribute transnationally, bypassing national distribution and, in some instances, regulatory controls. A more nuanced account of the political economy of world television and its cultural impact follows in Chapter 3 but, overall, this study considers TV3 to be a distinctive period arising from a conflation of influences (cultural, technological, industrial, social, aesthetic) with particular implications for TV drama forms and their production, distribution and reception under new circumstances.

As with attempts at the periodisation of the medium, critical approaches in the slowly emergent field of Television Drama Studies have equally gone through phases which have looked in very different ways at textual forms and their impact on audiences. In the 1970s academy, the compositional principles of texts were rather assumed to evoke specific kinds of viewing response. A formalist critique, grounded in more or less overtly Marx-derived "Brechtian" aesthetics, decried television's realist narrative and "transparent" representational conventions (see McCabe, 1976). In contrast, as Feuer notes 'Fiske's work on television reception was widely influential during the eighties in shifting the emphasis away from how texts position the viewer and towards what the viewer does with the text' (1995: 4). Fiske's "polysemic" approach in turn militated against estimations of textual quality since, in Schroder's formulation, 'The text itself has no existence, no life, and therefore no quality until it is deciphered by an individual and triggers the meaning potential carried by this individual' (1992: 207). In the 1980s and beyond, the impact on the subjectivity of viewers has been a matter of variously theorised accounts. Ethnographic studies in the 1980s (Morley, 1980; Hobson, 1982; Ang, 1985) appeared to confirm the polysemy of texts by documenting a broad range of readings from socially differentiated reading positions. With the increasing fragmentation of the television audience, social subdivisions and individuals were shown to take different meanings from their viewing experience. Moreover, in the latter half of the 1990s and at the turn of the millennium, the pleasures of television came to the fore, both in its general visual attractions (Caldwell, 1995) and in the cult following of specific groups of dedicated fans (Hills, 2002).

An overemphasis on the openness of the text and the freedom of the reader to make or take from it what he or she will, however, has a number of implications for understanding the circulation of television. As Miller has observed:

> Active audience research … in its assertion of the absolute openness of transnational texts, similarly strips the concept of culture of its power in the limitlessness of meaning, while also stripping the vital political notion of 'resistance' of its power in suggesting that a local reading of a transnational text actively resists ideological elements of that text. (2000: 7)

The question of how a programme produced in one culture is received and read in another becomes particularly pressing in TV3 when developments in technology afford the ready circulation of programmes worldwide, as noted. In a situation in which American output dominates the export of programmes, it remains important to take into account what people at a range of local levels do with television. But a properly critical account of television's significance should not lapse into complacency simply because there is evidence that some people read and enjoy texts against their apparent ideological grain. Whilst my approach does not directly involve specific ethnographic study, it aims to understand the cultural implications of distribution and reception more broadly and, to that end, will draw upon the audience research undertaken by others.

As Cunningham and Jacka have pointed out, it would equally be a mistake to resurrect the 'cultural imperialism' thesis (see Schiller, 1969 and 1991) simply in respect of the volume of exports from the USA in the world television market. As they succinctly put it, 'Culture is much more than media even if media are part of culture' (1996: 6). As we shall see in Chapter 3, furthermore, a post-Fordist dispersal of media power and television production perhaps places the USA in a less dominant position in the world economy than in the past, even though it remains highly influential, particularly in "high-end" drama. Jacka and Cunningham note that, 'Up to 90 per cent of television fare in many countries is locally originated' (1996: 30), but they acknowledge that drama is much more likely to be imported than other television forms.[1] In respect of the very expensive "high-end" drama with which this book is primarily concerned, production typically requires co-financing and, in anglophone cultures, North America remains the most likely source of funding partners, though there are European and other initiatives.[2] The cultural specificities of contributing countries, particularly where one partner is dominant, may be eroded in the process of product development, as examples in Chapter 6 will explore. Cultural exchange in TV3 may be more a road network than a one-way street, to borrow Tracey's extended metaphor (1985: 23), but the influence of American television style, as much as ideology, remains significant, if only because of its familiarity across the world.

Another significant shift in the understanding of television cultures relates specifically to the political disposition of audiences. The 1970s critique of the "classic realist text" was made, as noted above, from a particular ideological position at a historical moment in which a belief was sustained in the capacity of media forms to make a counter-hegemonic intervention in the socio-political process. The Marxist perspective is, however, one of several modernist 'grand narratives' (*grands récits*) noted by Lyotard (1984) to be unsustainable in the postmodern condition. Social change from heavy to service industry in the economically advanced Western industrial nations is a key factor here. Politics as conceived on the basis of class up to the early 1970s has given way to a more fractured politics of the personal. Partly through a post-Watergate distrust of politicians and partly through a disillusion in the capacity of party politics to address the complexities of world issues, younger generations appear either to focus upon the direct targeting of specific issues (animal rights in scientific research, for example) or to take little interest at all in world political questions. The politics of identity, mobilised significantly by the various phases in the trajectory of the women's movement and other gender- and sexual-preference-based emancipatory movements has significantly overtaken class and party politics in 'standpoint epistemologies' (Williams, 2001: 10). In respect of the study of TV drama, commentators who address political implications today have located their accounts more in the politics of the personal than in the grand historical trajectories of class struggle (Creeber, 2004a).

Just as television research has led to a modification of the old inoculation model of ideological imposition, so too a more balanced conception of the engagements between texts and readers has emerged. Bakhtin's concepts of heteroglossia and dialogism, the multi-accented sign and its potential for variant readings, has been mobilised in this context.[3] His sense that meanings are negotiated in dialogues between utterances would seem at first sight to affirm Fiske's account of polysemy and the findings of 1980s ethnographers noted above. But Bakhtin's concept of dialogism, as Miller has remarked 'grounds polysemy in the actual political, economic, social and ideological statements that shape reception and meaning' (2000: 9). In discussing the interplay between the local and the global in this study, the potential for cultural influence of the dominant producers and distributors, notably American, will accordingly be acknowledged. In recognising varying degrees of "otherness" or varying degrees of "our-own-ness" in the dialogic negotiations between texts and readers, however, it is not assumed that a supposed semiotic democracy of "personal choice" has redressed imbalances of power across the globe. The more excessive postmodern notions of free-floating signifiers will accordingly be qualified in recognition of a degree of semantic commonality within and across speech communities, even whilst acknowledging that readings are inflected through the prisms of local cultures and microcultures.

This approach makes it possible once again to discuss the forms, compositional principles and implications of texts and to argue that they invite dispositions of viewers, even if they lack the power to determine responses. In evoking differing accounts of the impact of television upon viewers and the modes of engagement viewers might have with television, I prefigure a theme running throughout the book concerning the function of television and the possibility, not to mention the desirability, that TV drama might go beyond its evident capacity to entertain large numbers of people in their leisure hours. My aim, besides locating new products transmitted by fresh means to newly constructed target audiences, is to afford a critical perspective on contemporary television cultures and accordingly I have acknowledged "where I am coming from" in the Introduction. A particular concern will be the ability of national governments under global market circumstances to intervene to sustain the local product which viewers are known to prefer.

"Cinematic" television: a paradox to which the times give proof?

A concern with textuality is pressed by the most recent trend in TV Drama Studies towards analysis of textual aesthetics. This emphasis arises partly from the creative exploitation of the better quality of the medium's sound and image (see Chapter 5) and partly because, in an age of well-produced DVDs of major television series, it has become possible for close textual readings on repeated viewings, both by fans and academics alike. Above all, however, it is because the "high end" of small-screen fictions aspires to cinematic production values, as will be seen in the discussion of many of the examples in this book. The visual style, the "look", of TV drama texts has become another key aspect, besides narrative form and other principles of composition, to invite analysis.

The idea that TV drama is increasingly "cinematic" needs a brief commentary at the outset, and the distinctiveness of the television medium will be addressed shortly. First, it should be noted that the impetus to reconceive TV as film comes from the industry, particularly from HBO with its tag line promoting its output as Home Box Office, in which the engagement is on an economic basis like that of the movie theatre, requiring payment directly for a singular "cinematic" experience ('it's not TV; it's HBO'). Secondly, the term might imply an enhanced visual means of story-telling in place of the dialogue-led television play with its theatrical, rather than filmic, heritage. Today's high budgets for "high-end" TV drama approximate to (though do not quite reach) those of cinema, affording a single camera with post-production editing approach, using 16mm, and exceptionally 35mm stock (or now HDTV) for recording its imagery, rather than magnetic tape. High budgets also afford highly paid star performers, external and occasionally exotic locations and many extras to flesh out the *mise-en-scène*. Established film directors are being drawn into television (see Chapter 5) and bring a range of filmic vocabularies and grammars into play. Intertextual reference is frequently made to film, as well as television, products and in some instances, as we shall see, there is a conscious use of modernist European cinema techniques.

All this said, however, there are obvious factors which mark TV fictions from their narrative cinema counterparts. Digital technologies, in particular HDTV, are impacting upon both mediums but most on the television production process and its imagery. It remains a moot point whether the much-improved digital television image is the equivalent of that of film, or whether each retains its own visual qualities. But the most obvious difference lies in scope and narrative form, since films typically run for 90–120 minutes and follow a single narrative arc, whilst television series run for perhaps fifty hours over six seasons, adopting multiple narrative forms, and in some instances shifting significantly over time, to sustain themselves. Indeed, it is a doxa of US television that at least four series of up to twenty-two episodes are needed to maximise profits through syndication. Though the industry structure is itself changing (see Chapter 2), long-form series–serial narratives remain the mainstay of the television schedules. Thus, though they may aspire to cinematic visual style, TV dramas nevertheless adhere to a range of distinctive narrative forms. The "cinematic" tag, all too frequently and loosely applied to contemporary television series, might best be understood, therefore, as an enhanced visual style, since modern technologies have certainly afforded a denser visual image and more effective soundtrack (see Chapter 5). This note of caution should inform instances where I also use the term "cinematic" as a shorthand reference subsequently in this book.

Technological advance

In terms of cultural impact, the most significant development in television technology has been the consolidation of cable and satellite distribution by digital
means. Cable, the major innovation of TVII cracked the distribution bottleneck
in the USA but advanced digital–satellite technology has achieved its break-up in
TV3. Satellite beams have for some time been able to reach most of the surface of
the globe but satellite technology has developed significantly since its commercial
expansion in the late 1970s. Indeed, the feature which contributes to a distinctive
TV3 is the emergence in 1994 in the USA of a new generation of high-powered
direct-broadcast satellites (DBS) and sophisticated encryption achieved through
digital compression. Encryption devices, "digi-boxes", afford control over who can
receive the signal, and thus payment (by subscription or pay-per-view) can be
exacted for delivery of services. Together, these developments afforded control
over access to satellite signals and thus over distribution. In the UK a parallel
development occurred with BSkyB in 1998.[4]

The key impact of digital technology in TV3 lies, then, in distribution and
concerns bandwidth, the capacity to distribute content. Besides satellite, more information can be distributed digitally through existing channels (the electromagnetic spectrum and coaxial cable) through a technique of compression. Increased
means of distribution and more available space on existing bandwidth means
more channels, even where analogue remains the basic platform. Where digital
capability has emerged, new modes of communication in television are opened
up. At a domestic level, the fibre backbones to networks and the broadband spectrum facilitate interactivity, as with personal computers. Viewers are now frequently
enticed to press the red button on their remote handsets to access further information or a new angle on the game. Already, some people access services such as
e-mail through their television apparatus and increasingly the ubiquitous domestic small screens, through sharing digital technology, will become one.[5]

In the public sphere, the apparent expansion (through digital compression)
of the electromagnetic spectrum has effected a significant change in perception.
Where historically it was accepted that, for reasons of spectrum scarcity, the electromagnetic resource had to be held in public trust and managed by state regulatory forces, digital plenitude displaces this conviction. A more individual disposition
to the television medium and a privatised viewing experience displace the former
communal and public service ethos. Worldwide there has been a drift away from
public service to market-oriented television services. Indeed, in the UK there is a
question as to whether the government will reserve some of the newly available
digital spectrum for increased public service ends or sell it to the highest bidder.[6]

Technology is not, however, determining but functions as just one, albeit significant, element in a force-field. The major impact of the technological innovations above has been facilitated by political shifts in a parallel direction away from
a public service ethos towards privatisation in the Reagan–Thatcher eras in the
USA and Britain. Deregulation has afforded particularly horizontal integration

across the media industries transnationally and also, in the USA, vertical integration previously precluded by regulation (see Chapter 3). Thus several forces in the field combine to promote the noted culture of consumer individualism and to place primary emphasis on the pleasure of personal experience at the expense of other possible functions of television.

Industry contexts

Since a highly competitive environment of choices had already emerged prior to TV3, an increasingly commercial drift towards the fragmentation of audiences by targeting key demographics might be seen as part of a broader historical trajectory. In the American "network era", (TVI), the cartel of ABC, CBS and NBC had a stranglehold on distribution and operated the infamous LOP strategy to maximise the audiences for which they competed just amongst themselves. Cable and satellite began progressively to dislocate this comfortable arrangement in the course of the 1980s. At the beginning of the 1980 season, the cartel had an apparently secure base of 92 per cent of the viewing population. But, as Miller relates:

> By the end of the 1980–81 season, that figure had dropped to 81 percent; by 1988, only 67 percent of prime-time viewers were watching network programming … The most visible and plausible cause [of this decline] was the availability of new viewing options made possible by the spread of cable television. (2000: 169)[7]

It was not until TV3, however, that the networks' power further reduced by DBS satellite and cable with advanced encryption in a genuinely multichannel, digital environment to the point where, though they remain residually influential, the networks no longer call all the shots but are called upon instead to respond to new circumstances.

In the UK, the historic position of the BBC as guardian of the airwaves was significantly sustained for many years after the introduction of commercial television (in 1955), but 1990s deregulation and digital technology has opened up a multi-channel environment similar to that in the USA. To make a stark comparison, in 1982, shortly after the inception of Channel 4 (and S4C in Wales), there were just four terrestrial channels (BBC1, BBC2, ITV, C4). In 2002 there were six terrestrial channels (with the inclusion of Five and ITV2) plus the additional digital channels of BBC3 and BBC4 and some forty other Freeview channels, not to mention the 1500 cable–satellite subscription channels circulating in Western Europe alone. The massively increased provision, besides further fragmenting the audience, creates much airtime to be filled and offers new challenges to producers and schedulers.

Indeed, the technological conditions of TV3 when located in specific socio-economic circumstances, invite innovative approaches to making television programmes. When increased distribution possibilities afford fresh business opportunities, new players emerge such as, in the USA, new networks (e.g. Fox Television – see Chapter 3) and stronger satellite–cable subscription operations (e.g.

HBO and Showtime). The context of a highly competitive, multichannel, digital environment demands high-quality brands as a new kind of flagship to distinguish a channel. Subscription channels in particular seek to attract interest by exploiting their new freedom beyond regulatory frameworks. As Todreas concludes from his economic analysis, 'At the same time that this [TV3] shift is destroying value in the conduit, it will create value in content ... [Distributors] will offer more money to content providers at the expense of their own margins' (1999: 7). Todreas's point is illustrated in Home Box Office's achievement in the USA of innovative product (*Oz, The Sopranos, Sex and the City*), and the knock-on effect on "high-end" production elsewhere will be brought out in the discussion of examples as my narrative unfolds. The above developments of technology set in a socio-political context amount to a very significant change in the disposition to product of producers in some parts of the industry. In defiance of those who decry television and its alleged "dumbing-down" of culture, TV3 perhaps heralds a new era of quality production, particularly at the "high end" of TV drama production whose influence is then felt throughout more regular fare.

The influence of digital cameras and editing have made their impact on production methods since, whilst film stock itself remains very expensive, single-camera shooting with post-production methods historically associated with cinema have become increasingly common by digital means in television. Though much "high-end" production continues to be shot on film, HDTV is emergent and parallel shooting on a digital camera allows instant playback and saves time waiting for rushes to be prepared.[8] The shift away from the outmoded (for drama) television studio, with its cameras constrained in movement by cumbersome cables, has brought a new dynamism to television production in general, which now aspires to a "cinematic look and feel", as noted. Special effects can be inexpensively produced in digital post-production and appreciated on domestic apparatus, the sound and vision qualities of which are much improved by digital technologies (see Chapter 5).

Specificity of the television medium

Given the production disposition towards cinema, the advent of large-scale, wide-screen domestic monitors with digital surround sound and the technological means to eliminate the interruptions of advertisements in recording or distribution by DVD, the experience of watching television (for some people at least) increasingly approximates to that of cinema. Where, in the past, attempts have been made sharply to differentiate the mediums of film and television, Caldwell (1995) has suggested that these developments bring the viewing of fiction on television much closer to a cinema-in-the-home experience, giving a new twist to the old question about the specificity of the medium of television.

Raymond Williams's seminal concept of "flow" (1974: 93) situated any specific programme in the broader context of the medium perceived in terms of a continuous stream of programming, advertisements and continuity items. Thus a distinctive feature of the viewing experience was the inability to take any given output in isolation. TV3 affords various modes of engagement. More people perhaps now watch alone, or in a more concentrated way with others, perhaps with the lights dimmed, isolating selected texts and focusing upon the screen image. The dominant viewing mode, if not quite familial, probably remains collective and domestic in small groups, perhaps of friends, in a lit space promoting talk about the programme as it is being aired. Although, with the recent emergence of mobile viewing platforms, even this orthodoxy is in question. The broadened range of viewing modes, encouraged by the quality of both the domestic television apparatus and DVDs, suggests, however, that the "flow" is a typical, historically contingent feature of television rather than an essentially medium-specific characteristic.

Similarly, the relatively casual disposition towards the television monitor in domestic spaces characterised by Ellis (1994) as the "glance", as distinct from the concentrated "gaze" elicited by cinema, may likewise be reconfigured as a contingent, rather than an essential, characteristic of medium. In response to Caldwell's questioning of the sustainability of the notion of the "glance", Ellis sees 'no particular reason to abandon the force of the notion' since, he argues, television's 'styles of visualization and narration do not assume' (2000: 100) a concentrated "gaze" as cinema does. This debate is particularly relevant to the dramas under discussion in this book, since the greater attention given to principles of composition and production of contemporary "high-end" drama would indeed seem to reward a more concentrated viewing response. Besides visual style and the density of the image, there are implications for modes of storytelling, perhaps in defiance of high-temperature "flexi-narrative" (see Nelson, 1997 and Chapter 2). Furthermore, a different range of pleasures might be mobilised by texts composed with particular attention to visual aesthetics and designed to be viewed much more like film in the cinema than "moving wall-paper" in a domestic space in which, as audience ethnography has shown, a wide variety of distracting activity might be happening.

However, TV3 should by no means be seen as exclusively digital, transnational and cinematic. The medium of television historically has been conservative precisely because it has been inextricably bound up with the patterns of everyday living. As Cunningham and Jacka have noted, 'even where alternative services are available in superabundance, as in the US, it is still the case that old-fashioned terrestrial national television is watched for upward of 60% of the time' (1996: 18). In the UK, the key terrestrial channels as yet remain analogue and sustain substantial audiences, though at numerically lower levels than previously, owing to audience fragmentation.[9] For all the hype about *ER* (NBC, transmitted in the UK on C4) when shown in Britain, the long-standing, regular medical series, *Casualty* (BBC1) still draws a far bigger audience.

Residual viewing cultures will change only gradually over time, and the established preference of audiences for local product are likely to act as a brake on the drift of media conglomerates towards a truly global marketplace. Spaces also

currently remain at national, regional or, indeed, local levels for distinctive output which might be seen as progressive or even counter-cultural.[10] The political
series in the British social realist tradition, for example, survives in the form of
occasional mini-series (*State of Play*) and, more rarely, in one-off single plays or
TV films on the specific UK political scene (e.g. *The Project*, *The Deal*), sustaining
a cultural singularity in British TV drama (see Chapter 8) alongside American
imports which have long since enriched British television culture (see Rixon, 2006).
Nevertheless, that 'fact of watching and engaging in a joint ritual with millions of
others, which Morley believed to be distinctive of television and 'at least as important as any information content gained from the broadcast' (1992: 81) may be
dissipated as the audience further fragments and as programmes designed for
niche, rather than mass, markets come to dominate. The "as if live" of broadcast
television may also be undermined if narrowcasting results in increased time-
shifting and further audience fragmentation.

      In sum, as Carroll (2003) notes, the misconception of habitual assumptions
about the ontology of the television and film media are made evident by developments in TV3. Boundary distinctions between the two media as historically constructed are becoming increasingly blurred. As Carroll summarises, it was assumed
that:

> TV has an impoverished image (marked by low resolution and scale) versus film's
> informationally dense imagery; the TV image is less detailed, whereas the film im-
> age is elaborate; in TV talk is dominant, while in film the image is dominant; TV
> elicits the glance, but film engenders the gaze; TV is in the present tense, whereas
> film is in the past tense; TV narration is segmented and serial, but film narration is
> uninterrupted and closed; and, given the previous distinction, the object of atten-
> tion in TV is the flow of programming, while the object of attention in film is the
> individual, integrated, closed story (the freestanding feature of film). (2003: 270)

These alleged distinctions have broken down in TV3 though, as noted above, I
contend that there is still a difference in narration, though even this is not an
essential difference, as TV movies illustrate.

The territory: markets and audiences

Defined spatially, the territory of this book is the potentially global market-place
of contemporary world television circulation, though in practice its focus is primarily on an Anglo-American axis in that context. Today's multipoint satellites,
in contrast to their local predecessors, transmit – and retransmit – signals over a
wide area, transgressing national boundaries and affording a worldwide, high-
quality sound and image provision. Such developments have encouraged commentators such as Schiller and Boyd-Barrett to extend their historic cultural
imperialism theses to characterise new "electronic empires" (see Thussu, 1998).
Besides the technological widening of the service platform, there are indeed a
number of aspects of TV3 which might point in that direction. Horizontal

integration has turned major international players into vast media conglomerates with worldwide influence (e.g. Time Warner, Walt Disney Corp., Viacom, News Corp.). Co-finance, as noted, is typically required outside the USA in the context of "high-end" drama, and several previously national companies over the past decade have developed international production wings (e.g. BBC Worldwide and Granada International in the UK, Kirch Group in Germany and Mediaset in Italy). Across the internet, a close relative of digital world television, interest communities have come to have more importance for some individuals and social groups than geographical neighbourhoods. The *telenovela*, for example, originating in Latin America, is prominent in satellite services to European countries, notably Spain, Italy and Portugal, illustrating that language communities may override geographical boundaries.

That technology affords global reach, allowing people simultaneously to witness world events such as 9/11 on their domestic monitors, should not, however, occasion too easy a leap to notions of "globalisation". Acknowledging new negotiations of the global with the local, Ang, amongst others, has argued that we are not yet cohabitants of McCluhan's electronic global village. Emphasising sustained, and increasingly fragmented, local identities and exclusions, she speaks of globalisation as 'an always unfinished, and necessarily unfinishable, process because this single global place we live in is also a deeply fractured one' (1996: 153).

Amidst all the dislocations of TV3, there has, however, been a further industry shift in the conception of audience, away from the idea of a "mass" audience to one composed of microcultures conceived of and defined in terms of niche markets. An understanding amongst advertisers of a possible advantage in targeting the "blue-chip" demographic instead of the mass audience goes back in the USA certainly as far as the 1980s and possibly to the late 1960s. Miller relates that, 'at the end of the [1960s] decade, both networks and advertisers were speaking of demographics as the concept defining commercial practices' (2000: 34). But Fox Television particularly, as we shall see in Chapter 3, has taken this approach to new levels of sophistication. In the UK, the sense of a largely undifferentiated communal audience was sustained in the context of a public service ethos perhaps until the late 1980s. Indeed, as demographic targeting emerged, large, as distinct from mass, postmodern audiences came to be seen to comprise amalgamations of several microcultural groups within a national audience, each attracted by a different aspect of the programme (see Nelson, 1996). Following increased market segmentation, TV3 has witnessed another strategy to aggregate a large audience from different sectors. Audiences of viable size can be constructed through global niche marketing transnationally as the *telenovela* illustrates, finding a substantial audience amongst Spanish-speaking peoples across the globe rather than within the boundaries of a nation state.

Taking another approach, subscription channels, which need only to please a sufficient number of subscribers to balance their accounts, are untroubled by the tension for advertisers between overall numbers and "blue-chip" demographics. As they no longer need to please advertisers in their programming, subscription operators can aim entire channels (e.g. HBO Premium) at more lucrative demographics. Rather than focusing upon specific programmes or advertising slots, entire channels construct themselves as "quality", intensively to target specific niches with products made to appeal directly to a sense of superiority. In stark contrast to the LOP strategy in the "network era" aimed at preventing regular viewers from defecting to another network by avoiding anything out of the ordinary, subscription channels appeal to busy professionals who have little time for television-viewing. Given that wealthy demographics are likely to be college-educated, a more sophisticated product is required to attract them and "must-see" television accordingly replaces LOP. The capacity to bypass regulators allows subscription channels to offer a more risky television. Whilst in some instances this descends into pornography, an upside of the subscription channels' market position in respect of drama is distinctive, edgy series (see Chapter 4).

Television's pleasures

As the medium has become more diverse, the range of pleasures afforded by television has increased and the theory of the medium needs likewise to extend to take account of developments. Owing to its emphasis on scientific rationalism in the post-Enlightenment tradition, the academy has typically not been adept at dealing with pleasure and desire. As noted in the Introduction, consideration of aesthetics has constructed lofty notions such as the Sublime and *jouissance*, and deep psychological accounts of desire, all of which seem at first sight inappropriate for the everyday domestic medium of television. It is helpful by way of revisiting television pleasures to distinguish different aspects of viewing pleasure marking the ends of a possible spectrum.

On one level, watching television remains a social act in the rituals of everyday life. Regular viewing of a favourite soap opera (in the UK, perhaps *Coronation Street* or *EastEnders*) in the knowledge that millions of others are simultaneously watching nationwide and that narrative developments will be a topic of conversation with family and friends, either whilst watching or on the following day, affords what Silverstone has dubbed 'ontological security' (1994: 5). His account extends beyond the social act to narrative strategies which carry on the forms and functions of cultural myth from oral storytelling traditions, providing, 'a secure framework for the representation of the unfamiliar or threatening ... [and] articulating the endemic and irresolvable contradictions of the host society' (1994: 38). The treatment of the narrative myth of family in soap opera illustrates this point well as a tension between break-up and harmony remains in constant negotiation. Thus soap viewing, amongst its range of more specific pleasures to audience fragments (the gay community's appreciation of the representations of masculinity and femininity in *Coronation Street*, for example), offers a core space of 'ontological security' around which the concerns of a culture's everyday life may be negotiated. This kind of viewing pleasure perhaps goes a long way to explaining the disposition of audiences worldwide to prefer local resonances in television programmes. The soap format may travel but the detailed context of its narrative requires cultural specificity.[11]

The kinds of pleasure offered by formulaic television output offering 'ontological security' differ markedly, however, from those at the other end of the spectrum where viewers might seek aesthetic visual pleasure or the frisson of risk. Though there may be a pleasure of excess in the melodrama of soap opera, it is ultimately bounded by the familiarity of the form and its ritual viewing slot. On subscription channels, in marked contrast, there is no guarantee of limits, even those of the forces of national regulation, and thus, to those who seek it, there is a pleasure even in the anticipation of the transgression of social codes. Indeed, it might be claimed that they offer the pleasures of ontological insecurity, the precise opposite of the pleasures afforded by the knowledge of boundaries imposed upon other output and at other times on other channels. "Adult content" on subscription-channel output, the rich use of expletives, full-frontal nudity and the graphic representation of a range of homo- and hetero-sexual acts, signals to even the casual viewer that HBO programming, for example, is not regular television fare. Whilst some viewers may well take the pleasures of pornography from HBO, my own interest in this end of the spectrum is in the perhaps closely related pleasures of "the gaze" and in the surprise – and indeed occasional challenge – of "edginess" (see Chapter 4).

Fully acknowledging those pleasures of programmes offering 'ontological security', I am interested in this book to explore the extended space opened up in TV3 for the opposite pleasures of programmes which are innovative. In respect of the "gaze", the theory of its visual pleasures has extended beyond Mulvey's seminal concept of "to-be-looked-at-ness" (1975: 17) to embrace the pleasures of women looking at men and gays and lesbians ogling beautiful bodies of their predilection. Just as the agency of gender in the narrative has changed somewhat through time to offset the historical objectification of just one sex, so recognition of the sexual aspect of viewing pleasure has broadened. Social change has afforded open acceptance of a wider range of sexual preferences. The psychoanalytic approach to sexuality and viewing has typically been foregrounded in respect of cinema rather than television but, as (for some) the gaze displaces the glance in viewing habits as noted, such theory becomes relevant to television.

Beyond overt sexuality, moreover, there is in the "look" and "feel" of the aesthetics of much "high-end" contemporary television, visual and aural pleasures which are more difficult to locate but none the less experienced. Television aesthetics involve the textures of the imagery and sound, and the play between them. They may be in the performers and their performances and the way they are situated in visually rich locations. They might be in the lighting, the camerawork and the unusual angle or effect. They are perhaps in the wit, or even the obliqueness, of the dialogue. They can be in the editing, in the variations of pace and rhythm. In sum, they concern all those aspects with which Film Studies has historically been concerned but which, until very recently, have not been thought appropriate to television. TV3 affords products which stand up to such "cinematic" analysis and has demanded new theorisation of television as indicated above, to embrace the aesthetic pleasures of the television text.

Edginess of content as well as form is offered in a variety of ways by the products of TV3. In the UK, for example, *Spooks*, a seemingly regular spy-thriller series shown on a main terrestrial channel, BBC1, deals with contemporary political material which government, and some viewers, may find sensitive. *West Wing* (NBC) similarly invites reflection on the contemporary administration in the USA. Neither programme teeters at the ontological insecurity end of the TV3 spectrum and they might well have been made in other television eras. My contention, however, is that the 'great value shift from conduit to content' (Todreas, 1999: 7) is having a beneficial impact on television output in TV3, extending the range of texts and viewing pleasures on offer. The theory of television has begun to take account of why viewers are drawn to watch particular programmes, sometimes with devotion (see Hills, 2002; Johnson, 2005). Viewers' motives may lie as much in pleasures as in meanings.

Blurred boundaries: generic and cultural hybridity

Television in TV3 mirrors cultural shifts more broadly in being marked by hybridity at all levels. The dominant cultural forms of the contemporary involve mixes of genre, form, modes of expression, production and distribution, and even ontologies. First, at the macroeconomic level, the television industry structure is characterised by mergers of film/TV companies with entertainment empires (e.g. AOL-Time Warner; Viacom-CBS). As Todreas observes:

> Until now the communications industry has been divided into categories; each had its own economic logic as well as its own regulatory framework. The telephone business had nothing to do with television, television was distinct from radio and radio was unlike print … Technology is now sweeping these distinctions into the dustbin of history. (1999: 5)

In Holt's parallel summary, articulating a similar breach of formerly firm distinctions, 'Boundaries between production, distribution and exhibition have collapsed to the point that the old edicts no longer apply' (in Jancovich and Lyons, 2003: 12). TV dramas are frequently international co-productions or directly linked with a sponsor by branding in ways that are not as crudely product-related as in the past (e.g. Renault Velsatis with *Six Feet Under* and *Shameless*).[12] On the domestic front, the television apparatus now approximates to the cinema screen in dimension, aspect ratio, image and sound quality. The distinction between TV drama, made-for-TV movie and TV movie is increasingly blurred in terms of the technical quality of product.

At a theoretical level, the influential intellectual force of poststructuralism has produced a perhaps dominant mindset in culture involving a softening of conceptual boundaries in the wake of Derrida's *différance/différence*, the endless deferral of closure in a chain of signification. And this is not just an abstruse theory expounded in the ivory towers of the academy. Its resonances may be felt in all aspects of daily life, and particularly in popular culture, from fusion music to fusion food. The shift from an industrial to a service economy has resulted in social change which blurs clear boundaries between formerly discrete working and 'middle' classes (see Harvey 1989; Nelson 1997). Indeed the academy in Britain has itself been drawn out into the market-place, and to open up its doors to those formerly excluded and to industrial concerns. An influx of taste formations has brought high culture up against aspects of popular culture, and hybrids are the result. Even in judgements of quality, a modernist negation aesthetic has arguably re-emerged in HBO, the acme of commercial television (see Chapter 7).

Texts combine previously disparate genres: amongst American product, *The Sopranos* is part action-adventure, part gangster movie and part psychological drama; *Buffy* is teen drama, new age, gothic horror and more; *Ally McBeal* is courtroom drama meets romance meets MTV; and *Friends* has been dubbed a 'dramedy'. In the UK, *Cold Feet* oscillates between comedy and dark social or psychological moments of intense emotion whilst *Shameless* combines comedy with "serious" social realism in a hybrid of serial narrative and sitcom form. "Reality TV" makes TV drama out of quasi-documentary in a collapse of any firm distinction between fiction and fact in a medium which increasingly offers 'television history as amnesiac fiction' (McCarthy in Jancovich and Lyons, 2003: 99). These hybrid forms will be explored through specific examples in the book, but it is helpful here to raise a key question about the relation between the parts.

Mixes of different genres are not new. As Johnson (2005) has ably demonstrated, for example, *The Prisoner* was innovative in the 1960s in mixing action-adventure with the political and philosophical dimensions of more serious programming to produce what she dubs 'Serious Entertainment' (2005: 42 ff.). Indeed, drawing upon Todorov's notion of 'hesitation', she proposes that 'This mix of the "serious" and the "popular" functions precisely to heighten the sense of hesitation, to create a world in which generic conventions cannot be relied upon as secure indicators of knowledge and expectation' (2005: 61). Thus, in Johnson's account, *The Prisoner*, an exceptional programme in its time, prefigures a phenomenon which has become commonplace in TV3 in a mix of genres to create new forms which retain something of the appeal of the established, contributing genres. Where, in the 1960s, the more formally experimental episodes of the *The Prisoner* caused an outcry, with McGoohan remarking that, though they say they want something new, 'basically people like a good story that ends up the way it should' (cited in Johnson, 2005: 62), today's viewers, brought up on television, are not only steeped in its various conventions but are also consciously aware of them. Thus there is greater potential for play with and between genres in TV3 programming and it is not surprising that *The Prisoner* has re-emerged to develop a cult following.

Moreover, in some instances, the way in which the genres are juxtaposed may indeed open up a space for dislocation which might be theorised in the Russian Formalists' sense of "the shock of defamiliarization" (*ostraneniye*) or specifically in Todorov's notion of "hesitation", or even Brecht's theory of "distanciation" (*Verfremdung*).[13] Where Johnson focuses upon telefantasy, this book illustrates that frictions and dislocations may be mobilised through the principles of composition across a wide range of today's mixes by combining elements such that they are not fully integrated or harmonised into a new whole, but collide with each other. Some fusions (in music and in food) blend styles and ingredients such that the discrete elements are effaced. Partly perhaps because genre in television historically has been a useful way of informing and attracting viewers, and audiences might today be built by combining different genres which appeal to different market segments (see Nelson, 1996), some television mixes leave things in play. Thus "hybrid", if it is taken to imply a construct in which mixed ancestry is fused, is a less accurate term to denote the genre juxtapositions of some contemporary television products than "paratactics", indicating a setting-side-by-side which leaves the primary genres clearly visible but in play with each other.[14] Moreover, in the plant world, hybrids are typically sterile whilst my claim is that paratactics might be productive.

Parataxis has been associated with postmodern principles of composition and it may thus seem ironic to associate such a strategy with impacts such as hesitation and distanciation which were formulated by modernist formalists (Todorov, Brecht). But the construct here does not assume a political effectivity, it merely indicates that, in the frictions created in the play between one element and another, new ways of seeing may be mobilised. The principles of textual composition need to be analysed and located in the historical context of their transmission, as attempted in the discussion of specific examples in this book.

Quality issues

As the television apparatus has gone digital, with widescreen aspect ratios and digital surround sound, few would argue with the claim that TV production values generally have improved beyond the imaginings in the early days when a barely discernible black-and-white image on a twelve-inch monitor meant that television was scarcely more than vaguely illustrated radio. Beyond production values, however, any consensus in value judgements remains in dispute. As audiences, and their differing pleasures, have increasingly been seen to be a matter of niche markets rather than common currency, fragmentation of viewpoints has been emphasised in Cultural Studies more often than the common good. However, the debate about public service in relation to the commercial sector remains alive, particularly in the UK where the public service ethos is deep-rooted, if dislocated in recent years. Strong claims have recently been made, as noted, for "American Quality Television" in a highly commercial context. In marked contrast, John Caughie has recently (2000) re-made the case for at least being less dismissive about Adorno's negative aesthetic than Cultural Studies has typically been (see Chapter 7). Thus, the time is right for considering again the range of claims for quality and the bases of evaluation.

The principle of selection of examples in the book is one of "quality", not necessarily in my judgement but in claims made about each of my examples for different reasons by different constituencies. The selected examples have all been adjudged to be "quality" by groups and individuals, as will become apparent as the chapters unfold. Attention will be paid in particular in the discussion of examples in this book to the qualities of the texts – dramatic, cinematic and cultural. In Chapter 7, the overall question of the worth of TV dramas will be revisited with a view to bringing out more abstract issues of contemporary estimation. Though my starting-point differs from that of Caughie in that I look to explore the possibilities of "quality" TV drama in circumstances which are inescapably commercial, I share his avowed purpose of encouraging critical debate to afford 'a way of imagining a television and a television drama which still has the possibility of being other than it is' (2000: 233).

Summary

Overall, this book is concerned with identifying emergent aesthetic and cultural forms in TV3 and offering an account of the force-field of influences in which they arise: production and distribution circumstances, textual forms, reception and cultural values. Whilst recognising the impact of visual style, attention is paid to narrative forms as well as aspects of drama, as traditionally conceived. Structurally the book intersperses chapters discussing specific textual examples with chapters affording deeper consideration of contexts and issues. For reasons of space, the emphasis is on the Anglo-American axis, but the broad context of contemporary television production is recognised to be globalising in tendency. One of the tensions at the heart of the discussion, however, is that audiences worldwide are known to prefer local product, given the choice. Thus the book considers the possible capacities in drama output to continue to address the "national", "regional" and "geocultural" as localities in a market whose forces are increasingly transnational. A second core tension is between a narrative of loss and a narrative of plenitude. A digital–satellite, multichannel environment offers more programmes to those who can afford to access it, but whether if offers more choice and as varied a diet as possible remains in question. A diminution of quality in increasingly commercial circumstances is not, however, assumed at the outset. Rather the starting-point for investigation is that, ironically, TV3 may encourage quality product at the "high end" of drama output. What "quality" might signify in this context remains a question open for consideration.

Notes

1 In the Czech Republic, for instance, the two public service channels of *CeskaTelevize*, CT1 and CT2, are working to shake off their association with state-run television of the Soviet

era. Two commercial channels, Nova (since 1994) and Prima TV (since 2000) have introduced a broader range of programming, including some foreign imports, but are also investing heavily in home-produced drama (see www.radio.cz/en/issue/58027. As yet, satellite and cable penetration is limited to 8.9 per cent and 19.3 per cent respectively (see *Monitoring Television Across Europe: Czech Republic*) but foreign imports have proved attractive to viewers able to access them.

2 For example, 'Television without Frontiers' an EEC directive, dating from 1989, updated in 1997, and under review in 2005, requires television channels to reserve at least half their broadcasting time for films and programmes made in Europe.

3 For a discussion of these key concepts, see Holquist, 2002.

4 For further discussion of the impact and penetration of new satellite and encryption technologies, see Grant and Wood, 2004: 329 ff.

5 There are technological differences to be addressed: the television image is currently composed of interlaced lines of electrons whilst the computer screen image uses sequential lines. There is little doubt, however, that convergence between the two mediums is inevitable in the shorter, rather than longer, term.

6 At the Oxford Media Convention (19 January 2006), Andy Duncan, CEO of Channel 4, made a strong case for free digital spectrum (paralleling free analogue access) to be made available to Channel 4 as the second public service provider, besides the BBC.

7 Caldwell (1995: 288) suggests a reduction from 91 per cent to 63 per cent.

8 In the UK, for example, the BBC's new version of the classic serial *Bleak House* (2005) was shot on HDTV and the opportunity of the Summer 2006 World Cup was taken to intensify the marketing of HDTV-ready television sets, even though the encryption boxes were in short supply.

9 Tessa Jowell, UK Secretary of State for DCMS, has announced the phasing in of analogue switch-off between 2008 and 2012.

10 Local TV has increased potential as understanding of how to make a TV programme becomes commonplace and digital kit becomes increasingly cheap and easy to use. In the wake of Enzenberger's guerrilla video movement of the 1970s, there are new opportunities for more mainstream, but nevertheless contentious, uses of local TV. Across Europe, there is a City TV network which affords space for voices expressing alternatives to hegemonic political views. In the UK, Local TV experiments are under way (in Hereford, for example, see www.ruralmedia.co.uk). They are currently under the auspices of the BBC but may find increasing independence in the future.

11 This does not mean, of course, that soaps do not find favour beyond their culture of origin but that the pleasures taken might differ in different contexts. The seminal ethnographic work of Katz and Liebes (1985) and Ang (1985) on *Dallas* suggests different meanings and pleasures circulate in different cultural circumstances. Alternatively there may be a cultural resonance between producing and receiving culture as, perhaps, in the British preference for Australian soaps (e.g. *Neighbours* and *Home and Away*). Even where there is cultural resonance, the meanings and pleasures taken are likely to be differently inflected.

12 Where, in the past, a more direct relationship was evident between advertising and programming, as in the sponsorship of *Inspector Morse* by Tetley Tea Bags, association today is more by brand position than overt resonance. The top-of-the-range Renault Velsatis does not wish to be identified with the sink housing estate which is the location of *Shameless* but with the cutting-edge drama brand for which the series is taken to stand.

13 Todorov offers three conditions of the literary fantastic: 'First the text must oblige the reader to consider the world of the characters as a world of living persons and to hesitate between a natural and supernatural explanation of the events described. Secondly, this hesitation may also be experienced by the character, and at the same time the hesitation is represented, it becomes one of the themes of the work … Third, the reader must adopt a certain attitude with regard to the text: he will reject allegorical as well as poetic interpretations' (cited in Johnson, 2005: 59). For an account of Brecht in a postmodern context,

see Wright, 1989.

14 'Parataxis', literally, is a grammatical term denoting the juxtaposition of clauses in a sentence without the use of a conjunction.

2

Distinctive product: three kinds of quality
The Sopranos, Shooting the Past, Shameless

To open up – and to begin to ground – this study's concern with the worth and qualities of distinctive drama recently on television, this chapter takes three very different examples of TV3 drama output and considers them in turn, first from the point of view of their textual features and then in respect of the bases on which they might be valued. Such an approach involves a consideration of the text in terms of its qualities as drama and – in the light of the discussion of medium-specificity in Chapter 1 – also its visual and sonic presentation (even as quasi-cinema). Though the examples to be discussed, *The Sopranos*, *Shooting the Past* and *Shameless*, are very different, they do have features in common, each being inherently concerned with values, both televisual and cultural. Each develops in a new, sophisticated way the mixing of narrative form and genre characteristic of "high-end" drama in TV3. Each resonates with television culture and a broader cultural moment in television history and displays a self-reflexive awareness of television codes and conventions to appeal to a contemporary media-savvy audience. Collectively, the examples thus support and illustrate a contention that a broad characteristic of "high-end" television drama to have emerged in TV3 amounts to a distinctive contemporary televisual mode, discernible in very different manifestations.

Commentators have found contemporary TV drama not only difficult to classify but, at times, problematic in terms of viewing response. Extending the series–serial narrative hybrid, "high-end" television drama has evolved into a sophisticated dramatic mode, not just through its mix of stories with episodic closure and continuing serial stories but also through integration of formerly distinct televisual, musical, and cinematic modalities. By blurring the boundaries between what has been perceived historically as the appeal of soaps to women and the appeal of action-adventure to men (see Fiske, 1987 for example), *The Sopranos* successfully combines different modalities to create an advanced cultural form. *The Sopranos* has a strong soap-like, continuing family-narrative dimension and yet enters into dark psychological territory in exploring character whilst at the same time having an explicitly violent and sexually macho action-adventure disposition. *Shooting the Past* offers a wistful, some would say nostalgic, vision of a more humanist way of life and its values. But it is refracted – literally and metaphorically – through the camera lens of Oswald (Timothy Spall) as he documents his attempted suicide. Spall brings to the series by association with his previous television roles (notably as Barry in *Auf Wiedersehen, Pet*) a popular comic eccentricity which plays against any sentimental retrospection. *Shameless*, taken as a sitcom, has made many people laugh, but its social realist aspect has made them equally feel uncomfortable about what they are laughing at.

Though, as noted in Chapter 1, it could well be argued that historically there have been occasional examples of complex and even mixed-mode dramas, the disposition towards distinctive drama under the production circumstances of TV3 exploits advanced paratactics and hybridity, as illustrated by the three very different examples for consideration. Even though the primary production impetus might be commercial in terms of targeting markets or aggregating different microcultures through aspects which appeal to each target segment, the times are disposed towards complexity and sophistication at the "high end" of contemporary TV drama.

In respect of the second aspect of this chapter, various evaluative traditions will emerge from the discussion, some related to what might be seen as features of traditional drama (storytelling based on character in specific circumstances), some related to different cultural–aesthetic traditions (for example, the American predilection for glossy romance and action-adventure as compared with the British tradition of social realism), and others emergent in TV3 (hybrids of cinema's visual narrative modes and/or popular music with historically distinctive televisual use of word, sound and image). Taking a step further back to a critical distance, it will become possible ultimately to locate these specific qualities and criteria in broader traditions of evaluation, but that wider view will not fully be achieved until Chapter 7.

The Sopranos (HBO, 1999–2007)

Textual mode and form

In form, *The Sopranos* (*Sopranos*) is a generic hybrid of the mafia gangster movie genre with psychological drama and soap. Akass and McCabe have noted that *Sopranos* brings into play a gangster genre traditionally hostile to women (constructed in terms of the angel/whore binary) with other narrative spaces involving strong, complex women, notably psychologist Dr Jennifer Melfi, and Carmela, Tony Soprano's wife. They note a collision of the gangster genre with the soap opera in a series in which 'the mobster finds himself in unfamiliar generic territory characterized by mundane chores and domestic worries … The narrative structure demands that Tony relinquish mob violence and function within feminine – and feminising – spaces' (2002: 147).

For some time, both cinema and television have aimed to achieve future success by taking the box-office attractions of two or more modes and combining them. Some television hybrids in particular have been commercial successes by this means, despite being critically questionable (see Nelson, 1997 on *Heartbeat*). Indeed, a commercially, rather than artistically, motivated form of the hybridity disposition is satirised in Robert Altman's *The Player* (1992). However, given appropriate production circumstances, there is no reason in principle why generic and narrative hybrids should not develop paratactically into sophisticated new modes, and *Sopranos* affords a case in point. Taking one of television's most successful narrative forms with opportunities for strong female roles and combining it with one of cinema's most successful macho genres, not only does *Sopranos* offer a broad appeal across genders but, by bringing two traditionally gendered narrative forms in tension, it invites an interesting narrative mix affording complex characterisation and challenging thematic concerns.

A further distinctive feature of *Sopranos* – and perhaps the dimension which bridges the two apparently opposite genres – is the series' exploration of the psyche of its protagonist, Anthony (Tony) Soprano, in greater depth than the texts of any of its gangster influences. In very early episodes, signs of a disturbed consciousness are evident in Tony's excessive anger and self-questioning remarks and his state of mind is further foregrounded through the device of him visiting a 'shrink', Dr Jennifer Melfi. The scenes of analysis take *Sopranos* into territory beyond the mob movie and, in terms of depth of character, beyond most soaps. Indeed, the key aspect of hybridity to distinguish *Sopranos* is its capacity to sustain a mobster-movie dynamic and yet explore character – particularly in the case of its protagonist – to considerable psychological depth. Since, echoing the nineteenth-century realist novel, *Sopranos* locates the agency of its protagonist in social structure, that of the New Jersey mafia, it might afford Tony Soprano's development in response to experience. However, whilst there are shifts in his attitudes, any fundamental change in character would undermine the premise of the series. Industrial constraints on the television form might thus militate against substantial character development, privileging instead an unresolved play of one element against another. The latter feature is mobilised in *Sopranos* by the strong women who, as Akass and McCabe have noted, claim narrative space of their own in conflict with the macho mobsters. The mix moves the series into the territory of a particular kind of "quality TV", allowing existential shadows to play across its surface gloss. Amidst the well-shot suburban New Jersey affluence, Tony frequently expresses a deep anxiety about the purpose of life. 'If all this shit's for nothing', he remarks to Melfi, 'then why do I got to think about it?' ('Denial, anger, acceptance', 1: 3).

The narrative economy of soap, as Jane Feuer has long since remarked, involves a tendency towards 'integration into a happy family … a balance between harmony and disharmony but no one couple can remain in a state of integration' (Feuer et al., 1986: 113). The televisual success of the soap form lies in its capacity for open, continuing, multiple-plot, serial narratives and, historically, in its association with matriarchs. In mobster movies, in contrast, the alpha male *capo* heads the family and the stories, in cinematic mode, are complete in themselves. Thus, in combining the two forms, there is an integral conflict over who heads the family and between narrative closure and continuing seriality. Though *Sopranos* has a clear protagonist in Tony, his character is set at the head of two families, one a close, if conflicted, kinship family particularly involving Livia, Tony's mother, Carmela, his wife, Meadow and young Anthony, his children, and Janice (aka Parvati), his sister. The Italian–American kinship family primarily affords the soap environment, with the domestic tension between Carmela and Tony structurally built in. But family tensions are replicated in the second, extended family – Tony's mafia crew.

Part kin, part "work-friends" family, the crew affords, in the context of *Sopranos'* particular television hybrid, some domestic aspects as well as gangster action. Internecine feuds between different mobster factions are a characteristic of the movie genre and there are such challenges to Tony's leadership within *Sopranos*. But one of the key malcontents to dispute Tony's right to be *capo* is his ageing uncle. Indeed, rather than there being two discrete strands, one playing out gangster tropes and the other domestic, there is a continuum between the two as, on one level, Tony's crew is a family. Indeed, it includes his close blood relatives Uncle Junior, Tony's father's brother, and Christopher Moltisanto, his nephew. Some of the business of both families is conducted in Tony's New Jersey home and the recognisable, up-market suburban domesticity of the one family lends credibility to the movie trope of the other, as they intermingle. Tony endeavours to keep the less savoury aspects of his "waste disposal" business away from his close family, particularly his children, but it has a tendency to seep back. Some emphasis is placed upon relationships along the continuum, including everyday loyalties and betrayals. Thus, in developing the hybrid, the soap elements have not simply been juxtaposed with the gangster elements but, since both have a family basis, aspects of the narrative mode of the former have readily folded back into the latter.

Sopranos undoubtedly has a heritage in cinema, perhaps owing more to *Goodfellas* than *The Godfather*, as has been argued (see Pattie 2002). But, as a long-running, multinarrative, drama, *Sopranos* takes advantage of television's now highly developed series serial hybrid form, which elsewhere I have dubbed "flexi-narrative" (see Nelson, 1997). As Creeber has remarked:

> With its combination of a continuous narrative structure contained within a clearly defined narrative arc, it [the series-serial hybrid] allows television to exploit its tendency towards 'intimacy' and 'continuity' yet without dispensing with the power and possibilities offered by its gradual movement and progression towards narrative closure and conclusion. (2004a: 9)

Thus, over time, regular viewers can build up a sense of an intimate knowledge of Tony and Carmela Soprano as their marriage comes under strain and falls apart in the wake of Tony's destructive tendencies, such that there is a strong, close-up, continuing serial dimension to viewing, offering a version of the pleasures of soap intimacy. The soap elements are sophisticated dramatically in that the scope of the continuing serial narrative is used to explore character in depth, and the relationship between Tony and Jennifer Melfi, and the comparative reactions of Jennifer and Carmela to Tony, have proved particularly fascinating to many viewers (see Akass and McCabe (eds), 2002: 152–157). Though many everyday soaps have developed this capacity to be used from time to time, their place in the competitive schedule, and the drive for ratings with which they are typically associated, tends towards melodrama and the foregrounding of rapidly rotated narrative segments over character. The production treatment and the distribution outlet of *Sopranos* (see below), in contrast, have afforded the development of a regular television form to new heights of sophistication.

In becoming on one level a sophisticated soap, however, on another level *Sopranos* retains the attractions of a gangster movie. As one viewer might derive continuing serial-narrative pleasures from *Sopranos* as noted, a more casual viewer might catch one episode and primarily experience a story arc, complete in itself, involving high-action mobsters, and have a quasi-cinematic experience, as if they had watched, say, *Goodfellas*. For one aspect of *Sopranos* does sustain all the elements of the Mafia-gangster genre: male bonding; a sense of community; strong, but questionably reliable, loyalty amongst the crew; unpredictable violence, some of it arising from internecine feuds; sexually available women; a sense of style; family values in an Italian Catholic tradition; strong cinematic imagery. The generic pleasures and the pleasure of closure are available. But a significant difference from its cinematic predecessors, is *Sopranos'* characters' overt knowledge of those movies which gives the series a self-conscious quality. Indeed, a sense of the loss of the former days when the secrecy of *omertá* and adherence to a strict code of conduct and values was notionally sacrosanct is articulated through the older generation's veneration for *The Godfather I and II*.[1] Having watched again the DVDs of the movies prior to a sentimental visit to Naples, the less perceptive of Tony's generals try to sustain the myth of the old school in an episode entitled 'Commendatori' (2: 17).

'Commendatori' focuses largely upon mobster business and issues and involves a story arc complete in itself shaped by the trip to Naples which ends with the crew's home-coming. In Naples, Tony Soprano is outraged that he has to deal 'with 'a fuckin' woman boss' ('Commendatori', 2: 17), but he knows in his heart of hearts that things are not – and perhaps never were – as they are constructed in the ideal cinematic representations of Mafia mythology. *Sopranos* typically points up such contradictions obliquely, as it does in this episode. For example, discovering that the prostitute he has hired in Naples comes from his ancestral village, Paulie Walnuts does not himself see the situational irony in his claims to kinship with her when he remarks that 'our families probably knew each other' (Commendatori, 2: 17) but the irony is made available for viewers to pick up on. Set in the context of the overall soap structure in which many viewpoints – and, particularly in the context of gangster genre, those of women – are made available, the regret expressed in 'Commendatori' for a lost time when women might be constructed as passive recipients of the male gaze rather than as agents, is subverted in the very process of it being reaffirmed. Thus, even in an episode predominantly set in Naples which focuses upon Mafia, rather than domestic, action, a counter-perspective to the macho disposition of most gangster movies is also in play.

A reading is possible from an entrenched, traditional male position which might take some comfort from the articulation of resistance to the effacement of the macho–masculine values in this episode. Such "masculinity" may be reinforced by the more summary achievements of goals through the violent assertion in *Sopranos* of male ego and power in many episodes. But the achievement of this reading position could only be at the expense of playing down another strand of the 'Commendatori' episode. Whilst the mob is away in Naples, Carmela is involved in another narrative aiming to persuade her friend, Angie, not to pursue a divorce. Hugging Angie, Carmela asserts, 'In the end, I know you're not going to leave him' (Commendatori, 2: 17). Whatever the marital outcome, however, Carmela knows that the romantic ideals of love are a sham, just as Tony has recognised in this episode that the myth of Naples is empty. Once again, this is obliquely conveyed – there to be read, rather than overtly stated. In a final close-up, Carmela's sad expression is ironically juxtaposed with the strains of an aria from a romantic opera.

A wide range of music is used both diegetically and non-diegetically in *Sopranos*, though the emphasis is on the judicious use of popular music tracks ranging from Frank Sinatra to the Eurythmics. The beat – of the signature soundtrack, for example – lends an energy and cutting rhythm to the series but music is otherwise seldom used merely to underscore the dramatic mood. The relationships between the soundtrack and the visuals is complex and frequently multilayered, typically functioning either ironically to comment on the action, or to point up a character's interior thoughts and feelings of which at times they may be unaware. Thus the soundtrack is an element in the overall multitracking of the production, consciously played like the various narrative modes against other elements. Indeed, the wistfulness of Sinatra's 'It was a very good year' played at length over a protracted sequence of relative inaction is only sustainable because it has a range of possible resonances apprehensible by viewers rather than the characters themselves. Similarly, Carmela's love of opera cannot be taken simply to express romantic aspirations which the reality of her life with Tony does not fulfil (though it does function on that level) but, as in the example above, her assertion of values in defiance of her knowledge of the world is more complicated. Carmela knows of Tony's infidelities, she knows of the Bada Bing dancers, she knows that there are circumstances under which even a Catholic wife may not be able to stay with her husband such that the heartfelt emotion of opera arias cannot be taken as a naïve means of escape. As with her express adherence to a Catholicism which rings hollow in her New Jersey circumstances, it is as if Carmela posits values where none can be assumed.

The subtlety of the use of music is part of *Sopranos*' distinctive production style which extends to the visual treatment. As noted, the fast pace and high temperature of today's television drama is achieved largely through the rapid intercutting of several storylines in any given episode. Assuming an advanced level of television literacy, cuts are made from high point to high point in each narrative to keep up the overall temperature. By intercutting the different modalities of the gangster genre, soaps and psychological drama, *Sopranos* is able to sustain intensity of interest but vary the tempo. Scenes of high action with a highly mobile camera are juxtaposed with domestic moments or sessions of analysis based in dialogue in shot-reverse shot. The Mafia environment and ambience are conveyed by the roving camera such that glimpses of half-naked women are cut in almost in passing as characters move across the Bada Bing space, the strip joint which is the front for Tony's office. Likewise, the overt showing of sexual acts is frequent but not dwelt upon, being swiftly intercut as part of the camera's restless roving through the New Jersey territory. Sequences such as these, and those involving travel in cars across the neighbourhood, are used to inject pace in counterpoint to the more static scenes of dialogue in the counselling room, home, office or restaurant. With its cinematic aspirations, HBO funds *Sopranos* at a level to achieve the stylishness of the carefully composed and edited film. In editing, very sharp cuts are made from the core of one scene slap into the high, often violent, action of another.

The dialogue itself is as sharp and streetwise as the camera style, arguably introducing a greater level of realism than hitherto. Above all, it is low-key and oblique, with the characters unable to articulate that understanding of themselves and their predicament which marks more regular, formulaic drama which feels the need to be explanatory. *Sopranos*, in contrast, trusts its target audience to be teleliterate and to gain pleasure from working things out and dealing with ambiguities rather than having everything narratively and ideologically closed. A particular feature of the dialogue is *Sopranos'* demotic use of the expletives in New Jersey speech patterns which the constraints of broadcast television have previously kept from the small screen. But with subscription television sitting outside the regulatory framework of broadcast TV, free rein is given to ripe language. Common phrases such as 'fuck you, you cock-sucker' are not merely reserved for the gangsters, being used even by Dr Jennifer Melfi when her own counsellor gets too near the bone (in 'Big girls don't cry', 2: 18). The dialogue is on occasion overtly witty and by no means politically correct, with Tony Soprano afforded some of the sharpest lines. When Richie Aprile takes up again with Janice (Parvati) Soprano, having served his time in jail, he tells a sceptical Tony that he and Janice 'got history together', to which Tony quips, 'Yeah. Israel and fuckin' Palestine.' When he visits a pulverised Beansie held together by a kind of scaffolding in hospital, Tony asks, 'Pick up the BBC on that or what?' ('Toodle-fucking-oo', 2: 16). But Tony does not have a monopoly on drollery. In the same episode, Uncle Carrado 'Junior' Soprano remarks of the Feds' avid pursuit of him, 'They're so far up my arse, they taste Brylcreem.'

Televisual and cultural values

To describe *Sopranos*, David Lavery adopts the metaphor of an elephant, an organism difficult to see as a whole but apprehensible from different angles by different observers. Though, evidently, *Sopranos* has meant many things to many people coming at it from a range of angles (see Lavery, 2002: xi-xviii), and acknowledging that actual readings of any television are made from historically and culturally situated reading positions, it is nevertheless possible from a critical distance to identify features of a text likely to resonate in given socio-historical circumstances and *Sopranos* will be addressed below in these terms. Though it is not possible to point to the textual features of any given example and to infer its "meaning", it is possible to impute that there are limitations to the potential of texts which are formulaic and produced in standard modes without any particular style, wit or innovative modality. That is not to say, as noted in Chapter 1, that standard fare is not pleasurable, entertaining and worthwhile. It is to say that sophisticated textual forms are constructed in ways which create space for "writerly" (Barthes's 1977 term) negotiations. Such texts do not follow the tendency of formulaic television to close down readings and contain them within a frame of normative social values but invite a dialogue which, at best, requires viewers to refocus their own ways of seeing by disturbing their bearings. It has often been assumed that the medium of television is poor in this capacity but the aim of this book is in part to contribute to dispelling such a myth.

Most episodes of *Sopranos* interweave several story arcs in parallel in a long-established method of multiple-plot drama. For example, 'The happy wanderer' (2: 19) runs the story of Tony's taking over his father's and Uncle Junior's 'executive game' of high-stakes poker (featuring Frank Sinatra Jnr) intercut with the story of Meadow's appearance in the school show motivated by her aim of achieving a place at a good college. Other arcs are on-going, for example Tony's feud with Richie Aprile and his consultations with Dr Melfi, resumed towards the end of Season 2. Structural features of this mode of storytelling invite thematic comparisons. Davey Scatino, a childhood friend of Tony, bumps into the Sopranos when he accompanies his son, Eric, to a college open day just as Tony is accompanying Meadow. Davey owes Richie Aprile significant sums of money but he nevertheless muscles in on the 'executive game' where he loses heavily and finds himself seriously in debt to Tony who is doubly angry with Davey since he did not want him to get involved in a game out of his league. In desperation to find repayment cash, Davey gives Tony his son's truck in part-payment and Tony, in turn, gives it to Meadow. Her rejection of such a tarnished gift does not assuage the anger of Eric, who refuses at the last minute to sing a planned duet with Meadow in the school show. Ironically, Meadow gets to sing a solo as she had always wanted and the episode ends with this, causing Davey and his wife to leave the auditorium to the seemingly inappropriate soundtrack of 'The Happy Wanderer'.

Earlier in the episode in his session with Melfi, however, Tony refers to a guy whistling as he walks down the street with a clear conscience as 'the happy wanderer' and, later, Melfi reminds Tony that he does not describe himself as such. The inscribed connections between the strands of such multinarrative episodes, pointed up as they are by the soundtrack, visual ironies or intertextual resonances, give the sense that the episode is more than the sum of its parts, though they by no means amount to either narrative or thematic closure. Those readers who take some deeper significance from *Sopranos* are encouraged so to do by this sense of a deliberately constructed textual weft, even though no single "message" is offered.

Any formal narrative closure in an episode of *Sopranos* typically remains in tension with broader thematic uncertainties which lend the text its not fully articulated, but perhaps dominant, trope. When the text is set in the reading context of late twentieth- and early twenty-first-century Anglo-American culture, the disquiet of affluent life in a postmodern world lacking sincerity and shared values resonates throughout the series. This disquiet may be differently inflected for different viewers. To pick up on the binary gendering with which this discussion opened, traditional "masculinity" has been undermined by the emergence of women to relative power. Like the AB1 males at whom *Sopranos* is perhaps primarily aimed, Tony Soprano apparently has it all. He is extremely affluent. He has family. He lives in a mansion with a swimming-pool, he eats in the best restaurants and he drives expensive cars. He has a stack of cash in his pocket which he unrolls as necessity arises. He carries all the hallmarks of success as defined in the USA. And yet he is unfulfilled, unhappy. His doubts, like those of many males with established careers based on making money at the expense of others, concern the apparent pointlessness of it all and a fear of death without achievement. 'I'm not afraid of death, not if it's for something', he remarks ('Denial, anger, acceptance', 1: 3).

Tony's anxieties manifest themselves in his behaviour. His anger, as Carmela points out to him, is always dangerously close to the surface and excessive when it erupts. Tony admits to Melfi, 'I'm not a husband to my wife, I'm not a father to my kids, I'm not a friend to my friends, I'm nothing' ('Isabella', 1: 12). At worst, his condition renders him dysfunctional. He has panic attacks in which he cannot breathe to the point where he passes out. His situation is life-threatening in that he has blacked out whilst driving and was lucky to escape alive. There is a substantial irony at the heart of *Sopranos* in that the life of a Mafia boss is in greatest danger not from those many people who have scores to settle with him but from his own anxiety syndrome.

In inviting a comparison between Tony Soprano and his counterpart successful males in the target audience, I do not suggest that the viewers are gangsters but that an important resonance of the TV series is with their plight at the turn of the twenty-first century. The very economic system of global pan-capitalism which informs the making of television in TV3 impacts powerfully on the AB1 males whom *Sopranos* aims primarily to attract. The pressures to perform economically create precisely those tensions experienced by Tony Soprano, at the same time as a traditional sense of "masculinity" is eroded. More time needs to be spent at work being more competitive in order to succeed in business, at the expense of spending quality time with wives and families. To make a profit in highly competitive markets, successful business people are obliged exponentially to squeeze their customers.

In Harvey's (1989) analysis, late capitalism functions by circulating, at an ever-increasing pace, services which must, of economic necessity, be satisfying only in the short term. Though the series offers one causal account of Tony Soprano's anxieties as being inherited from his father, the elusiveness of the syndrome might resonate with the audience as a metaphor for the contemporary life of AB1s. On the one hand affirming a feeling of "male" power through the imagery of expensive clothes, cars, sexually available women and swiftly executed "justice", *Sopranos* offers a counterpoint narrative of pressure and failure in terms of those very values on which social success is notionally modelled. Though appearing to be in control, Tony Soprano and his target viewers 'want to be in total control' ('Big girls don't cry', 2: 18) and know full well that they are not and cannot be. In contrast to the macho affirmation offered by traditional gangster movies, the prime target audience has found in Tony Soprano an anti-hero for its times, but in a vehicle which is nevertheless similar in many respects to its predecessors.

Despite their treatment at the hands of their men, the key women in *Sopranos* afford, in contrast, positive role models in that, by various means, they achieve a significant measure of control over their lives As Akass and McCabe summarise: 'Carmela has got her own way; she is the real power behind Tony Soprano. Far from being trapped by the all-embracing patriarchal structures, she has found solutions that work to her advantage' (2002: 154). Carmela's position resonates with post-feminist times, just as Tony's predicament resonates with contemporary maleness. Though Tony, in the vein of a typical bourgeois father, reminds Meadow that, 'everything in this family house comes from the work that I do' ('The happy wanderer'), Carmela accepts her economically dependent status but uses it to her advantage. At different times, she uses whatever means are at her disposal – money, sexuality or her position of power derived from being wife to the *capo* – to get what she wants. Whether, as Akass and Mccabe see it, her 'conscience is cleared by her Catholicism' (2002/ 155), she seems less in self-doubt than her husband. Indeed a key difference between Tony and Carmela is that she seems able largely to live by inherited values that she knows have little provenance, whilst Tony cannot accept a world without immanent values. Hence her relative calm and his seething anger. In the terms of the philosopher Richard Rorty, Carmela is able to posit values in a context of postmodern relativism whilst Tony remains tortured by a modernist existentialist angst, unable to take a leap of faith.[2]

Shooting the Past (1999, BBC1)

Textual mode and form

Shooting the Past (*StP*) is not obviously a generic hybrid like *Sopranos*, though it would appear challenging to classify. One internet DVD sales site (IMDb) classifies it as 'History/Drama' whilst another (Rotten Tomatoes) offers 'Mystery/Suspense,

Drama (General), British Television'. Whilst there are elements of mystery and suspense and a sense of history, it is perhaps the last characteristic, 'British Television', which best affords a clue to the textual mode and form of *StP*. In the context of this chapter, it also marks a contrast with the idea of "American Quality TV". For, if one characteristic of the latter is the dynamic pace of action-adventure or at least a snappy editing rhythm and a highly mobile camera, *StP* exemplifies the opposite, since Stephen Poliakoff consciously aimed to make "slow" television. In a BBC profile of the writer/director entitled *Shooting the Present* (directed by Louise Turley, BBC, 2001), Poliakoff reveals that in making *StP*, he had been 'interested in how short scenes had become on television' (BBC, 2001). He is well aware of the tendency towards the fast-moving, high-temperature TV drama, characterised as "flexi-narrative" (Nelson, 1997), and proposed instead to 'slow television down to the point that it stops … [with] scenes so long that they seem ridiculous' (BBC, 2001). Indeed, *StP* includes a number of long, conversational scenes reminiscent of old-fashioned theatre in their requirement of the actors to realise them in a single take. In addition, it includes a number of sequences involving Close-Ups of black-and-white, still photographs.

Poliakoff's aim was to draw viewers into the narrative, hoping 'to compel people in that way' (BBC, 2001) and, in the words of a *Sunday Times* review, he produced a 'meditation on the nature of photographic images, a celebration of old-world English eccentricity at threat in a world of high-technology glossiness, and a reminder that nothing in our heritage is sacred'.[3] The idea of English eccentricity coupled with the classification 'British Television' above, invites an exploration of *StP* in terms of its lineage in British TV drama which, historically, has been valued for its one-off single plays, innovative in form or strong on social realism, with space to explore in depth the idiosyncracies of character. We shall return to this estimation below, having marked that *StP* may have a taproot in the theatre heritage of the single play. First, what might be termed Poliakoff's dramatic method and his cinematic treatment needs to be unpacked.

StP is a three-part mini-serial drama, shot on film on location, telling the story of the threat of dissolution to a photographic library located in an eighteenth-century mansion just to the west of London. Establishing shots of the house surrounded by a deer park briefly evoke the television genre of "period" or "heritage" drama. However, in *StP* it is not the furniture and fittings, the bonnets and the couture which ultimately create visual interest but still photographs in black and white. The library's photographic collection has developed piecemeal from the days when a philanthropic insurance company founded an educational establishment. It has continued to run on a small-scale commercial basis until the present moment, 21 December 1999, when the insurance company has finally sold the estate. An American foundation has bought the building and plans quickly to convert it into a cutting-edge business school, 'the American School for Business for the 21st Century'.

Despite its proximity to England's capital city and its links with the contemporary media industries to which it supplies images, the library appears to inhabit a past age. The pace of its life and its antiquated customs are evident, for example, in the catering service: where many contemporary professionals have time at best to snatch a lunchtime sandwich at their desks, the library staff sit down together for 'a full, sit-down service', multicourse lunch on a daily basis. A breakfast service is also available on their arrival at work and there is time reserved for 'elevenses' and tea in the afternoons. The small staff comprises the librarian Marilyn Truman (Lyndsay Duncan), her chief assistant Oswald Bates (Timothy Spall), an ageing secretary, Veronica (Billie Whitelaw), two younger assistants, Spig (Emilia Fox) and Nick (Blake Ritson), and Garnett (Arj Barker), the head of a small group of catering staff.

The catering provision serves iconically to represent a past, more leisured, age, preserved from the outside world until the American buyers arrive in their digital interconnectedness with laptop PCs, mobile phones and pagers. They bristle with efficiency in their dark suits and striped ties, aiming to keep to a hectic schedule. They are welcomed and ushered by the team – including a dishevelled Oswald Bates, shuffling in white plimsolls (sneakers), his shirt half hanging out of his trousers – into a large, book-lined room. The grand dining-table is laden with 'a full elevenses' including Californian wine and doughnuts for the occasion. The Americans, whose mind-set is business-oriented and who want to get on, are unimpressed. Thus one dramatic conflict at the core of *StP* pits an apparently shambling old world against the new spirit of a contemporary business school with a digital knowledge base and systems management. This is in marked contrast with the library's card-based, idiosyncratic records system which depends to a large extent – as emerges when the narrative unfolds – on Bates's detailed knowledge of the library's contents and his visual memory. Besides the visual presentation, the dialogue points up the impression of outdatedness, with Marilyn Truman remarking, 'What sleepy people we must appear', and Bates subsequently observing that they must seem like 'pathetic, dusty people who have just stepped out of an Ealing Comedy with Margaret Rutherford'. As with much of Poliakoff's work, however, first impressions mask a more complex scenario to be unfolded.

It rapidly emerges, in an interview between Marilyn Truman and Christopher Anderson (Liam Cunningham) and his assistant, Styeman (Andy Serkis), that the Americans plan to strip the building within days. Letters confirming this situation and the expectation that the library has been packed up ready to be disbanded have apparently been signed by one Oswald Bates, unbeknown to Marilyn Truman. Bates denies all knowledge of any such letters. Thus the dramatic conflict between two worlds is sharply focused by the Americans' insistence that the library must go within four days and Miss Truman's absolute refusal to break up the collection and sell off only the most valuable photographs. At one point she is afforded just five minutes between mobile phone calls to resolve the dilemma.

The situation seems impossible but Bates announces over lunch that he has a plan. Drawing on the historical precedent of an incident at Austerlitz, he suggests that they 'do something truly perverse to make them doubt our sanity'. When the Americans return for an answer to the dilemma, he proposes, they should find the staff 'still here, eating a formal meal' such that they recognise that 'they are dealing with irrational people'. His theory supposes that business people thrive on the fear involved in 'deadlines, hirings and firings'. If the library team 'remove fear from the equation' by continuing serenely with their formal lunch, the Americans will be unnerved because, Bates says (in a mock-American accent), 'those assholes: they could do anything'. As it happens, when the Americans return, the team are taking tea in a plant-fringed conservatory. In the absence of other options, Bates's plan appears to be operating by default.

By the end of Part 1, Marilyn Truman has secured a week over the Christmas period to find a buyer for the collection by impressing Christopher Anderson with its worth. Bates – despite having astounded Anderson by producing within five seconds of the request a photograph of Anderson's street, Lemonia Avenue, in his hometown, Emporia, Virginia – is required to leave the building never to return. To some extent, his strategy of appearing to be 'a fruitcake', along with his ambiguously comic threats to burn down the building, has worked. He apparently has to go but, as he observes, 'That's what they think!'

On the face of it, a three-part mini-series of almost 180 minutes' duration about the closure of a library is scarcely the kind of project to excite television executives or draw schedulers to the edge of their seats. In a contemporary television world it is axiomatic, as noted, that viewers' attention must be grabbed in the first forty seconds and then held with fast-moving, high-temperature action. For Poliakoff, then, *StP* is effectively a dramatic experiment in the humanist, individualist tradition, the content of the piece being imbricated within its form. The power of Bates's human knowledge and visually retentive and connective brain is pitted against the forces of a new technological milieu championing instrumental efficiency of performance over idiosyncratically insightful humanism. Though *StP* is not ultimately nationalistic in the manner of Old England standing firm against American incursions, the conservative aspects of the library and its culture are intended to evoke aspects of a British culture under threat. Similarly, the treatment of the material is, as noted, consciously in conflict with the trends of contemporary TV drama which might be said to be influenced by the USA (see Chapter 5).

Defiant of easy postmodern assumptions, Poliakoff contests the received view about limited attention spans that 'life moves so fast now and people can concentrate for less' (BBC, 2001). Indeed, the aim of *StP* is to demonstrate that audiences can still be gripped and held by good stories about characters who become increasingly interesting as their narratives unfold because their backstories or interior lives complicate the first given impression. As Timothy Spall remarks, there are 'people you think you recognise … certain types … but they completely confound your expectations' (BBC, 2001). In respect of character, Poliakoff works not with the glamour and celebrity which particularly typifies most high-profile "American Quality television" but with the superficially ordinary. He has a strong conviction, as he remarked in respect of *Perfect Strangers*, 'that there are at least three good stories in every family' and he is himself particularly interested in 'characters who are trying to be individual' (BBC, 2001) in resisting forces of change with a homogenising tendency which threatens to rationalise their specificity. As he puts it, he values 'people who resist being dragged into the world of mass culture' (DVD *StP* feature).

The treatment of character in Poliakoff effectively amounts to a distinctive dramatic method. Unlike more formulaic drama in which character traits are re-affirmed for the sake of clarity, characters are revealed throughout Poliakoff's work to be other than they at first appear. In *StP*, Oswald Bates's shambling eccentricities of appearance and behaviour belie a highly intelligent individual with exceptional qualities of observation and a capacity for making imaginative connections which fuse poetry with Holmesian deduction. In spite of his deceit in concealing the correspondence from the Americans which precipitates the library crisis and his policy of resistance through a dogged non-compliance, he ultimately saves the photo collection through his extraordinariness. The avowedly unworldly Marilyn Truman rises by degrees to the occasion as she attempts against all odds to find a buyer for the entire collection of photographs and almost succeeds in persuading a thrusting advertising executive of its worth. Though she cannot agree long term to Bates's more devious strategy of concealing the most valuable photographs in the collection, she is equally as adamant as he is that the collection cannot be split up. Obliquely challenged by Bates, she ultimately finds in herself a power of storytelling sufficient to persuade Christopher Anderson that the collection must be saved. As Anderson remarks of the shy librarian in a recognition illustrative of Poliakoff's theory of character, 'You're great. A very passionate person – and a wonderful story-teller' (Part 3). Indeed, where *StP* is successful in drawing viewers in, Truman's powers of narration within *StP* bear out those of Poliakoff in the piece overall.

Part of Marilyn Truman's capacity is reciprocally to recognise in Anderson himself qualities beyond his surface appearance as a typically go-getting American businessman, smart and polite but not allowing anything to stand in the way of his sense of progress. Once the intrigues of his grandmother's past have ultimately been revealed to him (Part 3), Anderson undergoes a Damascus moment when there surfaces in his very being a dimension of which he had been vaguely aware but never fully conscious. The power of narrative has unsettled his being and when he observes 'Out of nowhere, I have a new history' (Part 3), it is clear that his future life will be fundamentally different as a consequence of the story he has just heard. Poliakoff's philosophy of character and narrative is thus made manifest in *StP*. Through Anderson's experience, Poliakoff demonstrates the power of narrative within the frame and lends conviction to the improbable on a small, but highly significant, scale. Beyond the frame he aims to hold a television audience and convince its members of the worth of specific individual lives and, indeed, the potential narratives in us all. As Spall puts it, 'Poliakoff is the great dramatist of "I've got a story to tell"' (DVD *StP* feature).

But, whilst *StP* does depend substantially on its own humanist–narrative compulsion, it would be a mistake to overlook other, more media-savvy, strategies adopted in its compositional principles. Instead of grabbing the audience with a fast-edited summary of backstory or a prefiguration of episode highlights, *StP* opens, after the "heritage"- establishing shots noted above, with Timothy Spall's direct address to camera in close-up. Spall brings with him a reputation of strong performances of fascinatingly eccentric characters as well as in the art house projects of Mike Leigh. In another instance of "serious entertainment" (see Chapter 1), his presence connotes popular comic as well as "serious" drama, potentially attracting viewers from across a broad spectrum.

In a framing device, Bates actually addresses the television camera directly since, as he relates, he does not own a video camera. He is documenting 'the last afternoon of [his] life' through audio recording on an old tape machine and intermittent still photographs, taken remotely with an SLR camera. Thus Bates captures the viewers' attention and sets up a narrative tension with the notion that he is about to commit suicide as a result of the 'extraordinary events that have happened'. Bates implicitly confronts the perceived need for TV drama to start at high temperature, asking viewers, 'A chubby man wearing a cardigan, talking into a tape machine -how can that be urgent?' Why should we care? Or rather, why should you care?' Having posed viewers this direct challenge, Bates answers his own question: 'Anybody who has suddenly lost their home or business, or been overlooked for promotion … this is for you.' Poliakoff, then, whilst defying the fast-action, attention-grabbing openings of most contemporary TV series, finds his own equivalent means of arresting and keeping the viewers' attention in the opening moments. Subsequently, the device of Bates talking directly to camera is used to develop the narrative and comment on the action as well as extending an intimacy with his persona and predicament.

Casting Lindsay Duncan opposite Spall on the one hand and Liam Cunningham on the other, though it might avoid the charge of celebrity box-office attraction, is designed to draw audience. Duncan, like Spall, has an association with "serious" drama but with a popular edge. Telegenic as ever, her vulnerable but sexy, blonde image is impressively juxtaposed with Irish-born Cunningham's tall, dark figure. Both performers have the sensibility to convey depth of character as they are required to do in *StP*. Building on his primary casting, Poliakoff both exploits and subverts another dominant aspect of popular drama, namely romance. It would be too simple to say that the attraction between Marilyn Truman and Christopher Anderson is primarily sexual, though there is a frisson from their first meeting as they engage in an underplayed battle for power over the situation, Truman playing for time and Anderson demanding immediate closure of the library. The closest the narrative takes them to a sexual relationship is towards the end of Part 2 when, having failed by a narrow margin to convince the advertising executive to buy the collection, Truman invites herself to dinner with Anderson and, in her own understated, middle-class English way, dresses to impress, if not to kill. At dinner, Anderson remarks on Truman's desirability and acknowledges that, despite being a happily married man, he finds her attractive. A commercially oriented, mainstream drama could scarcely have resisted the opportunity for a sexual affair, but the point of Truman's seduction lies elsewhere: she wants Anderson to buy the collection.

Poliakoff, in an interview, admired *West Wing* amongst "American Quality TV" for avoiding sex after Episode 1. He takes a particular satisfaction as a writer/director in holding an audience without resorting to the overworn tropes of sex, or even romance. When Truman and Anderson finally embrace towards the end of Part 3, the moment is densely layered emotionally and dramatically. Following the extraordinary revelations about Anderson's family past, the moment is triggered when Anderson learns by telephone that Oswald Bates has not in fact died – as Truman believes she has overheard – but has actually shown some improvement. Truman's relief in an admixture of elation, sorrow, guilt and pleasure simply has to be shared physically in an embrace with another human being, as if reaffirming the very force of life. Though undoubtedly a level of sexual attraction between Truman and Anderson remains, it is buried at the bottom of this palimpsest of other human feelings which at this moment in the drama have a far greater importance and, Poliakoff would seem to infer, might have in drama more generally.

Beyond the main trio of characters, Poliakoff is astute in including two young assistants, Spig and Nick, alongside the ageing Veronica and Styeman, the insensitive assistant to Anderson. As a perfomer, Billie Whitelaw has a career and reputation, beyond those of even Duncan and Spall, for avant-garde and popular work ranging from Beckett's *Not I* to Kay Mellor's *Playing the Field*. Though her role in *StP* is a cameo, she subtly extends a perhaps archetypically English dramatic trope, namely that, in defiance of appearances, indirection and gentle forgetfulness may well yield results, when she assists Truman in just about recalling Anderson's grandmother's birthplace, Skibereen. This is the key which unlocks the final puzzle leading to the revelation of Anderson's extraordinary family background and ultimately to the saving of the library. In this respect, the character of Veronica balances and offsets that of Styeman, whose leaden, though digital, efficiency markedly lacks soul.

The dramatic function of Spig and Nick in *StP* is similarly quite limited but significant. Nick, who is taciturn to the point of preferring not to speak, does make the connection with the advertising agency which almost buys the collection, and Spig tries to coach Truman in such ways of the contemporary world as mobile phone usage in order to maximise her chances of success. Given that they are not essential to the plot beyond fetching and carrying, it might be surmised that their inclusion primarily serves to afford access to younger viewers who otherwise may not be drawn by the library-closure narrative. Nick is a conventionally good-looking young man and Spig draws attention by her striking red hair and colourful dress and her habit of lounging around, louchely smoking a cigarette. Early on, she appears in a waisted three-quarter-length coat in bold checks of lime green, mauve and cerise and later she wears leather trousers and a plum-coloured sweater, both outfits clashing strikingly with her hair. Visually, Spig, in particular, serves to offset the impression that the photographic library is an entirely fusty place, disconnected from contemporary reality. Nick and Spig's commitment to the collection serves also to convey its relevance to the contemporary.

It is in large measure the interrelations of the main trio of eccentric, attractive and intriguing characters, each revealing through gradual exposition dimensions beyond what at first appears, which sustains interest in *StP*. Though presented in a very different vehicle with different compositional principles, it should be noted that *Sopranos* also revolves around a trio of fascinating characters, Tony, Carmela and Jennifer Melfi. Just as with Gandolfini, Falco and Bracco, the screen presence and acting ability of Spall, Duncan and Cunningham is an important aspect of the attraction and retention of viewers. By differing, though parallel, oblique storytelling means, both vehicles draw on the traditional Western drama's mode of character in conflict to hold viewers' interest in the serial narrative, even though they might afford other attractions simultaneously.

StP is beautifully lit and shot. The stacks of boxes and folders of still photographs which mark the geography of the library create tunnels for interesting long-shot viewpoints. Rows of photographs pegged up on strings augment the shadowy interior, against which focused pools of light create an atmospheric chiaroscuro. Any colour – as, for example, in Spig's costumes or Duncan's blonde hair – stands out in relief against the grey-buff backdrop. The most striking effect of the visual treatment of *StP*, however, is the use Poliakoff makes of the black and white still photographs, many of which are stunning in themselves. Although it might seem paradoxical in a motion-picture medium, Poliakoff adjudges that 'when a film camera looks at a photo for a split second, it's always interesting' (BBC 2001). Building this one-off impact into densely layered sequences, Poliakoff, on several occasions in *StP*, allows the camera to offer a point of view – within the narrative most often that of Anderson, but also that of the television viewers – of a sequence of individual stills glimpsed rapidly in succession against an affective soundtrack (see Chapter 5 for sequence analysis). The angle of vision is also changed by close-ups of details in photographs – a face, the angle of a hat, a pair of eyes locked in an intense gaze.

Still photographs ultimately hold the key to the overall narrative and they are used seductively to draw Anderson and the television viewers into the unfolding of a mystery. It turns out that Bates, before taking the overdose, has discovered a visual trail leading back to the shady life of Anderson's grandmother as a member of a nightclub band in Paris. Banned from the library and not wishing to succeed its demise, Bates takes the overdose but leaves oblique clues for Truman to discover the trail leading to a remarkable revelation. Truman and Spig literally lead Anderson through the alleyways of the library stacks as if drawing him deeper into a tarantula's web, at the core of which he will be entrapped. The lure is comprised of photographs, each set adding a scrap of evidence to a case which is finally irrefutable when Anderson as a very young boy is pictured with his mother visiting his wayward grandmother in Paris.

Though *StP* is in many ways theatrical, it is also highly arresting visually. Film director Charles Sturridge who worked on Poliakoff's film *Soft Targets* (1982) observed that Poliakoff's early plays 'brought cinema into the theatre' (BBC, 2001) in their dynamic visual storytelling. Although in *StP*, Poliakoff deliberately slows scenes down to an almost dialogue-led, theatre pace, he sustains a cinematic dynamic, though patently not at the pace of *Sopranos*. Both *Sopranos* and *StP*, superficially as different as the proverbial chalk and cheese, might be seen as innovative blends of theatre and early television's dialogue in close-up with cinema's widerscreen, visual dynamic. Like *Sopranos*, *StP* uses musical soundtrack to great effect. But in *StP*'s case it is not popular music but a minimalist score which has great impact. Specially composed for the drama by Adrian Johnston, the score works intricately with the visual and other narrative elements, foregrounding a haunting piano phrase, repeated with minimal development and no ultimate resolution, to evoke a paradoxical mix of mellowness and angst.

Televisual and cultural values

In the interviews with Lindsay Duncan which feature both on the BBC Poliakoff profile (BBC, 2001) and, re-edited and augmented, as special features on the *StP* DVD (BBC, 2003), she remarks that he 'is very modern man: a man who makes connections'. Curiously, but not inappropriately, this remark seems to refer on the DVD to Oswald Bates but on the broadcast to Poliakoff himself. Indeed, Poliakoff does appear to share much with his character, Bates. Michael Gambon has remarked that Poliakoff is 'like a boy, just an eccentric' (BBC, 2001) but, in spite of appearances, both are modern men who make connections. Although, in *StP*, Poliakoff deliberately evokes old-fashioned, "slow" television, his concerns resonate with contemporary debates about both television and culture more broadly. The celebration in *StP* of the capacity of the human mind to make allusive, creative connections, as distinct from a computer's bigger database but inability to connect other than through a code of zeros and ones, raises pressing questions in contemporary culture. In the headlong trajectory towards cyberspace, it may be that the distinctive and extraordinary qualities of humans are being overlooked. The final images of *StP* show Marilyn Truman talking to Oswald Bates on a bench by a duck-pond. Bates has survived, his brain has been damaged by the overdose but he has not quite lost his sparkle. Such an image might be taken as a metaphor for the struggle of the human imagination to survive the incursions of the posthuman.

The sympathy elicited for Bates's character, through its foregrounding in the narrative and in the treatment overall, is emotionally affective – at least, it brings a lump to my throat each and every time I view *StP*. When I ask myself what I am moved by, the answer is not clear, but there would appear to be several factors in play. On a narrative level, there is empathy for somebody who has stood up to a threat to his livelihood. At the outset Bates directly tells viewers who might have 'suddenly lost their home or business, or been overlooked for promotion' – anybody, in fact, whose personal dignity has been trampled upon by the instrumental rationalism of an institution which affords no concern for the small life, a mere cog in the mechanism – that this TV drama is for them. Thus Poliakoff shows himself, like Bates, to be a modern man making connections, since the serial, though obscurely set in a fusty library, actually taps into a key issue in contemporary culture of the individual suffering at the hands of a drive to ever-greater economic efficiency under advanced capitalism (Anderson is building a business school for the twenty-first century).

Though it would be oversimple to cast such sympathy for the socially oppressed person in an exclusively British dramatic tradition – after all the small guy is similarly featured in American drama – there is in British culture a long-standing championing of the underdog. So, behind the empathy for the individual in the moment of denouement, there may well be in me (and no doubt others) an enculturated sense of pleasure in the triumph of small resistances against the odds. So, where *Sopranos*, in my analysis, connects with contemporary gender politics in a postindustrial age, so *StP* resonates with a parallel contemporary concern. The peculiarly English aspect of this phenomenon might just lie in the manner of its achievement, an eccentricity which defies the standardising tendencies of social normativity. But this aspect might also be located in a cultural, if not overtly political, tradition, that of humanist liberal individualism to be discussed in Chapter 7.

Shameless (Company Productions for Channel 4, 2001)

Textual mode and form

Shameless is accredited to writer Paul Abbott who devised the drama and wrote much of the first series and is one of its four executive producers. Abbot does not, however, sustain with his productions the detailed writer–director engagement of an *auteur* like Poliakoff. Indeed, he devolves the writing of episodes to others since he is used to working in writer teams. Abbott's situation differs markedly from Poliakoff's in that he does not come from a privileged educational background and theatre heritage but, more typical of contemporary television writers, he learned his craft through the industrial process of writing for soaps. In Abbott's case, his apprenticeship was with Britain's longest-running, continuing serial drama, *Coronation Street*. Though his approach to the writing–directing process is in consequence less individualist than Poliakoff's, Abbott has nevertheless been personally associated with the concept of *Shameless*, particularly since he has acknowledged that he drew significantly on the context of his family upbringing on the fringes of Manchester in devising it. *Shameless* is by no means autobiography, but Abbott – like Poliakoff and, indeed, many writers – draws indirectly upon his own experience and family history for his ideas and his way of seeing.

A comparison between Poliakoff and Abbott gives rise to questions both of industrial practices and of value in respect of TV drama. Poliakoff is at pains to convey his distinctive authorial vision and demands maximum control over the processes of production to achieve it. The discursive position of Abbott, in contrast, is initially located in a dominant form of televisual and popular culture, namely soaps. Accordingly, he seems to be comfortable with the idea of a collaborative creative process, even to the point of devolving the writing, once the vehicle is established. Some commentators attribute an alleged lack of distinction in "post-golden-age" TV drama to the pressures of commercialism and its attendant industrial – as opposed to individually crafted – modes of production. Though, in respect of *Sopranos* and other examples in this book, it will be apparent that a commercial context and industrial production mode typical of the American system by no means entails mediocrity, the value attributed to authorial signature might not apply in the way it does with Poliakoff. Ironically, however, *Sopranos* is strongly associated with David Chase and *Shameless* is biographically associated with Abbott and, though the episodes of each series may be uneven, they appear to sustain a distinctive discursive mode which might be termed authorial vision. These questions of textual value in relation to production context will be taken up in Chapters 3 and 7. Meanwhile, this chapter focuses upon *Shameless*, as devised and sometimes written by Abbott, in the first series.

The unusual textual mode of *Shameless*, another kind of hybrid, has its roots in aspects of soap, and particularly perhaps *Coronation Street*, in terms of its mixture of social realism with melodrama and excess. From a general description, *Shameless* might be taken to be a work of social realism, even a documentary. The drama concerns a family living in challenging conditions on a "sink" estate in the outer suburbs of Manchester. The mother of the six children in the Gallagher family has walked out and Frank Gallagher (David Threlfall), ironically the patriarch of the family, is perpetually drunk or stoned. The eldest daughter, Fiona (Anne-Marie Duff), has become the family carer by default, and the other five children – Lip (Jody Latham), Ian (Gerard Kearns), Debbie (Rebecca Ryan), Carl (Luke Tittenson/ Elliot Tittenson) and Liam (Joseph Furnace) – muddle along as best they can, despite their useless father. Such a situation in British television tradition might have warranted a docudrama treatment with the aim of touching the nation's social conscience about the plight of Britain's forgotten youngsters, those who, through no fault of their own, can scarcely cling to the edge of the poverty line. And, indeed, these facts of a real (though fictional) contemporary situation are evident in *Shameless*. But the treatment makes the series also very funny.[4]

In terms of dramatic form, *Shameless* resembles a sitcom as much as a mini-serial drama. Though it traces through time the experience of the characters and there are some continuing narratives – for example, Fiona's developing relationship with boyfriend Steve (James McAvoy) in the first series – the episodes all begin in the same way with Frank Gallagher's voice-over introducing the life of his family on the Chatsworth Estate, the name itself carrying a heavy comic irony in its comparison with the stately home of that name. In the mode of sitcom characters, Frank never changes, whatever his experiences in the previous episode, and the situation does not change: there is apparently no way out of the Chatsworth predicament. There is a loose continuity of narrative across episodes but incidents which are central in one episode, are not typically followed up in the next by way of consequences, as they might be in a serial narrative. Each episode comically treats an aspect of Chatsworth life, focusing upon one of the characters. In Episode 2, Frank is nowhere to be found and this is a cause for alarm only because it is giro day and Frank can be relied upon only for matters of fundamental self-interest such as collecting his cash. A neighbourhood search yields nothing and, when a body surfaces in the canal, fears genuinely grow. But Frank turns up in Calais with no passport, no money and no clue as to how he got there. This is a 'Frank story'.

Episode 4, written by Abbott, is a 'Debbie story' and perhaps best illustrates the extraordinary tone of *Shameless* which disturbs viewers. In this episode, Debbie, similarly to Frank, disappears mysteriously. She is soon revealed to be safe, but she has kidnapped a toddler to whom she has taken a shine because, she claims, he was left outside at a local party with nobody taking any notice of him. The boy's parents are shown actually to be frantic as to his whereabouts and Frank, picking up on the local 'kid snatched' furore, winds up the narrative tension in his over-dramatised concern about the safety of the missing youngster, in ignorance that the young boy has been kidnapped by Debbie, his daughter. With his fellow self-appointed vigilantes, he becomes increasingly manic in his accusations of – and indeed physical attacks on – anyone who might be constructed as a 'pervert'. An alleged 'drug-head', himself a recent father, is beaten up in passing as the vigilantes roam the streets, and, as Frank later relates, 'The lads have just kicked a confession out of ice-cream, Alex'. Frank, mouthy as ever, rails in tabloid phrases at the police and the 'scumheads', uttering platitude upon platitude but doing nothing helpful: 'You'd die for your kids'; 'Your only son! Can you imagine?'; 'God be with you'; 'I can't eat, Sheila' (uttered while stuffing his face). These clichéd expressions of concern, picking up on the declaimed mythologies of the working-class in his voice-over at the top of each episode (likening Chatsworth Estate to the 'Garden of Eden', for example) are patently at odds with Frank's actual lack of concern for, and mistreatment of, his own children. Indeed, Debbie's disturbed behaviour in taking the boy and dressing him up as a girl may well be seen as a consequence of Frank's parenting deficiencies.

The ironies are subtly pointed up within the episode. When it emerges that Debbie has actually planned this kidnap and lured the toddler with chocolate, Steve upsets Fiona by remarking that 'Debbie's a kid with a problem.' Though the process of returning the toddler without Debbie's actual behaviour being discovered involves a range of fantastic and comical manoeuvres involving all the Gallagher kids in devious behaviour to construct a false trail, it is motivated by a real concern that the family will again be split up if Debbie is found out: 'and if Social Services find out Dad's moved in with Sheila, they'll have a field-day splitting this lot up. Look what happened last time' (Episode 4). As Fiona thus vents her very genuine concern, photographs of each of the children looking out of place in ill-matched foster families flash across the screen. Ultimately 'The Plan' works and the toddler's parents are persuaded that Debbie has found and rescued the child. In another underscoring irony, Debbie is showered with money by grateful parents and friends for her efforts. The apparently final shot sees Frank grovelling on the floor to pick up the confetti of cash, saying, 'It's like that scene from *Gone with the Wind*'. Thus the sitcom format reaches closure with the social implications of the episode left hanging, but there is a coda.

In a different kind of serial drama with a social purpose, the consequences of Debbie's behaviour might have been further explored. Though this episode affords a potential insight into a psyche disturbed by her experience of unconventional parenting which is otherwise only glimpsed in her idiosyncratic compulsions in other episodes, no major attempt is made in this or any subsequent episode to bring out in more depth either the personal and social implications of Debbie's character or the political circumstances which give rise to her plight. In the coda to the episode, however, a number of the less-attractive sides to life on the Chatsworth Estate are juxtaposed by way of a trailer for future episodes. The motive of Sheila's teenage daughter Karen's seduction of Frank is revealed to be jealousy as she indicates to Lip when she tells him that since Frank moved in with her mother she has been sidelined. Frank waits for Sheila, virtually comatose on her cocktail of drugs, to nod off to sleep before going to Karen's bedroom and, in the process of warning her of the dangers of older men, ends up 'shagging' her. Frank's continued sexual liaison with his new partner's daughter, his eldest son's girlfriend, is the pivot of further upset in the next episode.

Also in this unusual coda, with reference to 'all that business yesterday' with Debbie which is evoked by the haunting music from the musical box, the family and neighbours clear Frank's room (since he is now at Sheila's) and refurbish it in pinks and mauves for Debbie. They give her a cot furbished in pink with a life-size baby doll as if it were to replace the kidnapped toddler. As Steve explains in voice-over, 'People round here with good imaginations get bored when nothing happens … Round here, though, therapy's an unfamiliar word: blackmail and bribery are tried and tested techniques' (Series 1: Episode 4). The trick works insofar as Debbie becomes very attached to the doll, indeed too much so as she claims she has to miss school to attend to it.

That is as far as *Shameless* goes to deal with consequences but the pointed ironies noted are designed to prevent viewers from reading *Shameless* simply as an anarchic sitcom. Where political points are made in *Shameless*, they are made obliquely; they are conveyed by implication rather than preached. This point is certainly not made as a criticism but implicit comparison with other forms and modes of drama which fall more neatly into established categories, to mark the kind of hybrid drama that *Shameless* is. In contrast with a more overt piece of old-fashioned social realism aiming to convey a message or invite a specific attitude in response, *Shameless* works obliquely to make viewers uncomfortable whilst also making them laugh out loud. In Episode 5, Debbie's behaviour is obliterated by Frank's liaison with Karen. But even as he tells Karen that he cannot continue with the casual sex with her, he manages to impute blame to everybody but himself, a man of honour. As he says, 'A man has got to look his son in the eye; I held him [Lip] the day he was born; If your granddad was here, he'd be saying the same' (Episode 5). The sitcom aspect of *Shameless* demands a comic treatment and its conventional narrative closure entails the avoidance of pursuing the consequences of any given episode on the characters. Sitcoms typically work by sustaining dominant characteristics in the protagonists which, when located in different situations likely to antagonise them, give rise to comic effect. Abbott's (and his writers') particular comic treatment takes *Shameless* towards the plot contortions of farce, creating opportunities for excess, for example in the farcical play with the Superman/Captain Curtis costumes as the Gallaghers and friends frantically try to replace the toddler's outfit shrunk in the wash by Debbie in the episode above. Frank Gallagher is the anchor character who remains the same, his feckless self-interest being the characteristic out of which black humour can repeatedly be drawn. The other characters, however, because they are struggling to survive, also partially inhabit a different mode of drama, serial social realism, in which the consequences of character in situation are more typically explored, rather than obliquely implied. In *Shameless* episodes, however, social issues are touched upon just sufficiently to register, as noted, but left unresolved. Perhaps owing a debt to *Coronation Street*'s distinctive mix of melodrama and realism, Abbott contrives in *Shameless* to leave sit-com and serial drama hanging in the balance. Overtly, the sitcom format and the comic treatment licenses some viewers to laugh, but the potential of serial implications in the reality of the social circumstances leaves other viewers uneasy.

Because he is drawing on his own experience of growing up in a chaotic household, both his parents having left home, Abbott writes as an insider on the social experience rather than as an outside observer. As a consequence, perhaps, he represents the situation more as a participant observer merely documenting things as they happen rather than viewing them from a distance through a political or ethical optic. Abbot's position is not entirely neutral, however, but in part is celebratory because, as he observes, there was a positive side to his home situation:

> The deserting parents, the teenage pregnancies, the lack of legitimate income, the criminal sentences ... Chaos became the norm and our threshold for tolerating upheaval was tested to the nth degree. From this accelerated growth spurt came the rewards of accelerated life skills – we could all cook, clean, decorate a room at three in the morning, strip a bike (someone else's) down to its basic components without leaving forensic traces, and the ones of us who hadn't got pregnant or got anyone else pregnant, knew more about contraception than we needed to. Bits of that life were unmissable. (interview on C4 website, October 2005, 1)

Abbot's sense of the very ordinariness, the everydayness, of the kinds of experience and behaviour which inform *Shameless* is at odds with the sense of the outsider, the sense of the middle-class viewer that it is unacceptable. Steve, Fiona's boyfriend, is used to afford this latter perspective on events. As the writer, moreover, Abbot is aware of that gap and ,through his dramatic method, he exploits it. As he remarks, 'I hung on to the title *Shameless* for its irony, the kind of accusation outsiders would have chucked at my family back in the 1970s ... We'd been loud, aggressive, primitive and anarchic. But I never once recall us feeling ... *Shameless*' (interview on C4 website October, 2005, 1).

Many, but not all, of the performances are deliberately excessive in their presentational style. Threlfall's Frank Gallagher is a case in point and the performances of Maxine Peak's Veronica, and Sheila Jackson's Maggie O'Neal, are equally stylised versions respectively of busty, blonde "front" and agoraphobic designer-drug dependency. The Gallaghers' neighbour, Veronica, purports to be a nurse when in fact she works as a cleaner in a hospital, whilst Sheila, having escaped a loveless and sexless marriage to take up with Frank Gallagher, lives in a prozac-fuelled romantic haze. Whilst avoiding out-and-out caricature, both comediennes exploit their roles to the full. However, other characters, notably the Gallagher youths, are more realistically performed such that, amidst the comic mayhem, they can command sympathy. Lip is momentarily shown in tears, deeply feeling the sense of betrayal and hurt caused by his father's 'animal' behaviour with Karen. The format does not allow it to last too long, but the feelings are portrayed with sufficient conviction to have impact. As Lip remarks to Steve, deflating another of Frank's myths, 'Honour thy father; it takes some doing.' (Episode 5). Likewise, the treatment of Liam's homosexuality and his relationship with married, Muslim shop-owner, Kash (Chris Brisson) in Episode 3, for example, whilst not without its comic moments, allows the complex feelings of a young gay man on the Chatsworth estate to have affect. When Frank finally dumps Karen giving her a crumpled fiver and saying, 'Get yourself an E or something', she too is momentarily shown to be hurt.

The textual self-awareness marked by the presentational excess of *Shameless*, though it denies that it is an account of "things as they really are" in the British social realist tradition, nevertheless does not prevent darker aspects of social reality and the feelings the characters have about their plight from registering. Indeed, it is the very play between dramatic modes – and consequent shifts of response demanded of viewers – that distinguishes *Shameless*. Like *Sopranos* and *StP* it invites a complex seeing, similar in kind but different in specific from my other two examples of distinctive contemporary TV drama.

Televisual and cultural values

Shameless, in its concern with an underclass, might well be located in the British social realist tradition. Though it is seldom visible in TV drama, an underclass typifies the social structures of late capitalism. The eminent economist, J. K. Galbraith (1992), for example, offers a simple model of a two-thirds:one-third society in an analysis of Western democracies in which the majority prospers whilst the minority remains outside the normal political processes of that society. People in that under-class do not vote at general elections as their experience suggests to them that there is no point in doing so because their plight does not change with any new administration. They manage their lives amongst themselves as best they can. The situation of the Gallagher family in *Shameless* resonates with the idea of such an underclass in contemporary Britain. Fiona, for example, remarks , 'We don't need the police fighting our battles for us' (Episode 4) as if this microsociety functions beyond the usual social agencies by its own internal laws of survival rather than any external legislature.

The defeat of expectations by the blurring of generic boundaries in the treatment of the social material in *Shameless* is ultimately what gives rise to the uncomfortable viewing experience noted. Arguably, such a dislocation of normative television bearings is more affective than a worthy docudrama which, by more overtly addressing a social issue, may put people off by a sense of preachiness in the telling. As viewers laugh in *Shameless* at the undoubtedly funny and (by television standards) outrageous antics of the episodes, however, they are equally made to sense the more serious implications which, if critical commentary is anything to go by, are what seem to linger with viewers. Several journal articles when reviewing *Shameless*, for example, recall *Boys from the Blackstuff*, a drama mini-series more overtly located in the British social realist tradition even though it does have a black comedy (but not a sitcom) dimension.[5] If Paul Abbot's aim had been to expose the plight of "sink" estates in contemporary Britain and to invite action to remedy their ills, the series would indeed be placed in such a tradition. But, as noted, the sitcom dimension of *Shameless* primarily invites laughter rather than sympathy or concern. Otherwise, the treatment of social life resembles more traditional nineteenth-century naturalism as espoused by Zola to document the processes of life dispassionately observed. Where feelings are invoked, they tend, if anything, to be feelings of admiration of the capacity to cope with – and indeed enjoy – life under challenging circumstances.

But some viewers, particularly those with working-class origins, have declared their discomfort in watching *Shameless* because they feel they are being invited to laugh at their own class.[6] Thus, on the level of social realism, they seem to be convinced by the underclass world of the series but they sense that they are not being invited to see it as an exposé of a social problem needing attention in the manner of *Cathy Come Home*, but as a mockery. For such viewers, Abbot's disposition to treat the material with a mix of naturalism and humour – because his own experience of it allows him to see and portray it as full of colour – is disturbing. If, as Creeber has remarked, 'traditional social realism takes the colour out of working-class life', Abbott restores it in a new hybrid of styles. Creeber also questions whether the hybridisation and upbeat treatment typical of contemporary television dilutes any potential political impact.[7] Patently, the anarchic comedy of *Shameless* differs from the "serious" docu-drama treatments of earlier examples of social-issues television. But there is a case for seeing it otherwise.

First, in today's television environment, it is unlikely that a more dour social realism would attract viewers. If nothing else, such a treatment would seem old-fashioned, belonging to another age. Secondly, viewers are more sophisticated in respect of television as a medium than in the past, more aware of its constructions and manipulations and more sceptical of authorities which purport to tell "how things really are". Thus, even if it were accepted that a social or political motive for production might be sustained, the treatment of a drama would need to be different. Furthermore, an entertaining treatment which acknowledges viewers' awareness of codes and conventions and invites viewers actively to pick up on the ironies pointed up by a gap between mythologies and actualities may be more politically effective as well as more compelling television. Viewed in this light, the impact of *Shameless* may be all the greater for making people just that bit uncomfortable. In not aiming to be a *Play for Today*, *Shameless* might offer a new political viewing experience.

Small signifiers in the text afford levers for prising open the ironic gaps. When, in Episode 3, Kev, to avoid being hassled by girls in the pub, tells them he is getting married, a half-cut Frank overhears and spreads the news. Before he knows it, Kev is at the centre of one of *Shameless's* anarchic parties and has been sold a second-hand wedding suit. A casual cutaway to a newspaper headline announces 'Council house sell-off' and, later in the episode, having unexpectedly inherited some cash to fund the wedding, Veronica suggests to Kev that instead they take up the opportunity to buy a house. Another cutaway to the billboard of a newsvendor, however, reads 'Buy your own house; betray your class'. How such small but deliberately included signifiers are to be read remains an open question. Are viewers meant to see the absurdity of a tabloid headline in the light of the vitality of amusingly attractive characters trying to get by in a world that has little to offer them? Or are viewers meant to respond to an absence of the political awareness of the former generation of an industrial working class, to whom collective action to address structural inequities was preferable to individual escape into the middle class, as indicated by the billboard? The snatch of the theme tune from *The Great Escape* over this moment is just one example of the use of a range of musical styles in the series, often ironically to comment on the action. There is no debate on this housing issue in the dialogue and it is not further highlighted in any way in the episode, but it is there to be read when, because it is otherwise extraneous, it might easily have been omitted. Thus there appears to be a conscious intention at least to float a political question, the end of which is left open.

Similarly, whilst the Gallagher family has gathered to eat fish and chips on a Friday night in Episode 3, there is a rare moment of quiet which allows the television to be heard reporting on the rise of poverty and an extended call upon benefits in Tony Blair's Britain. Steve, the relatively middle-class outsider, appears to pick up on the report but nothing is said and the others continue eating. Once again, it is patently deliberate – the moment of quiet is contrived for the purpose – without any further textual indication of how the signifier might be read. On one level there is a consonance between the visual image and the verbal report, confirmed by the Gallagher family being ostensibly funded by Frank's giro. But it remains open whether a Daily Mail 'dole scroungers' attitude is invoked or a *Play for Today* concern invited about social injustice and the failure of the political system. In the context of contemporary television practice and contemporary theory of dialogic negotiations of text in context (as noted in Chapter 1), however, an open and playful text with the potential to disturb viewers into active engagement with a text (as distinct from receiving a political message) may be more politically effective for the twenty-first century. For the politically committed, the downside of this approach is that it does not guarantee any particular insights. But at least they are available to provoke a way of complex seeing not always elicited by more regular TV fare.

Abbott is committed, as his televised Huw Wheldon Memorial Lecture (September, 2005) attests, to high-quality drama on television. He has faith in the sophistication of audiences for TV drama and is offended by them being sold short. He does not propose any specific mode of drama, valuing good writing and production whatever the vehicle. Being steeped by his apprenticeship in the conventions of popular television, however, he is able to draw upon them but to turn them through several degrees to make them into something else. His strategies include oblique dialogue making viewers work harder to engage, subtle play with devices to acknowledge the audience's awareness of television conventions and the mixing of dramatic modes and generic codes to make something new, but in a way which draws upon the audience's familiarity with those codes.

Summary: *Sopranos, Shooting the Past, Shameless* as distinctive product

The three examples of distinctive products of contemporary TV drama discussed above differ considerably in their textual modes and forms and in their discursive positions. In my estimation, moreover, they are to be valued according to different criteria in different traditions. To admire both the pace of *Sopranos* and the slowness of *Shooting the Past* might seem contradictory and I acknowledge accordingly that I am adjudging each from different value perspectives. Both examples are, in my view, good of their kind and effective vehicles in contemporary television, confounding those critics of the medium who, as Bianculli (1994) has fully expounded, can see no good in it at all. Where *Sopranos* is a distinctively American product, *StP* and *Shameless* are distinctively British, but in different ways. *StP* sits in a high-art tradition of *auteurism* which has resonances with *Sopranos'* modernist-cinema aspirations, whilst *Shameless* draws on popular television forms (soaps and sitcoms) but also has affiliations with the British tradition of social realism.

All my examples share an understanding of contemporary television's codes and conventions and take television seriously. To a greater or lesser extent, each acknowledges within the text an awareness of the audience's understanding of TV the generic codes, narrative modes and conventions of TV drama, an understanding encultured by viewing as much as by the extended inclusion of Media Studies in formal education. Each example mixes modes of television and some mix genres or narrative forms. In doing so, they pick up on the disposition in contemporary television – and in contemporary culture more broadly – for hybrids and fusions. Whether this is attributed to the commercial impetus to repeat successes but not in quite the same way, and to maximise viewing potential by mixing one genre with another ("it's like *Goodfellas* meets *Dynasty*"), or whether it is seen as a recycling of established tropes as in Jameson's (1993) version of postmodernism, hybrids have come to characterise and to dominate contemporary TV3 (see Chapter

5). What is distinctive about my examples, however, is that each treats this disposition to fusions in a way which creates something new in the mix.

I do not suggest that there is a similarity between the products (though there are some resemblances, as noted) so much as a similarity in treatments and in the viewing experiences of complex seeing which they might elicit. By both subverting and confirming generic expectations, all my examples demand, as argued, that viewers work harder to negotiate the features of each code, following moments of Todorovian 'hesitation'. Mixing the discursive "feminine" of the soap genre with the macho action of the discursively "masculine" mobster genre, *Sopranos* invites the negotiation of two apparently incompatible codes which it makes accessible by drawing on the overlapping features of each in their family orientation. *StP* uses a range of devices to draw a potentially wide range of viewers into the drama, overtly acknowledging at the outset that the context might seem televisually uninteresting, but challenging viewers to disengage whilst drawing them into a narrative web. The shock of recognition here, if it works, is that a simple story well told in one seemingly fading dialect of the television medium can be compelling. *Shameless* effects a "hesitation" by looking, from one point of view, like one thing (a social realist drama) and then turning out to be another (a sitcom). The ambiguity refuses to allow viewers to settle into a familiar reading disposition by subtly asking leading questions. When creative people who take television seriously address the forms of contemporary TV drama, distinctive product results. The circumstances in which this might happen are the subject of the next chapter.

Notes

1   For a discussion of the characters' differing readings of *The Godfather* movies, see Pattie (2002).

2   Rorty suggests that, even if no basis for solidarity is to be found in "human nature", the core self of human beings, it remains possible to posit values (see 1989: 192ff.).

3   Cited on www.methuen.co.uk/shootingthepast.html.

4   The development of my thinking about *Shameless* in what follows owes a debt to papers by Glen Creeber and Amy McNulty at the *Cultures of British Television Drama* Conference, University of Reading, 13–15 September 2005.

5   See, for example, Millington and Nelson (1986).

6   To offer some anecdotal evidence, this point, when made by Glen Creeber at the Reading TV Drama Conference, on 15 September 2005, resonated with members of the audience, and Alan Fair, a Film Studies colleague at Manchester Metropolitan University, explained his refusal to watch the series in these explicit terms.

7   Creeber, in a presentation given to the Cultures of British Television Drama Conference, Manchester Metropolitan University, 13–15 September 2005.

3

State of play: the TV drama industry – new rules of the game

Production conditions for distinctive product

Those readers primarily interested in the TV dramas themselves might think the industry background to be less compelling. But, properly to understand why we get a particular kind of TV drama to appear on our screens at any given time is not just a matter of creative people coming up with fresh ideas. Moreover, the dramas behind the scenes are just as intricate and fascinating as those on the screen. First, here, I look back at circumstances in the past which have given rise to innovative drama, with a view to establishing any similarities with those which have facilitated the distinctive drama of TV3. Taking a retrospective, long view of television-drama history, it appears that programmes which have been perceived to be of exceptional quality, canonical even, have typically emerged under circumstances in which the "creatives" have had either exceptional control over the production process or an unusual level of commitment to it. Early examples of the former are rare, but might include *Hill Street Blues* in the USA and the products of the Loach–Garnett partnership in mid-1960s Britain.

As is well documented, despite being, 'possibly the lowest-rated programme ever to be retained' (Hoblit cited in Feuer et al., 1984: 25–26), *Hill Street Blues* (NBC, 1981–1987) survived a disastrous pilot to become one of the most celebrated dramas in American television history (see Feuer et al., 1984 and Gitlin, 1994). When network ratings began sharply to decline under threat from cable and satellite (as noted in Chapter 1), network executives were prepared to give exceptional creative freedom to Bochco and Kozoll to create a new police series which they hoped would halt that decline. The writer–producers took full advantage of the control they gleaned in setting up the deal and, in spite of network executives' insistence on some modifications following the pilot (see Nelson in Creeber, 2004b: 100–105), they effected a radical shift in the form and style of TV drama series. In a similar, but even earlier, challenge to 1960s regular TV fare in the UK, Loach and Garnett, having wrought a concession from BBC management, famously took the new lightweight 16 mm cameras out of the studio in which TV drama production had hitherto been hidebound and static and into actual environments. Making a film version of Nell Dunn's novel in *Up the Junction* (1965), they took an improvisatory approach based on scenarios drawn from the book and used a documentary shooting style. As a result, in defiance of the executive producer and BBC management, they created a new dramatic form with a greater sense of immediacy than had previously been possible beyond news gathering (see Cooke, 2003: 69–75).

A well-known British example of a programme which achieved success through the exceptional commitment of its creative team is *Boys from the Blackstuff* (1982) towards the end of the period of the BBC's English Regions Drama. Executive producer, Michael Wearing, had to fight for funds for the series and ultimately find creative solutions to a budget shortfall. In consequence, there was a strong sense of commitment to the series on the part of the creative team generally, augmented for some by a specific commitment to its social context and political impact (see Millington and Nelson, 1986). The point with these landmarks of television history, and other similar examples, however, is that they are exceptions to the norms of regular TV fare produced under television's established production circumstances in the American "network era" or what might in the UK be called the PSB–terrestrial age of television. The quality of these programmes, in line with Thompson's formulation of "quality TV" in the "network era" is that 'they are not "regular" TV' (1996: 13). Indeed, they are distinguished by being different from the norm and were typically achieved by undergoing, in Thompson's phrase, 'a noble struggle against profit-mongering networks and non-appreciative audiences' (1996: 14). In contrast, the examples discussed in Chapter 2 are distinctive in themselves, under circumstances where there is no longer a simple norm.

Where in TVI, the "network era", the stranglehold of the 'big three' American networks over distribution led to the LOP strategy, the political economy of TV3 is very different. There have been significant changes in market conditions worldwide, with particular ramifications for each nation. Developments in satellite technology have played their part in the emergent new circumstances, as noted, and have led in turn to a radically different approach to profit-making in the television industry. Instead of securing profits through control by oligarchies over a distribution bottleneck on the back of constraints on bandwidth (in both the USA and the UK), profit is to be made through distinctive programme content, with additional income gleaned through dissemination across media platforms in a vertically and horizontally integrated, multidimensional environment. There has accordingly been an extended shift away from a conception of the audience as a mass to be sustained by avoiding offending viewers. Niche marketing, the contemporary approach to audiences, has become much more refined in a general shift of capitalist economics from Fordism to postmodernity. Several fresh approaches to audience-building have been taken in this period of transition, as noted, but they are typically based on audience segments, microcultures rather than masses.

In its various distribution modes, contemporary television has placed more emphasis upon the branding of distinction rather than regular fare (although, of course, the latter continues to be a staple of the schedules). It is evident in strands (e.g. NBC's "must- see" Thursday night), in channels themselves (e.g. HBO and Showtime) and in specific products for "must-see" television (e.g. *Sopranos*). And this is not just the case in the USA or amongst the US-based media conglomerates. Continuity now (November 2005) flags the schedule for BBC1, the UK's main public service channel, as 'the one to watch', using this phrase to imply both the channel itself and selected programmes constructed as "Event TV". The programming flagged on the night of 27 October 2005, for example, was not new in kind – it included the first episode of a "classic serial", *Bleak House*, followed by an established political spy thriller, *Spooks* – but it was the approach to branding which was novel. Channel 4 is currently seeking to brand itself again in terms of a public service channel (see below).

The BBC, furthermore, is currently branding itself as a producer of epics to rival American appeal to cinema heritage. Launched on terrestrial channels in the week commencing Sunday 30 October 2005 were the first episode of a three-part drama of the epic struggle to find Tutankhamun's tomb under the banner title *Egypt* (BBC1, BBC with WGBH Boston) and the first of an eleven-part blockbuster chronicling the birth of the Roman Empire under the banner title *Rome* (BBC2, BBC with HBO). Both series tap more into cinematic legacies (*Raiders of the Lost Ark*, *Ben-Hur*) than televisual traditions. Co-productions of the BBC with WGBH Boston have a long history, particularly for period dramas based on adaptations of classic novels which, besides airing on UK terrestrial channels have been destined also for the PBS channel in America. But a co-production of the BBC with an American cable channel is innovative, with HBO putting up the majority of the $100 million production budget for twelve one-hour episodes. Though there is a British connection with *Egypt*, through the involvement of Lord Carnarvon with Howard Carter in the story of the search for Tutankhamun's tomb, and though *Rome*, for contingent reasons,[1] uses British actors in all the leading roles, both productions deal in material with transnational appeal rather than specifically British or American material. This is an indicator of some big-budget productions in TV3 and may be a sign of the future.

Global–transnational media conglomerates and transnational vision

A feature of TV3 is the rise to dominance not just of big players in television drama production but also of companies with truly transnational reach, their television interests being horizontally integrated with other media interests. Most are centred in the USA and they include Time Warner, Vivendi-Universal, Walt Disney Corp., Viacom, Liberty Media and News Corp. The companies gain their critical mass by having portfolios of television interests allied to holdings in mixes of the press, radio, film, internet, telephone, music production and related media and communications products. Time Warner, for example, includes America On-Line (AOL), Home Box Office (HBO), New Line Cinema, Time Inc., Time Warner Cable, Turner Broadcasting Inc., Warner Brothers Entertainment, Time Warner Investments and Global Marketing. The last company publicises and facilitates the others in the overall corporation context. It illustrates how a corporation as large and diverse as Time Warner can, with an integrated marketing strategy, make its products distinctive through devolved branding. As Global Marketing's website announces, they 'push brand awareness to a new level': 'A catalyst for collaboration across the company, Global Marketing fully develops customized, idea-driven programs for its marketing partners by capitalizing on Time Warner's wealth of content, media platforms, consumer relationships and marketing infrastructure worldwide.'[2]

Besides dispersing risk amongst a range of business interests, such conglomerates as Time Warner have the critical mass to invest in infrastructure and in specific expensive products such as TV drama (as in *Rome*, through HBO). Though they may be located in the USA, the media conglomerates have a decentred, transnational outlook in terms of markets and business opportunities. For example, to take advantage of low wages and tax breaks afforded by different national governments, television (and film) production, formerly located largely in Hollywood, now moves around the world from Prague to Berlin to Australia, as the project or production conditions demand. With regard to audiences, the typical aim is to appeal to targeted segments of a worldwide market.

Though national borders have not been entirely eroded, as we shall see, it makes little sense in the context of a global market-place to consider the political economy of any specific nation in isolation. Today's production and distribution is vertically and horizontally integrated within the "culture industries" on a global scale. Little more than a decade ago, however, systems of finance, regulation and production were organised nationally, even though there was evidently some exchange of product and limited co-production. Generally speaking, apart perhaps from in the USA, dissemination was conceived primarily on a basis of national cultures and consumption. Exports were desirable and brought additional profits but they were not typically inherent in the conception of projects. Building on significant changes in the 1990s, TV3 is characterised, in contrast, by national industry deregulation which effectively facilitates bigger companies with transnational vision and reach. As Kimmel notes in his study of the emergence of FOX television (to be featured below), 'There's no question that without the help of the Federal Communications Commission, Rupert Murdoch's task of launching a fourth American television network in 1986 would have been infinitely more difficult, if not downright impossible (2004: 175). Given this book's illustrative emphasis on the UK as well as the USA, however, it is illuminating to consider developments in Britain in the context of Europe and the world to see how individual nations are adjusting to new circumstances.

Rewriting the rules of the game

In the early 'noughties', following a review of exports in the communications and media industries published by DCMS in *Building a Global Audience: British Television in Overseas Markets* (1999), a trade deficit in television programmes was perceived. The core tension between production to suit the needs of the domestic market and production for export was recognised in this report but not regarded as insuperable. It proposed that the government should 'consider the need for international competitiveness when framing policies for the domestic home market' (1999: 41). Though other reports (see Steemers, 2004: 57–61) countered the television underperformance argument, the New Labour government, in its broader review of the UK communications industries, continued to pursue change with a view to keeping British companies competitive in the world market-place.

Since the USA is a particularly difficult market to penetrate, some attention has also been paid, in spite of language barriers, to European opportunities. As Grant and Wood record:

> In 1984, the European commission produced a discussion document entitled 'Television Without Frontiers'. Its primary thrust was to encourage the development of a continental market for small-screen entertainment: in its own words, the opening of 'intra-Community frontiers for national television programmes'. (2004: 205)

Various attempts have since been made to encourage a European approach to television. The decision to remake *Dr Zhivago* for Granada's first-ever European co-production is significant, illustrating the disposition towards European collaboration and a transnational vision. The 2001 adaptation for television of *Dr Zhivago* was, 'shot in English in the Czech Republic, it had an Italian director (Giacomo Campiotti), an international cast (Sam Neill, Hans Matheson, Keira Knightley), Russian literary provenance and a British writer, Andrew Davies' (Steemers, 2004: 158). Granada and Carlton both developed international arms separately but, with the blessing of government deregulation in 2002, they would become better placed as a larger single company to function on a European and world stage.

Though the American conglomerates are dominant with a share of almost a 70 per cent share of the world television market, European countries and companies are able to operate in a transnational market-place but typically by coming together, either through merger within or across national boundaries, or through co-production strategies. As noted, critical mass appears to have become a necessary condition for competing in today's global television industry. Within the UK, the BBC, which historically has been seen as the cornerstone of British broadcasting and culture, has become, through its subsidiary company, BBC Worldwide, the only significant UK player in a global context. In Steemers's analysis, 'In 2002, Worldwide sold 40,000 hours of programming to over 550 broadcasters in sixty-nine countries underlining its position as Europe's largest exporter of television programmes' (2004: 84). The commercial television companies in the UK have accordingly responded to a pressure to combine to achieve a sufficient critical mass to compete. The various independent terrestrial television companies which successfully bid for regional licences in the wake of the 1990 Broadcasting Act have gradually joined forces over the past decade, finally resulting in the latest merger of Carlton and Granada, to provide a single commercial television provider, Independent Television (ITV).

The draft Communications Bill, of May 2002, emphasising a global context, proclaimed, 'In this world, it is essential that the UK reinforces its position as one of the most attractive places for communication companies to do business. Unnecessary regulation needs to be removed wherever possible.' (DTI/DCMS, 2002: 03). Granada and Carlton needed to merge not only for reasons of critical mass within the UK but also, arguably, to be attractive for take-over by a global media conglomerate. Prior to 2003, foreign ownership of British media interests had been restricted to 15 per cent of audience share. Relaxation of this constraint following the 2002 Communications Bill, however, has set up ITV for possible purchase by one of the US-based corporations. Though some commentators have seen this move as an unwarranted government intervention detrimental to British cultural interests, it is arguably not a conspiracy beyond the workings of advanced, global capitalism. From another point of view, as noted, national governments have simply perceived the need to make regulatory adjustments to facilitate industry change in TV3. But this difference of view represents what still remains a key question to be addressed: the place of public service broadcasting in an advanced market economy.

A parallel example in the USA in respect of vertical rather than horizontal integration, is the change made to the Financial Interest and Syndication (Fin Syn) rules. Under the Fin Syn rules dating back to 1970, the American networks were prohibited from the prime-time scheduling of products in which they held a major ownership stake. This effectively required the networks to obtain most comedy and drama series from independent third parties. The "prime-time access rule" also reserved a key hour in the various American time zones for programming acquired by local stations and not provided by the networks. These regulations were introduced with the aim of increasing diversity in programming by preventing the "big three" of the "network era" from dominating the market (see Holt, 2003). Ironically, they may have had the opposite effect, since, in Holt's view, these regulations, strengthened in revisions of 1976 and 1980, 'prohibited vertical integration of production, sale and distribution of programming, preventing the networks from creating a schedule that privileged their own products' (2003: 15). Arguably, then, the Fin Syn rules, whilst they appeared to be militating against market monopoly and opening up opportunities for independent television stations and producers, may have been detrimental to creativity. They could not help an innovative programme if the response to the pilot were unfavourable since a network was unable to hammock a promising new series with established successes to afford time for audiences to become accustomed to its new angle. Even in the "network era" innovation was needed, if only to keep the industry fresh, but in TV3, as noted, distinctive, branded product is the order of the day.

When, in the 1980s, network audiences began to decline under competition from early cable and satellite, the powerful core industry sought redress. The subsequent FCC deregulation allowed networks to schedule their own productions in primetime. Since it has long been recognised that it takes time for audiences to adjust to new forms but that, given time, they may well grow to like them very much (*Hill Street Blues* is a case in point), the relaxation of Fin Syn thus gave a boost to innovative product. New opportunities opened up for companies to nurture new product, with NBC, for example, able to create its Thursday night "must-see TV" strand. Innovative programming produced by a network or one of its substantially owned subsidiaries might by such means initially be supported by its juxtaposition with established brands. But it was not the only novel development in the USA. Ironically at a moment of network decline, a new network, Fox Television, emerged at the dawn of TV3 to take full advantage of the new circumstances. Rupert Murdoch and the Fox executives defied history and all television wisdom to establish a fourth American network, the first since the closure of Dumont in 1934. To achieve their end, they challenged most of the orthodoxies of the established American television environment and contributed in considerable measure to the emergence of TV3. A brief sketch of Fox's key strategies is instructive.[3]

Fox Television – a case sketch

With an initial mix of ninety-nine affiliated independent stations and cable TV outlets, Fox, though much smaller than the 'big three', just about had the prospect of a viable audience, and its achievement exemplifies the advantages of horizontal and vertical integration. Not technically defined as a network (though presenting itself as one), Fox could use its own production studio to keep costs down and it drew upon pump-priming financing from Murdoch's global media interests to muscle in on new markets. For example, Fox persuaded the National Football League to shift its television coverage from CBS to Fox by pitching its youth demographic, and Murdoch was prepared to pay over the odds to break into sport (see Kimmel, 2004: 163–164). The audience analysts at Fox pushed the use of demographics further than in the past.

Though niche marketing was by no means new, niches in global marketing for all kinds of goods have become more viable in a postmodern economy of dispersal and fragmentation. Advertisers were persuaded that they needed to get to the younger demographics, especially 18–34- and 25–49-year-olds where there were more potential buyers. Indeed, Fox executives effectively rebranded youth itself, working 'to sell [advertisers] the values of 18–34 and how they were very sophisticated and upgrade' (Fessell cited in Kimmel, 2004: 117). Fox Television's successful programming appeal to youth has had an impact worldwide. As Fox market analyst, Fessel recounts:

> There was a very strong theme of very repetitive complaints about the three networks that indicated to us that if we had innovative programming, if we had

programming that focused on particular age groups, if we had programming that pushed the edge ... then we thought we could really appeal to a very strong interest and need. (cited in Kimmel, 2004: 22)

Fox thus recognised that bland LOP programming had had its day and that innovation and risk-taking aimed at younger demographics was the way forward.

Where the 'big three' served all with bland LOP, Fox proclaimed, 'We're NOT the Establishment', 'We're the Alternative', 'the most popular network amongst adults 18–49' (see Kimmel, 2004: 235). Because of the young, urban, counter-cultural feel of its programming, Fox also appealed incidentally to African-American viewers, 'not only because of the black performers, but also because of the sharper, edgier content compared to the white-bread fare on the Big Three' (Fessell cited in Kimmel, 2004: 118).[4] The alternative programming, such as the teen drama *21 Jump Street* (which discovered Johnny Depp), *Beverly Hills 90210* and *The Simpsons*, was aimed at capturing the elusive target audience of younger males with disposable income.

Amongst notable drama successes appealing to the broader 18–49 segment, *Ally McBeal* affirmed the Fox brand as quirky and eccentric, but *The X-Files* proved innovative and enduring, affording Fox a franchise to exploit related merchandise.[5] As Greg Meidel sees it, *The X-Files* is:

created in-house. It becomes the number one hit on your network. It then becomes a number one hit in syndication on your cable network. The week-end runs are number one on your owned-and-operated stations. It's number one on B-Sky-B [in Europe], it's number one in Asia, it's number one in Latin America. It's the epitome of vertical [*sic*: horizontal?] integration. (cited in Kimmel, 2004: 16)

For capitalism to accelerate its growth (see Harvey, 1989), the former Fordist conception of a mass market needed to be refunctioned in television, as elsewhere, to address microcultures. In competitive, multichannel environments, both national and transnational, the branding of products, programme clusters and indeed branded channels themselves have become increasingly important since Fox Television led the way. Fessler observes that 'the other networks were trying to be all things to all people', and Roth adds that Fox instead was 'daring, distinctive, different' (cited in Kimmel, 2004: 211). The launches of new features need to serve, in McMurria's view, as 'strategic attention-grabbing nodal points within increasingly crowded television schedules that are now "geared" for international audiences' (2003: 66). "Event TV" inevitably has implications for the kind of output produced and disseminated, implications to be addressed in discussion of specific examples. But first, the different approach that TV3 has taken to audiences must be further unpacked.

Audiences: commodities

As noted, a feature of TV3 is its use of niche marketing strategically to attract a specific kind of audience. One approach, taken by Fox, is to target an audience which advertisers are especially interested to catch because it has proved elusive. Young people – particularly young males, with significant disposable incomes because they are as yet free from family responsibilities – are attractive to advertisers because of their spending power, but they are elusive since they do not typically stay at home and watch television. Thus programming which attracts such an audience, as Fox discovered, could serve as the basis on which to build both an audience and, indeed, a network. The opportunities afforded by vertical integration allow a company to build upon a specific audience base by scheduling an evening's viewing around a banker product. Indeed, Fox's capturing of the younger male market, in Holt's summary view, 'spawned a new age of niche marketing in broadcasting and with it, a new universe of advertising capital and incentive for investors' (2003: 19).

Even though the audience is fragmenting both within television and between television and other media outlets such as the internet, a volume audience still remains attractive to advertisers. It is likely to continue to do so under the new market conditions if only because television as yet remains a much more efficient way of reaching a large audience than its new rivals, though in time this may not prove to be the case. Advertisements placed with NBC's Thursday night "must-see TV" schedule, for example, have reached huge numbers of 18–49-year-old males. Much greater investment would currently be needed to reach an equivalent number in this desirable market segment through the internet. Even in a context where overall viewing figures are falling slightly, then, television advertising currently remains attractive to key investors. In the UK, ITV still sees its future as a volume channel, though it recognises also the need for impact.[6] Reliance on advertising for the funding of television, however, may prove a risky strategy in the longer term.

There is increasing concern within the industry that new technologies, such as TIVO and Sky Plus boxes, which allow audiences to time-shift and bypass television advertisements altogether might, in the foreseeable future, see advertisers investing their money elsewhere. Indeed, Phil Redmond, executive director of Mersey Television, told the Oxford Media Convention in January 2003 that commercial television in the UK 'is heading for a funding black hole'. At that time, the British commercial sector's audience share had fallen from 30 per cent to 24 per cent and ITV revenues had fallen from £2 billion per annum to £1.7 billion. In this light, it is not surprising that the two largest independent companies, Granada and Carlton, have been facilitated to merge as noted. In 2005, Redmond's own company has been taken over by All3media under an apparently irresistible economic imperative to merge into larger organisations. Should Redmond's prediction be proved right and the advertising market go into meltdown, however, revenues may be insufficient to sustain distinctively British commercial, terrestrial television companies, adding further weight to the imperative to go global. Given that Britain's national policy for television since 1990 has been tied to the market in spite of its strong historical public service ethos, the future of the BBC and the national licence fee is of even greater significance. But slow-grinding mechanisms of the institutions and the behaviour of viewers, as illustrated by the rituals of viewing and channel loyalty (or disinclination to shift), suggests that change will be gradual rather than overnight.

Risk in drama production

Grant and Wood (to whose research this account is indebted) have dubbed the contemporary media industries context the "*nobody knows*" (2004: 48) environment. In respect of mobilising the production of any given vehicle, the risk is huge but drama poses particular challenges because it is so expensive to produce. Improved production values, aspiring to cinema, have inevitably raised the stakes for the gatekeepers, those who ultimately make the decisions about what will be produced. But, though they adopt a number of strategies aimed at reducing risk, they know they are ultimately involved in a lottery.

Ratings information and demographics are, as noted, much more sophisticated and are perceived to be more important than ever. The market analysts thus have a voice in determining the kinds of programmes made by identifying demographics in particular scheduling slots at which the company overall is aiming. For all the market analysis, however, it is impossible accurately to predict success. As Grant and Wood note:

> This was dramatically confirmed in a study published in 1994 on the selection of television drama by the US commercial networks. Despite the use of a number of indicia (for example, well-known talent, track record of the creators, focus groups) in deciding which pilot series to select for the season's schedules, none of these indicia had any statistical ability to predict which series would actually succeed. (2004: 48)

In the USA, Fox Television, as noted, has drawn the entire television industry towards younger demographics and "edgy", urban programming, but it achieves this by focusing on the preferences of the demographic desired by advertisers and persuading them that Fox products would attract them. Similarly, in the "network era" of volume audiences, it was the "Peoria factor", whether or not the show would appeal to "middle America", which determined programming. Though the multi-channel context of TV3 appears to offer greater diversity, it still privileges the profitable and thus does not appeal to all segments of society and to some extent marginalises the less advantaged.

The risk environment encourages strategies thought to bring success. For example, the use of A-list stars is deemed a prerequisite for American television series, as in the film industry. Similarly there is a pull towards repeating previous successes or, in postmodern times, fusing elements of one successful product with those of another. Franchises of successful formats figure increasingly, even in drama where it is particularly difficult (see *Queer as Folk*). Marketing and publicity often consume budgets equivalent to those for production, aiming to make the product visible in an overcrowded market-place. Against the forces of conservatism are those of the horizontal integration of today's industry structure which affords maximum capitalisation on any success to offset the losses incurred in failures. Companies such as HBO and Fox Television have shown, however, that greater risk may promote, rather than inhibit, success.

Other economic forces militate against innovation. Beyond the USA, it is more profitable to buy in television programmes than to home-produce. As Grant and Wood summarise the British context in the late 1990s:

> By comparing audience, advertising revenue and program cost, they [David Graham & Associates] estimated which programs returned most to the broadcasters' bottom line. Predictably, long-running soap operas like *Coronation Street* or *East-Enders* were the most profitable. But, after those were accounted for, acquired foreign programs, despite attracting smaller audiences than independent UK productions, were routinely more profitable for the broadcasters who aired them. (2004: 132)

In this light, it is not surprising that there has been an increase in soap output in Britain and that the relatively cheaply made dramas such as *The Bill* (Thames for ITV) have shifted emphasis towards the on-going serial narratives of soaps, particularly with romance-interest storylines involving core characters. What needs further explanation, however, is why companies in Britain, or elsewhere, continue to pursue expensive "quality" drama output which is destined to make a loss. And this is where factors beyond crude market economics and the balance sheet enter the equation.

The case for intervention: new strategies for new times

"Market failure" indicates 'the failure of the market as a whole to do what markets are presumed to do best, that is lead to the best possible outcome for the greatest possible number of participants' (Grant and Wood, 2004: 58). In a context where transnational media conglomerates have the potential to dominate world markets and to make only those products which yield them most profit, and where home-produced television drama in all countries other than the USA is loss-making, market failure is an issue. As illustrated by the case of Fox Television, for example, a company can be commercially successful in targeting just the most profitable sectors of the market when broader cultural factors may demand a wider appeal. Articulating a worst-case scenario, Grant and Wood suggest that, 'the megaphone of the blockbuster increasingly drowns out the whisper of the independent, the alternative, the local and the marginal' (2004: 20). As they see it, the:

> relative handful of conglomerates and even the more ubiquitous calculus of maximum return quite rationally seek to eliminate all but the most highly profitable of creative expression from circulation. Mere value to an audience or even merely modest profits do not measure up against maximising value to shareholders. (2004: 18)

The case for regulation and for public ownership (such as with the BBC) rests on a recognition that cultural products are different from "widgets", and to achieve a

diversity which addresses all social needs requires a measure of political intervention. In the view of Grant and Wood, 'Free access to the fullest variety of expression is not a social luxury. It is the very substance of freedom' (2004: 20).

Cultural goods produce experiences. 'What we value', argue Grant and Wood,
'is the ephemeral transfer of an imagined life from the author's mind to our own,
the few minutes of emotion provoked by a song, or the hour and a half we spend
in another world conjured up by coloured light moving across the screen' (2004:
21). Where niche markets within one nation's boundaries might be insufficiently
profitable, it is possible with some kinds of television fictions to build a bigger
audience transnationally. The *telenovela*, cited in Chapter 1, offers a case in point;
TV movies, as distinct from the relatively low-budget made-for-TV movies of
yesteryear, afford another. In an informative account of Hallmark Entertainment's
strategy based on TV movies, McMurria reports that the Hallmark Network:

> broadcasts sixteen different feeds in twenty-three languages as of 2001. Each chan-
> nel typically premiered thirteen to twenty TV movies per month, and 70–80 per
> cent of total programming came from the Hallmark library, with the balance con-
> sisting of locally acquired programmes. Each feed contains a single programming
> stream, with space for up to six different language subtitling tracks. Regional offices
> in London (Europe, Middle East, Africa), Miami (Latin America) and Hong Kong
> and Singapore (Asia) execute sales and marketing campaigns and co-ordinate sub-
> titling/dubbing. (2003: 81)

Transnational means of dissemination by a mix of cable and satellite television
distribution networks have thus created an international audience for long-format
TV fictions, expensively made, high-profile mini-series and TV Movies.

Yet another approach in TV3 to funding big-budget TV drama productions
and making them profitable actually bypasses revenue from advertising. Subscription channels, such as HBO, rely primarily on the income from subscribers. Thus
they have to offer, to a target audience with excess disposable income, products
which are typically unavailable elsewhere and to keep the audience happy such
that they will renew their subscriptions. The pornography market is one aspect of
these channels in this context. But, in respect of TV drama, since they are trying to
attract a "blue-chip" demographic which is likely to be college-educated and thus
have the more sophisticated taste formation of those with cultural as well as economic capital, they may invest in "high-end" products. The evidence of HBO Premium is a case in point. Whatever view is taken of any individual programme, a
portfolio including *Sopranos*, *Oz*, *Sex and the City* and *Six Feet Under* is broadly
impressive in these terms. A much more direct relationship is created between
producer and viewer for such programming than the former indirect relationship
between them, mediated as it was through company executives negotiating with
advertising agents. According to Simon Sutton, President of HBO International,
power has shifted to those who control the programmes' brands and, having proved
that audiences are drawn to quality, the strategy of HBO Premium will continue
to be to produce signature series with 'a strong, unique creative vision'.[7]

Under earlier circumstances, the tendency was strong, in contrast, to construct viewers in terms far more conservative than they actually were and to adopt an LOP approach to both audience and product. In TV3, a much more direct relationship between viewers and audience is often set up, not just by market research but also by means of the internet. Joss Whedon, producer of *Buffy the Vampire Slayer*, for example, has acknowledged that he takes feedback very seriously and allows it to inform the development of the programme. Other producers and channels actively encourage instant internet feedback and reciprocally offer chatroom sessions with production personnel and website information. Television in TV3 cannot be taken in isolation from other media, particularly the internet, since, at the macro-economic level, the major corporations have interests, as noted, across all media. It is not surprising, therefore, that they encourage links between them which they utilise to their mutual advantage

Global sales of subscription programming and the marketing of related merchandise through the owning conglomerate's horizontally integrated networks inevitably brings in additional revenue to offset costs and yield substantial profits over time. Whatever the downsides of the economic changes in TV3 might be, Todreas's claim, cited above, positing a 'great value shift from conduit to content' appears to be borne out. Thus there is a case for saying that the TV3 environment gravitates towards distinctive, "quality TV" product in contrast with the formerly in-built industrial disposition towards mediocrity in former eras. The American networks and British terrestrial channels are forced to compete both in terms of audience strategy and to produce that "quality" product the economically desirable audience segments are coming to expect. Even large institutions or companies may, however, have to look beyond in-house funding to do this: hence the BBC's co-production with HBO on *Rome*.

Besides the "high-end" output, which is the focus of this book, a broad diet of programming also remains available on television, and mainstream institutions within any given nation (the networks in the USA, and the BBC and main terrestrial ITV channels in the UK, for example, remain very significant players). It should not be forgotten that, despite the huge success of subscription channels in the TV drama sector, many people habitually follow the home-produced soaps, either in preference to the subscription channels or in conjunction with them. Alongside the research (cited in Chapter 1) suggesting that most viewers, given the choice, prefer home-produced programmes, there is some evidence to indicate that there is also viewer loyalty to the single-figure numbers on the TV dial or remote. That is to say, there may be a significant residual and conservative culture in television viewing habits precisely because it is a domestic everyday medium which militates against too fast a change. That is partly why TV3 is a preferable term to a global–digital age since, taking a synchronic snapshot of current practices, there are several systems at work.

It is, however, the diachronic market and cultural trends of development which I am trying to capture here. The argument is that, since "high-end" TV drama has always been expensive to produce, and since production values continue to be pushed up by both technological developments in the distribution and reception apparatus and audience's teleliteracy and expectations, it is becoming increasingly challenging for anybody but the big institutions and media global conglomerates to produce. Co-productions involving conglomerates are also subject to their influence. The conditions of a fragmenting overall market might seem fundamentally to threaten "high-end" TV drama by diluting available funding, but in fact they have mobilised some strong forces which pull in the opposite direction. Market conditions, to repeat, have 'shifted profit from conduit to content' (Todreas, 1999: 7ff.) and allowed some key producers to focus more directly upon "blue-chip" demographics, resulting in a more lavish, more sophisticated drama to appeal to that market. Where HBO leads, furthermore, the networks have been drawn to follow. Networks need to have impact as well as retain substantial audience numbers, and NBC's *Desperate Housewives* owes a debt to *Sex and the City*.

The viewers' relationship with television is changing fast. In the future, the means by which people receive television and the means by which they become accustomed to paying for it will be crucial. Subscription, or pay-per-view, television addresses the problem of diminishing advertising revenues by bypassing them. The increasing capacity to download television programmes – or at least sections of them – from the internet, taps in to the now-established means of downloading music. Given internet access, an MP3 player or i-Pod and sufficient money (pence rather than pounds; dimes rather than dollars), it is already possible to download for personal use any number of music tracks.[8] In principle, the same economy is feasible for television drama. It is after all already operating to an extent for clips and, through subscription and pay-per-view, for theatre films distributed through television. Download opportunities, or direct broadband digital access, will become increasingly possible as national televisions go thoroughly digital following the analogue switch-off. Indeed, part of the current strategy in preparation for a more fully digital age of even the relatively conservative BBC is to make its vast library of programming digitally available to all. The question of the funding method, through a sustained annual licence fee or by the kinds of commercial means noted above, remains in question, as does the readiness of people fundamentally to change their viewing habits.

As the effectiveness of spot advertising diminishes, product placement and direct sponsorship have become increasingly important means of sustaining some commercial funding of television.[9] In turn, the outcome of the licence-fee decision in the UK will impact on British television culture. Continuance of a licence-fee would sustain at least some sense of a national television, most likely in the case of the BBC with a sustained public service remit. A fully commercial provision may allow those with the means to pay access to the 'global cornucopia of programming and nearly infinite libraries of data, education and entertainment' predicted by Rupert Murdoch but, again, there are implications for the commodity form as well as national cultures.

The British dilemma

It will now be evident why I suggested above that it makes little sense to deal with one nation's television institutions or culture since the context of TV3 is already global and likely to become increasingly transnational in outlook. Former national concerns about the ownership of the means of communication have been challenged by new technologies, with regulatory frameworks, as noted, playing catch-up to meet the new industrial circumstances. Even in continental Europe, where language barriers obtain and where countries such as France have fiercely defended national cinematic cultures in the past, the privatisation and growth of European television in a transnational context has led to increasingly international production and the dissemination of an inevitably anglophone television output (see Coleman and Rollett, 1997). Though I now return to the British context, to raise some of the implications of change, the challenge to national culture and identity applies to most nations worldwide. In particular, the noted tension between the global and the local is a common and crucial issue. For "high-end" TV drama at least, lavish and sophisticated programming is likely to remain available, but it may lose the local (national or regional) specificity that it has had in the past.[10] Given that viewers are known to prefer programming perceived to be culturally specific to them, this would appear to be an issue for all concerned.

At the macroeconomic level, it is understandable that governments have facilitated the adjustment of regulations to allow their national television production and distribution industries to remain economically viable. But, in so doing, they inevitably concede ground to the global market at the expense of defending national communications culture. This aspect is particularly resonant in the UK since Britain historically has had the strongest public service ethos in the world. In respect of a whole range of values, the BBC has been regarded since the introduction of commercial television and a mixed economy in 1955 as the yardstick which, in Michael Grade's resonant phrase, 'keeps the rest honest'. Though it has become a genuine international player – particularly through its commercial dimensions, BBC Worldwide and BBC Enterprises – the BBC has largely been perceived to be a public service broadcasting icon in the UK. As its audience share diminishes along with those of all other formerly mass-broadcast institutions in a fragmented, multichannel environment, however, a crude economic argument to sustain its Charter and funding by a national licence fee weakens.

There are, however, a range of cultural arguments – beyond the scope of this book to explore in detail – which might be mobilised in favour of sustaining both charter and licence fee. As Grant and Wood succinctly put it, 'Local cultural expression can be impoverished if it is not open to foreign ideas. But it can equally be impoverished if it is dominated by the voices of another country' (2004: 5).

In the context of "high-end" TV drama, the benchmarks of quality might now be located elsewhere, but a sustained BBC with a distinctive ethos would at least keep some perspectives in the global mix, possibly on a world stage, which might otherwise be all too readily effaced. Chapter 6 looks at issues of the global and the local in relation to specific examples of TV drama product.

Another consideration in the contemporary British context is the place of small independent production companies. Many of these emerged in the early to mid-nineties in the wake of the 1990 Broadcasting Act's requirement for the main terrestrial channels to include 25 per cent of overall broadcasting to be made by independents. These requirements were intended to militate against any monopolistic tendencies of the big institutions (in particular the BBC) and to bring fresh ideas into the industry. In the past decade, however, many of these companies have either gone out of business or merged with others to make bigger corporations (as in Mersey TVs incorporation by All3 Media noted above). Their problem, in the developing context recounted here, is a lack of critical mass. Their growth has been hindered, furthermore, by the way in which their productions have typically been commissioned by distributors. By fully funding their productions, the big commissioners (e.g. the BBC or Channel 4) have retained secondary rights where the substantial profits (assuming success) are to be made. In Steemers's technical summary:

> the cost plus system delivered low returns from production fees and back end share and no assets, making it difficult for independent producers to attract venture capital or develop alternative revenue streams from secondary exploitation that would allow them to grow, diversify and invest in other productions. (2004: 66)

In sum, even companies with good ideas and consequently successful product could not grow significantly in a context in which size matters.

Following an ITC review of this situation, the Government agreed in January 2003 'that free-to-air channels should be subject to binding codes of practice in their dealings with independent producers, subject to approval and enforcement by Ofcom [the new communications regulatory body]' (Steemers, 2004: 68). Once again, this evidences a national government retaining a regulatory role but a largely reactive one in response to the impact of market conditions. This particular aspect of policy matters considerably to the account in this book, however, because a number of programmes cited as examples of quality TV drama (e.g. *Shameless* and *Queer as Folk*) have emerged from small independent production companies and thus their capacity to survive in TV3 matters. It may be that this sector will remain important by settling into a smaller number of larger independents, as the trend indicates, and that they will be able to take risks in programming.[11]

Though some popular drama, notably soap opera, is relatively inexpensive to produce, drama is typically more expensive than programming such as game shows, make-overs, or Reality TV. At the "high end" under current expectations of production values, drama is becoming increasingly expensive to make. For example, as Grant and Wood report, *West Wing* costs 'US$4 million per episode' (2004: 223) whilst 'In 2002, Fox committed an unprecedented US$6 million to a pilot for the series *Fastlane*' (2004: 106). In this heady context, only a few institutions can compete at the "high end": established public service corporations (such as the BBC in the UK, CBC in Canada, and ABC in Australia); premium subscription channels owned by media conglomerates (such as HBO and Showtime); production companies vertically integrated with distributing companies (as now in the USA); and substantial independents (making commissions for the networks and other publishing outlets). As noted, the American networks, though they may well produce distinctive work on occasion, will tend towards the "quality popular" end (see Chapter 7) of the drama- output spectrum, though they may invest in flagship productions to sustain channel impact. Similarly, the commercial channels in the UK – ITV and Five – are increasingly likely to seek volume rather than niche audiences and thus produce dramas with broad appeal. Whilst this does not preclude innovation, strong forces gravitate towards the "tried and tested with a new twist" rather than radical experiment. It is worth considering, however, the role of independents in innovative production.

In the UK, as noted, regulations require that 25 per cent of output transmitted on licensed terrestrial channels is drawn from the independent sector (indies). Thus, in theory, there is ample opportunity for a range of voices to be heard and a diversity of styles to be seen. In actuality, however, 10 per cent of this output is made by just three established indies and 25 per cent is drawn from just twenty-five companies. The whole indie sector in the UK is smaller than the BBC/ITV output taken together. There have been some 800 indies since the late 1980s but many have not endured. An expensive pilot not taken up for a series by the commissioning network can prove disastrous for a thinly resourced indie. Production conditions are such that only independents with a critical mass that allows them to be well resourced are assured of survival. As Grant and Wood observe, 'larger firms in the business of distributing cultural products possess significant advantages that present nearly insurmountable barriers to the entry of new competitors' (2004: 58).

Secondary rights ownership has become a hot issue in this context, since the bundling and buying of rights by the commissioning company effectively prevents indies from building a resource base by capitalising from secondary platforms when they do produce a success. In the current negotiations of future arrangements in the UK, PACT is aiming to ensure, as John McAvoy puts it, 'that in the UK the dominant terrestrials do not foreclose on competition'.[12] It still remains cheaper for the BBC to produce in-house on a marginal cost basis than to commission from indies and thus, in respect of its proposed WOCC (Window of Creative Competition) policy aimed to answer questions of capacity and transparency and to put in-house BBC production to the test of the free market, the odds may remain stacked in favour of in-house production.[13] Notwithstanding these challenges, a few independents have been successful with drama production, and some on the territory of challenging drama. Red Production Company is a case in point.

Case sketches in the UK context: Channel 4 and Red Production Company

Channel 4 (C4) was established in 1982 with a distinctive public service remit to address minority audiences and for innovation. It emerged in the UK at a time of worldwide channel expansion when, in the post-1960s, increasingly pluralist society, the remnant centrist authority of the BBC was being called in question. Indeed, as Ellis notes, C4 programme-makers, unlike their predecessors at the BBC, 'felt themselves to be excluded from the centres of power. Their self-image was one of being "anti-establishment" of holding liberal or radical ideas and being openly critical of many older cultural values. "Innovation" became the rallying cry of such people' (2002: 149). And, indeed, C4 has since gained a worldwide reputation as an innovative, at times overtly experimental, television service. Though a commercial publisher–broadcaster, C4 gained its revenue from advertising indirectly in its early years and was thus somewhat protected from the demands of advertisers which, as noted, have tended historically towards a maximising of audience by playing safe. A proportion of the income from an excess-profit tax levied by government on the regional ITV companies funded C4 and, in return, the ITV companies secured the right to sell advertising space on the new channel, retaining the proceeds, exempt from excess-profit tax. Thus there was an incentive to sell advertising space, but C4 itself was kept at arm's length from the market and could thus pursue its remit. A decade later, however, the Broadcasting Act of 1992 undermined this position by making C4 directly responsible for its own advertising revenues, thus exposing the channel to the market, arguably to its detriment in terms of its programming policy. Though it continued to be a commercial success, the full diversity of programming for which it had become famous was under threat.

The force of advertisers' requirements had tended to keep ITV – at least politically – bland and the BBC had striven historically to avoid political partisanship through its core concept of achieving "balance". As Ellis summarises British broadcasting policy orthodoxy, 'Whether documentary or drama, it should attempt a thorough articulation of a problem or a character, and avoid the partial, polemical, or tendentious. Balance … meant the avoidance of programmes which put distinctive points of view. (2002: 155). But C4 established itself under circumstances free from direct market forces and with a remit to be innovative Unlike the BBC, C4 was set up as a publisher–broadcaster and shaped a channel identity in line with its remit by commissioning interesting – and at times challenging – work from indies. Indeed, the setting-up of C4 saw a significant increase in the number of independent production companies, many comprised of personnel who had felt frustrated by the conservatism of the BBC and/or the outright commercialism of the ITV sector. Thus, as well as achieving diversity of programming and representations under its remit to address minorities, C4 developed in the full cry of a number of voices wanting – and having the opportunity – to articulate strong and alternative points of view. As Ellis characterises the emergence of what he calls the age of availability in the 1980s, 'Balance gave way to diversity. Television is no longer the arbiter of content but a forum for content. Channel 4 pushed the boundaries of what it was possible to see on British television, and hastened the process' (2002: 156). Unfortunately, the circumstances which afforded this period of innovation, challenge and diversification were not to last. In the

1990s, the move, in the UK and worldwide, away from public service remits towards market economics and privatisation in television disturbed the foundations of C4. Having to raise its own revenue directly from advertising and under the pressure of a diminishing audience share in a multichannel environment, C4 came to rely increasingly on American imports for its flagship programming.

As noted above, it is ultimately cheaper to import even prestigious programmes from the USA than to commission and co-fund home-grown product. In its bid to attract the elusive youth demographic, some programming went beyond innovation to outright shock (see Ellis, 2002: 158–159). Though it remained viable in its public service form and sustained some innovative programming, C4 felt the pressure of the 1990s, just as it had been infused by the early 1980s context. After the resignation as CEO of Michael Grade in 1997, his successor Michael Jackson appeared to go with the Thatcherite tide inexorably towards a thorough commercialism, questionably cancelling its bedrock soap, *Brookside*, and turning to Reality TV formats alongside American drama imports.

Since the arrival of Andy Duncan as CEO in mid-2004, however, the tide appears to be turning again at C4. As he articulated clearly in a keynote to the 2006 Oxford Media Convention (from which quotations below are taken), Duncan sees the future of C4 as a second British public service channel, using commercial means to a public service end, in healthy competition with the licence-funded BBC. In today's digital environment, he envisages 'public service plurality on every platform, not just network TV'. However, potentially returning C4 to its inaugural emphasis, he proposes 'more innovative, thought-provoking and trouble-making television'. Thus, in developing a carefully crafted multidimensional media brand, he seeks to resurrect 'remit impact', a space for the 'oppositional, a creative place for new voices'. Alluding to ITV's closure of its 24-hour news channel and anticipating ITV and Five's increasing withdrawal from public service approaches more rigorously to pursue commercial ends, Duncan recognises that, to have their voice heard, public service broadcasters need the strength that comes through scale. But he endorses thinking circulating for some time in government policy forums that competition is needed for the BBC in the UK environment. The old schism between commercial and public service values would appear in television, as elsewhere (in education and the Health Service), to be displaced.

Duncan points to C4's greater share than BBC1 or BBC2 of the 16–34-year-old audience, and notes that E4 is bigger than BBC3 and More4 bigger than BBC4. He points to drama productions (*The Deal, Hamburg Sector*) which have recently rivalled BBC output in terms of quality and popularity. For the near future, based on a healthy balance sheet, he proposes very significant investment in programming and publicity in excess of £80 million to make C4 'the leading shaper of contemporary culture in Britain'. In making this pitch for C4 to be an additional, but commercially based, PSB (public service broadcasting) channel, Duncan is conscious of both the commercial multiplatform competition and the rubric of Ofcom's policy consultation document which aims to 'maximise benefits to citizen-consumers' (in another conflation of terms which were formerly seen to be mutually exclusive).

The success of C4's bid depends on the allocation to it by the Government of a free digital spectrum equivalent to the analogue currently provided. This is by no means assured, as other companies will object to an alleged interference in the market, and the Government stands to make large sums from the sale of residual digital spectrum. The importance of the pitch in the context of this book's account of industry forces is that it illustrates the practical tensions in establishing industry policy. In the UK at least, the case for public service values and some, albeit light touch, regulation through quotas or subsidies to achieve that end remains in play. In respect of TV drama production specifically, a Public Service Publisher (PSP) channel with a sustained remit for innovation would afford commissioning of some of the more challenging writing and production which independent companies such as Red Productions aims to foster. Should C4 be successful in this current strategy, the balance between demand-led and supply-side approaches to production may be shifted sufficiently to contribute significantly to sustaining short-run, innovative drama reflecting local (regional, national) cultures on British screens, such as those emanating from Red Productions.

Now located back at Granada Studios in Manchester, Nicola Shindler left Granada Television at the end of 1987 to found Red Production Company from her kitchen. This was a bold move since the times were becoming uncertain. Though Shindler had a successful background as a TV drama producer which included work on BAFTA-winning *Hillsborough* and *Cracker* (Jimmy McGovern) and *Prime Suspect 5* for ITV as well as *Our Friends in the North* (Peter Flannery) for BBC, the future of Red Productions was by no means secure. Though many indies were suffering from commissioning drought and it might seem a particularly risky moment to start a new venture, Shindler had connections at C4 where former Granada colleagues had taken up influential posts (see Chapter 4).

Shindler was not, however, seeking an easy option in respect of product. She formed Red Productions to work with new writers on modern, innovative but entertaining dramas. Fortunately for the company, *Queer as Folk* (C4, 1999, written by Russell T. Davies), *Clocking Off* (BBC1, 2000, written by Paul Abbott) and *Bob and Rose* (ITV, 2001, also written by Russell T. Davies) were early successes. Thus Red Productions found outlets on all the main UK terrestrial channels to establish its base. It has since transmitted work on the new digital BBC3 channel (*Casanova*, 2005, written by Russell T. Davies) and the commercial digital channel, Sky One (*Now You See Her*, 2001, written by Matt Jones). Shindler and Red Productions might reasonably claim to have brought to notice two of the UK's recent writing talents in Abbott and Davies but they have also produced the work of other less-known Northern writers, some discovered by Red Productions through the Northern Soul script competition which it devised in partnership with C4. Red Productions thus not only illustrates a quite rare, successful indie, ranging across all major outlets in a highly competitive environment, but also an extremely rare indie producer of drama which is both writer-led and innovative in a manner which many commentators claim has gone out of fashion (see Brandt, 1981 and 1993).

Summary

From their wide-ranging study of the contemporary media industries, Grant and Wood (2004) conclude that, contrary to popular myth, digital and satellite technologies have not created a borderless cyber-universe. Though some transnational distribution appears to bypass nation states and thus national regulatory authority, in practice national governments have found ways and means to sustain some control over what is transmitted and to whom within the bounds of their responsibilities. As they wryly remark, 'Reports of the death of national cultural policy, to say nothing of the end of the nation state, turn out to be greatly exaggerated' (2004: 331). Indeed, although public service interests remain a factor in the interventions of national governments, financial interest emerges as the key factor in keeping boundaries relatively secure. As Grant and Wood conclude, 'Territories defined around national geography are a prime factor in determining how money is made from intellectual property. Financial interest, as it turns out, trumps technology' (2004: 331). If, therefore, for reasons of diversity of overall output or reasons of nurturing and protecting home-grown industry to meet the apparent preference for the local over the global, governments wish to make steering regulatory interventions, they can. Except in countries such as China, the cornucopia predicted by Murdoch to be on offer worldwide is unlikely to be blocked in the foreseeable future, but, to maximise diversity, it is likely that national governments will need – by means of subsidies and quotas – to continue to make small interventions. In the case of the UK, adding C4 as outlined by Duncan above to a sustained publicly funded BBC may go a long way to ensuring the distinctive British quality drama as defined and envisaged in this book.

This chapter has sketched the political economy of TV3 bringing out, by stark comparison with the circumstances of TV1 a changed approach to marketing (from mass to niche audiences) and products (from LOP to distinctive programming). The account has shown how, in the context of the postmodern economy and extended development of digital technologies, horizontally and vertically integrated media conglomerates have risen to dominance. National media companies and institutions have needed to respond, typically by means of commercial growth and merger. National regulatory bodies (governments and their agencies) have been obliged to deregulate to reposition home industries and facilitate change but may need to continue to steer through regulation to ensure the maintenance of diversity and to meet local needs. In respect of "high-end" TV drama, the new circumstances of TV3 with its 'great value shift from conduit to content' have foregrounded branding of distinctive product ("must-see" "Event TV") to maximise visibility in a crowded market-place with the aim of attracting a "blue-chip" demographic. The reduced need to appeal to advertisers has additionally facilitated risk-taking and promoted "edgy" television in some quarters, in contrast with the former tendency to normativity – and, at worst, mediocrity – built into the television industry. Some possible downsides of what otherwise look like promising conditions for the production of "high-end" TV drama have been flagged for subsequent consideration. If the network era might be characterised as repeating established formulae to avoid offending people, however, TV3, in respect of "high-end" drama might be characterised as a time to take risks and shock audiences with both content and formal experiment. The next chapter looks at the nature of some of these risks.

Notes

1 According to a *Radio Times* preview citing executive producer, Frank Doelger, 'We felt that British actors offered us significant advantages. American actors are for the most part perceived as contemporary performers, so when they're in a period drama, they don't come over convincingly to US audiences' (29 October–4 November 2005: 18).

2 (www.timewarner.com/corp/businesses/detail/global_marketing/index.html, accessed 2 November 2005).

3 For a book-length study of the emergence of Fox television to network status, see Kimmel 2004, to which this sketch is much indebted.

4 For a book-length account of Fox Television's relation with black audiences, see Brent Zook, 1999. Brent Zook argues that Fox changed the course of black television unintentionally. 'It inadvertently fostered a space for black authorship in television' (1999: 4).

5 For further discussion of Fox and *The X-Files*, see Johnson, 2005: 95–107.

6 Interview conducted by Robin Nelson and Stephen Lacey with Steve Bottomley and Jo Dunnington of ITV Network Planning at ITN, Grays Inn Road, London, 26 January 2006.

7 Simon Sutton speaking at the Oxford Media Convention, 19 January 2006.

8 Alex Graham CEO of Wall to Wall Television and Chair of PACT presented projections which demonstrated the feasibility of television downloads to iPod equivalents to the Oxford Media Convention, January 2005.

9 In the UK, payment for product placement remains illegal, though it appears to have become more widespread to judge by the regularity with which named brands appear even on the BBC. The question of whether or not money changes hands remains something of a trade secret according to Steve Bottomley and Jo Dunnington in an interview conducted by Robin Nelson and Stephen Lacey, ITV Network Planning at ITN, Grays Inn Road, London, 26 January 2006.

10 Local Television initiatives, such as the European Local TV City network and the 2005–6 BBC Local TV experiments, have been moderately successful but they remain low budget and tend to concentrate on factual programming.

11 The ITC review (2002), as reported by Steemers, noted , 'the fragmentary and "fragile" nature of the independent sector – with approximately fifty medium-sized companies accounting for a quarter of the market by share of turnover and a further 500 companies representing 10 per cent of the market' (2004: 66).

12 John McVay, Chief Executive of PACT speaking at the Oxford Media Convention, 19 January 2006.

13 For details of WOCC, see www.bbc.co.uk/commissioning/tv/network/wocc.shtml.

4

Pushing the envelope: "edgy" TV drama
Queer as Folk, Sex and the City, Carnivàle

Other than in the domain of art video, television has not traditionally been regarded as an experimental medium. Art video demonstrates that it is not the medium itself which imposes constraints but the social context of broadcast transmission.[1] As observed, the broadcast television industry historically has tended towards norms, and what has passed for innovative has frequently been little more than an established formula with a new twist. I repeat here that I do not wish to imply that mainstream fare is necessarily bad television. The domestic nature of the medium and its perceived prime function to entertain and make large numbers of people feel comfortable in their homes, however, has typically militated against radical experiment with either content or form. But, as argued in the last chapter, the TV3 era of branding, narrowcasting and "must-see" TV events demands the distinctive product which is my concern here.

The multichannel environment has afforded opportunities through new channels aiming only for relatively small audiences in the first instance to try out challenging production ideas. Even established institutions such as the BBC have been able through the new Freeview, digital provision with its new channels (BBC3 and BBC4) to test the water in respect of drama which might well not have been commissioned for mainstream channels. Russell T. Davies's *Casanova* (Spring, 2005) and Simon Ashdown and Jeremy Dyson's *Funland* (Autumn, 2005), transmitted on BBC3, are cases in point. Where mainstream, terrestrial channels are governed by regulators (FCC in the USA and Ofcom, the successor to ITC, in the UK), subscription channels are able to bypass the regulator and thus be even more daring, particularly in respect of "strong language" and "scenes of an adult nature". But the testing of boundaries by the subscription channel output gradually pushes the envelope for all television in terms of what is deemed culturally acceptable, and the range of possible content and forms is consequently broadened.

In respect of form, the tendency of the leading subscription channel, HBO, to align its products with modernist cinema might evoke the idea of the avant-garde, the fore-runners who, in the original military usage of the term, served as a cutting edge to breach the defences of the opposition. Though there might be something of this in HBO's challenge to the forces of regulation, in postmodern times the impetus for any formal innovation plays out more in hybrids than through distinctive artistic signatures, with the blurring of boundaries rather than their transgression and playing with ambiguity and irony, postmodernism's capacity, as Hutcheon puts it, 'to install and reinforce as much as undermine and subvert the presuppositions it appears to challenge' (1989: 1–2), has been successfully deployed in some examples of TV drama to mask some quite exceptional material on the pretext of its being merely playful. Rather than functioning in the spirit of a grand narrative of progress and the breaking of new ground in a linear trajectory of "progression", the hybrids of TV3 – as exemplified, for example, in *Shameless* – have found room for manoeuvre with a potential to unsettle the audience's bearings in political terms without the overt challenge of some of the early television dramas which consciously and defiantly challenged both televisual and Establishment norms.[2] Though they are more likely to engage with the politics of the personal than with the Marxist grand narrative in which the work of Jim Allen, for example, might be located, contemporary TV dramatists have found accommodations with commercial production which have allowed them nevertheless to introduce new perspectives. This chapter explores some examples of "edgy" TV drama in this light.[3]

A significant contribution to innovation in TV3 comes from gay culture. Over the thirty years since the decriminalisation of homosexuality in the UK and with the gradual emergence of a plural society, voices previously marginalised, or encoded, in broadcast outlets have been making themselves heard. My first example, *Queer as Folk*, created and written by Russell T. Davies, shocked audiences by bringing the sexual promiscuity and other aspects of gay life centred on Canal Street at the heart of Manchester's real-life 'gay village' to the small screen. It is, perhaps, the very everydayness of the depiction which had such impact, as we shall see. My second example is also informed by a gay aesthetic, although its focus is on the sexual, romantic and career lives of four female protagonists in New York. Though it is based on a book by Candace Bushnell, *Sex and the City's* creator and producer, Darren Star, like Russell T. Davies, brings a gay perspective and gay aesthetic to bear on the programme. Excess and a love of fashion and up-market lifestyles characterise key aspects of each series, along with a tendency to melodrama, and thus both *Queer as Folk* and *Sex and the City* hook into features of popular, spectacular television. Their disposition to shock, sometimes by the characters behaving in overtly provocative ways, and their explicit sexual content, however, pose challenges to mainstream television viewers.

My third example, *Carnivàle*, takes us more overtly into the realm of telefantasy, a distinctive and long-standing mode of television fiction which has been significantly retheorized in recent times to bring out not only its particular use of spectacle but also its disposition towards moments of Todorovian 'hesitancy' in its juxtapositon without harmonisation of disparate elements (see Johnson, 2005).

Though the narrative framing of *Carnivàle* sets up an old-fashioned Manichean conflict between good and evil, the treatment, besides being visually arresting, "cinematic" even, involves the layering of documentary montage with dream sequences, visions and the exercise of paranormal powers which, at the outset at least, are not afforded sense-making frames. Within the temporal setting in the American Depression of the 1930s, the experience of those under pressure at the margins of society are foregrounded. In very different ways, fundamentalist Christian and fairground freaks lie outwith the comfortable living of middle America and, whilst they are set at a historical distance, they resonate with the contemporary.

Thus, all three chosen examples adopt, above all, perspectives beyond petit bourgeois norms and, albeit in very different ways, unsettle established codes and conventions of television to dislocate habitual modes of TV viewing to invite new ways of seeing.

Queer As Folk (Red Productions for Channel 4, UK, 1999)

Queer As Folk (*QaF*) is "edgy" television which produced controversy when it was first shown in the UK because its representation of gay culture is bolder than previous efforts. For the first time in a British television series, all the principal characters are gay, the language is unusually ripe, even for Channel 4, and the physical relationships between the men are explicitly depicted, challenging regulatory constraints.[4]

Seen from one perspective, *QaF* represents the coming of age and the televisual 'coming-out' of writer Russell T. Davies, paralleling the development of the medium itself in respect of gay issues. As Davies explains in the booklet accompanying the 'Definitive Collector's Edition' of the series published on DVD in June 2003, his writing career prior to *QaF* saw a range of gay characters introduced at first in minor roles in television series with other agendas. Many of the programmes were for children. He introduced 'a Devil-worshipping Nazi lesbian' (2003: 3) in a children's TV thriller *Dark Season* (BBC1); a gay man and a lesbian vicar in *Revelations*, a soap opera; and two gay schoolboys in *Springhill*, 'a mysterious apocalyptic soap' (2003: 3). When producing the children's series, *Children's Ward* (Granada), he introduced an HIV story but 'wasn't brave enough to create children's television's first gay kid, and had to watch with envy and admiration when *Byker Grove* broke new ground' (2003: 3). Finally, in *The Grand*, 'an everyday story of 1920's hotel folk', the character of Clive, 'a working-class lad struggling to express his sexuality' (2003: 3), took over what was supposed to be an ensemble-cast series. Though Davies's preoccupation was something of a disaster for *The Grand*, which was axed following a slump in ratings, it was the germ of *QaF* in two important respects.

First, Davies realised that, although the Clive episodes were inappropriate for *The Grand*, the writing itself was a significant development for him. As he recalls, 'I'd resolved to find a new way of writing ... something closer to real life; a style where people don't say what they're thinking. And I'm only telling you this because it explains that strange cryptic quality that *Queer as Folk* has at times' (2003: 5).

The quality of the writing, to which we shall return, is not always enough to ensure television publication. The qualities of Davies's writing were, however, spotted by Granada producer, Catriona MacKenzie, who mobilised the second motivating force by advising Davies to follow his instincts. Inviting an interesting conflation of form and content, as Davies reports, 'In essence, she was saying, "Go gay!"' (2003: 7).

As noted above, when new ground is broken in TV drama by means of formal experimentation or challenging content (or both); production research reveals that some unusual licence had been given to the creative energies driving the project. Typically, a creative writer or writing team and imaginative producers come together to take advantage of a particular set of institutional circumstances. In the case of *QaF*, beyond the relatively chance occurrence of MacKenzie reading and appreciating the work of an emergent writer finding a voice, Nicola Shindler had, in 1997, just taken the adventurous decision to leave Granada to set up Red Productions (as recounted in Chapter 3). The kind of work with which Shindler had been associated – and which Red Productions has subsequently gone on to produce – is not regular TV fare likely to find favour with schedulers, but work aiming to push the envelope. *QaF* is a case in point. Mackenzie, however, along with Gub McNeal, had also recently left Granada to become Head of Drama at Channel 4, a channel with a minorities remit. Although the mid-to-late 1990s were an uncertain time in British television, with the BBC, despite renewal of its Charter, going through the quite fundamental changes of the Birt years, and overstretched advertising revenues squeezing all but the most popular formats in the commercial sector, the circumstances surrounding a particular production can sometimes defy the overall industrial odds. Thus, as far as *QaF* is concerned, as Davies concludes, 'If I believed in such things, I'd say the stars were in the right constellation in late '97' (2003: 6–7).

Though the way forward was clear to Davies following MacKenzie's advice, the journey from impetus to production in 1999 was nevertheless protracted. Davies's first ideas for a drama involving a gay man in love with a woman did not fire initially (though it subsequently emerged as *Bob & Rose*, ITV1, 2001) and he began to feel weighed down by a presumed responsibility to write the definitive gay series. Eventually, with the advice to 'go gay' prompting him to come out televisually, and given the freedom of locations rather than a studio in which to play, he thought, 'Fuck responsibility. I'm going to write what I want. A good story, with a good laugh, and the odd bit of heartbreak along the way. Just like any other story, and to hell with the agendas' (2003: 9).

The story that emerged, based on a pair Davies met in Manchester's Cruz 101, concerns two best friends who are in love without fully realising it. It is indeed just like many other TV stories in that it fits a well-established love-interest narrative pattern. Typically, such stories involve an attractive heterosexual couple where the narrative flirts with a chemistry between a central couple but precludes consummation (Sculley and Mulder in *The X-Files*, for example). Derived from the novel, it is a standard narrative hook of the contemporary serial television drama on which the audience is knowingly kept dangling. In *QaF*, the difference is just that at the start of the series the potential lovers, Vince Tyler (Aiden Gillen) and Stuart Alan Jones (Craig Kelley), are good-looking men in their late twenties, long-standing friends since their schooldays. Amongst the various men who enter into their life centred on Canal Street, the heart of Manchester's gay village, is fifteen-year-old Nathan Maloney (Charles Hunnam), perhaps a version of the schoolboy gay character Davies wished he had written earlier in his career. Besides this explosive element ripe for narrative development, Stuart also becomes the father of a baby in Episode 1. He has donated his sperm to Romey Sullivan (Esther Hall), the committed lesbian partner of Lisa Levine (Saira Todd), with 'the most expensive wank [he's] ever had'. A situation rich in social issues is not, however, much developed until Episodes 5–8, produced by Sarah Harding (see below).

It is the four opening episodes, and perhaps Episode 1 in particular, which establish the more dynamic and 'in-yer-face' televisual style with which *QaF* is typically associated. Produced by Charles McDougall and designed by Claire Kenny, the first four episodes have a distinctive visual style, and a dynamic rhythm which makes the most upbeat of contemporary television seem sluggish. It is high-impact production situated not in Santa Monica or New Jersey but in the formerly industrial city of Manchester in the North of England which historically has evoked the industrial revolution and, in the British tradition of TV drama, social realism, addressing issues of class and industrial struggle. The challenges in *QaF*, however, are more concerned with gender issues and the struggle for some (Vince) to 'cop off' compared with the ease of others (Stuart) to engage in casual sexual relationships ('shags'). A core structural feature of *QaF*, affording a sense of narrative progression when the initial emphasis is largely upon the creation of a lifestyle "feel", is the intercutting of Vince's experience with those of Stuart. The frequent mobile phone calls between them serve as a device to cut straight into moments of significant action and thus afford a state-of-the-art televisual means of keeping high the temperature of the drama.

Though many of *QaF*'s locations are actually set in former industrial redbrick buildings, Manchester, following its postmodern makeover, is lent something of the feel of New York. The series has a strong, almost self-conscious, sense of being visually designed. The light, precise, but low, emanates from blue neons for the exteriors (of the club *Babylon*, in the opening sequences), and reflected off white sculptured surfaces in the interiors. The dominant colour range is blue, black and silver-greys. The streets are blue, the hospital has blue-purple signs, Boddingtons brewery is blue, the fish tank and duvet in Vince's flat are blue. Stuart sometimes wears a mid-blue suit and his loft apartment has blue video and PC screens. The jeep (owned by Stuart's company but driven by Vince as well as Stuart) is black with silver alloys, and both men frequently wear black suits for work. Even the final shot of the episodes, a close-up of a TV monitor playing the end of an early *Dr Who* episode, leads us into the vortex through a receding silver-blue tunnel.

The hi-tech, postmodern environment is shot mainly at night, the ambient illumination against a dark sky iconically suggesting, as with New York, any dynamic contemporary city that never sleeps. Indeed, Nathan's friend Natalie remarks that, to Year Twelve at school, Canal Street is New York (Episode 8).

To soften this dominant look as the action or narrative moment requires, a range of creams through red-browns, and particularly bronzed fleshtones, are used. In Stuart's open-plan loft apartment, for example, the sanded oak floorboards and exposed wooden roof-beams offset the gadgetry and, when Stuart puts on a cream-yellow sweater from his range of designer outfits, the ambience is shifted. Much of the explicitly shot, sexual action takes place in Stuart's loft, the prime, though not the sole, location for satisfying his voracious appetite for 'shags' (when asked in Episode 8 by Nathan 'how many men have had sex in here?', Stuart laughingly replies, 'twenty-seven million'). There is no holding back on the clinches, which are passionate with greedy kisses and much tearing-off of shirts, but the sexual acts are beautifully shot in a visual tradition more associated with romance than pornography. When Stuart first seduces Nathan, for example, the moment is caught by a 180 degree revolving camera as the pair rotates in a dizzying embrace. Their naked bodies are lean and bronzed against the very white sheets of the bed. Though the physical placing of their bodies and the close-ups of their kissing with tongues and perspiration-glistened torsos leave little to the imagination, broadcast television's regulatory codes preclude overt shots of the genitals (though one or two fleeting shots are sneaked in) or acts of penetration. Overall, the presentation of sexual acts, whilst more explicit than ever before on British television, is subtly aestheticised, almost as part of the visual design of the series.

Sex is not, however, romanticised, most of the relationships being shown to be casual, and more stable partnerships ('boyfriends') being disparaged from the point of view of the predominantly young men depicted. Perhaps the most shocking aspect of the sexuality, the aspect which gives the series its "edginess", is its very ordinariness in this context. It's just what people do. The series' title derives from an old-fashioned Northern saying, "there's nowt so queer as folk', tolerantly acknowledging differences but coined before 'queer' took on its current resonances. The deadpan articulation of a recognition of differences in the phrase is in many ways remarkably apt for a series which does not set out to be shocking but to show a way of life in a manner more honest than the coy depictions of homosexuality in former TV dramas. The everydayness of sex (or the lack of it) in *QaF* is also conveyed through a great deal of humour in talk about sex and amidst the sexual action. For example, a mobile phone call from Stuart to Vince to announce the arrival of baby Alfred interrupts a potential liaison with a muscleman who has followed Vince home. Vince's repeated 'Oh My God's!' start as expressions of his astonishment at the new arrival but, as muscleman removes his kit to reveal first a stomach corset and subsequently a flabby paunch, the phrase functions on another level. Earlier, Phil has joked with Vince that he'd once had sex with a muscleman: 'it was like being let loose on a bouncy castle'(Episode 1). The humour is used in a number of different ways. For example, there is a running gag throughout the first four episodes that Vince never 'cops off'. A sharp, sometimes waspishly satiric humour is shown in addition to be an important part of gay culture. When Alfred is born, Stuart reviews his predicament, epigrammatically remarking, 'It's the exact opposite of childbirth: first you have the baby, then you get fucked' (Episode One). From a gay point of view, a straight pub is described as 'people talking in sentences without a punch line' (Episode 2).

In addition to the humour, *QaF* lets the viewers know, despite its realism in some respects, that it does not take itself overseriously by self-reflexively acknowledging a range of television dramas. *Dr Who* features largely in the series because Vince (not to mention Russell T. Davies himself) is an addict, even finding his potential sexual encounters diverted into watching the rare video copies in his collection.[5] Gay encounters are remembered by Vince and defined by their televisual, rather than their sexual, preferences, though there is an implicit connection between gay culture and certain programmes. At the very beginning of Episode 1, Vince describes an acquaintance as weird because he has 'every episode of *Juliet Bravo* on tape'. After another sexual moment is aborted because Jonathan, his 'shag', has 'Brazilian beach parasites living in [his] arse', Jonathan regales Vince with his acting stories, having spent 'two weeks with Duffy from *Casualty*'. Vince discusses *Coronation Street* with Rosalie Coller (Caroline Pegg), the young woman who works in the supermarket where he is a manager and who, initially not knowing he is gay, fancies him. After Vince has reprimanded Stuart, who makes to jump off the hospital roof when Alfred is born, saying it's soap-like behaviour: 'birth and death in one episode', he re-enacts with Stuart, in another popular culture reference, the iconic figurehead moment in *Titanic* (Paramount and C20 Fox, 1997). Ironically, as Vince observes, he always 'plays the Kate Winslet role'.

From the opening, upbeat guitar rhythms which punctuate composer Murray Gold's carnivalesque theme track – all steel band rhythms and breathy ullulations – the "feel" of the first four episodes of *QaF* is largely celebratory. There are some shadowy undertones but they serve mainly to counterpoint the general exuberance. Examples include Stuart rhetorically asking, 'Why doesn't anybody stop me?' near the end of the first episode, throwing briefly into relief a reckless lifestyle which has seen him indulge in numerous sexual encounters, become a father, take drugs the provenance of which he has no idea about, seduce a fifteen-year-old and, in sum, follow his every whim, even while his true friend, Vince, hangs around for him in the cold. In other shadowy moments in Episode 2, Nathan's mother becomes increasingly concerned about her son's behaviour, whilst Stuart shows himself to find baby Alfred an inconvenience, farming him out to whoever will take him in order that he can get back to Canal Street. Nathan realises with disappointment that he means nothing to Stuart as Vince disillusions him with very hard words about his closest friend: 'Nathan, he's a cunt. He doesn't give a toss about anyone' (Episode 2). Things get even darker when, having snorted cocaine in a casual encounter in Episode 3, Phil collapses and is left to die by the 'friend' who does not contact anybody but just steals his cash on the way out. After the funeral, Stuart and Vince find themselves clearing porn, 'the gay man's legacy'

(Episode 4), from Phil's flat so that his mother doesn't stumble across it. But these words and incidents, though given space, are left largely unexplored until the second four episodes which, as noted, open up broader perspectives. Episode 4 ends with Stuart having more fleeting sex with Nathan whilst declaring that he thinks Phil's death to be brilliant and saying, 'I want to die shagging.' It is a celebration which, though not quite sounding hollow, is beginning to be viewed from other perspectives.

It is Davies's, and the production's, disposition to tell it like it is and the oblique writing referred to above allows the series to steer a path between excessive, sentimentalising celebration and moralising. The action and the one-liners come fast and punchy and the series moves on. As Davies reflects on the first episodes:

> Charles [McDougall] injected those episodes with an energy and style beyond anything I'd imagined. You could take those same scripts and make a plain, ordinary, hand-held drama [perhaps in the British social realist tradition], but Charles pushes every element of design and lighting and composition, to produce something extraordinary ... The script of that first episode is disjointed, a little too gnomic and potentially very dark. Charles – and his editor Tony Cranstoun – made it a monument of light and sound. (2003: 13)

Davies's newly discovered way of writing, 'something closer to real life; a style where people don't say what they're thinking' (cited above), yields oblique dialogue, with loose ends left over from earlier drafts, and sets the basis for a documentary realism.

Inconsequential dialogue – in which the characters defy television's habitual disposition to be explanatory by not articulating exactly what they are thinking, indeed not knowing what is motivating them – has precedents, particularly in theatre. Chekhov famously developed a mode of naturalist writing which captured how people actually speak, in all its curtailments, non-sequiturs and surface inconsequentiality. Importantly, Chekhov's drama is noted for being non-judgemental, simply presenting the dialogue and action and leaving it to audiences to respond, but directors have often since intervened to treat the action in ways which might shape response.[6] The play between what we might call documentary material and dramatic treatments is equally interesting in respect of QaF.

The writing may convey a quasi-documentary sense that gay culture is simply being observed as it happens but McDougal's camera and the sharp editing play against this to create a hybrid form in Episodes 1–4. The direct address to camera by each of the three protagonists draws upon another device of contemporary documentary, the video diary. But each address is set against a vibrantly coloured backdrop, yellow for Vince, red for Stuart and mauve for Nathan. Indeed, it is the highly colourful design of the series, the mobile camera and the editing pace which ultimately preclude any sense of a documentary's invitation to make a judgement based on the evidence and create a primary sense of celebration in the first four episodes. In Episodes 5–8, the tone of the piece subtly shifts.

In Episodes 5–8, a broader range of perspectives on the gay community is brought to bear. The locus of interest moves away from Canal Street (though the latter continues to figure) and into broader contextualising environments. Scenes take place in Marie's house, Vince's apartment, Stuart's parents' bungalow (and garden), outside Nathan's house, and in Romey and Lisa's house. In short they are set in a range of domestic environments of heterosexuals and lesbians rather than gays. A family dimension is particularly dominant in Episode 6 which includes a long, slow sequence of Stuart helping his father dig the garden to plant a shrub, a sequence with Vince and Cameron visiting Hazel and Bernard, another languorous sequence with Alexander being deliberately ignored by his parents whilst out shopping in Manchester, and a slow, emotionally charged sequence when Stuart's father quite uncharacteristically visits him (and baby Alfred) at his flat. These environments set in relief the Canal Street venues and implicitly invite other ways of seeing the gay community.

More is seen, for example through Nathan's mother's eyes. She is shown not to be judgemental in respect of homosexuality but just concerned for her son when she is taken by Hazel, an habitué of the village, to a Canal Street club to experience the culture for herself. Nathan's father, in contrast, cannot accept his son's sexual preference and deliberately and repeatedly rams Stuart's jeep in anger (Episode 6). As the narrative develops, however, Nathan finally chooses to return home and his father, though still finding the idea of gay sex offensive and hiding his homophobia behind the guise of protecting Nathan's younger sister, does show the potential to become more understanding and accepting. A new narrative strand, beyond the gay village, sees Romey, Alfred's lesbian mother, agreeing to a marriage of convenience with black immigrant Lance Amponah (John Brobbey), to allow him to apply for British nationality. It is Romey's lover, Lisa, who hatches a plot to prevent this, calling on Stuart who 'owes her' to send to the Home Office a pack of love letters from Romey to her. Though he reluctantly agrees, Stuart literally seduces Nathan to undertake the task.

Not coincidentally, this extension of the social and geographical landscape also brought *QaF* an upturn in the ratings. In the first four episodes, the series is predominantly Stuart-centred and, as noted, largely celebrates his confidence in doing just as he pleases, giving little consideration to those around him or the impact of his actions upon their lives. Episodes 5–8 brought, as Davies acknowledges, 'a more intimate drama ... quieter more reflective' (2003: 14). His recognition that viewers 'needed an invitation to approach' (2003: 14) affords the insight that, though *QaF* attracted a gay audience (which had mixed feelings about the series), Channel Four, as a main UK terrestrial channel, has the potential for a broader audience which may well have felt shut out by the Stuart-centric point of view of Episodes 1–4.[7] Stuart's preoccupation with 'copping off' is viewed critically by a range of characters in Episodes 5–8. Marie, his sister, complains that he ignores his parents and her children; Romey tells him, 'It's all your fault 'cos you just shag'; and Cameron, Vince's would-be boyfriend, criticises his selfish treatment of both Vince and Nathan, telling him, 'It's sex: everything you do is sex' (Episode 6). Throughout Episodes 5–8, the camera is allowed to linger on Stuart's face in close-up, inviting us to read his thoughts. Though some of the sheer energy and front of the first four episodes is lost, Sarah Harding did Davies and the series a different service in developing its dramatic tone and extending its reach.

And Harding's approach does grow out of previous material, developing precisely some of the shadows which do little more than offset the bright lights and colour of Episodes 1–4. She does not fundamentally change the disposition of the series, avoiding any final closures of ideology or narrative, but her treatment does invite the formation of viewer opinion, if not shifting judgements. For example, Stuart's invitation of Rosalie to Vince's surprise birthday party is calculated for maximum upset. As Harding shoots it, viewers share Rosalie's shock at arriving late. Hopeful of making out with Vince, she is instead confronted by the excess of the party and introduced to Vince's boyfriend. As she ascends in the lift, her figure shot through the lift grating is juxtaposed with Alexander's flamboyant female impersonation. The perspective offered is not one of a final judgement on Stuart and gay culture, but deftly invites other considerations. It is made clear subsequently that Rosalie is not undermined by the experience and is able to remain friends with Vince, indeed encourages him to come out at work. But the treatment offers, if momentarily, an outsider's – rather than an insider's – eye on the gay scene.

Episode 5 brings out a possible motive for Vince's failure to 'cop off', let alone secure a more permanent relationship, when Cameron points out to Stuart that he is holding Vince under false pretences. Though Vince, furious at Stuart's behaviour over Rosalie, leaves his birthday party with Cameron he ultimately dumps him. Having apparently at last taken charge of his life, in the very final sequence Vince persuades Stuart against his disposition to dance on stage as if declaring themselves to be a couple. But the soundtrack, 'It's Raining Men', perhaps lends no conviction that they will remain romantically together. Indeed, on his way to the club, Vince has extolled the virtues of unrequited love which, 'never has to change, never has to grow up and never has to die' (Episode 8).

Sex and the City (HBO, 1998–2002 in the USA, six seasons)

Of all the examples in this book, and even amongst those of "edgy" television, *Sex and the City* (*SatC*) perhaps caused the greatest stir in the early 'noughties'. As reflected in the views of commentators from academic criticism to the popular press, viewers either loved it or hated it, but few regarded it with indifference. From the depths of Charlotte Raven's 'pile of swill' (cited in Akass and McCabe, 2004: 2) to the heights of articulating in art-cinema style the hopes and fears of a generation of women, *SatC* has evinced widely conflicting, but typically strongly felt, responses. The series focusing on the lives and loves of four thirtysomething female friends in New York broke new ground in its representations, often graphic and full on, of women's sexuality, at times blurring the boundaries with HBO's pornography channels, the commissioning and distribution channel of *SatC*. However, the elicited disposition of viewers towards the series, as we shall see, is what marks the difference.

Though it is more typically associated with postfeminism and postmodernism in respect of its context and treatment, *SatC* might be located on the modernist trajectory of the avant-garde in its breaking of new ground. It certainly uses shock tactics to invite fresh perceptions of sexual politics and, indeed, where HBO and *SatC* led, others quickly followed. In 2004, for example, NBC aired *Desperate Housewives* which, as listed by the official website, 'takes a darkly comedic look at suburbia, where the secret lives of housewives aren't always what they seem'.[8] Though it affords its own pleasures, however, *Desperates*, in comparison to *SatC*, is constrained largely to titillation by its position in primetime on a major network where it is subject to the regulators (see Chapter 7). In locating a group of sexually active female neighbours at the centre of a TV drama series, however, *Desperates* moved into territory opened up by *SatC*.

The challenge posed by *SatC*, its "edginess", is, in contrast, centred in its conscious breaching of taboos about women and, in particular, female sexuality. In several accounts, the series is seen, moreover, to empower women by subverting patriarchal discourse and celebrating particularly women's friendship and sorority (with a small 's') articulated through conversation. Its appeal may have been primarily to heterosexual women – and possibly more specifically white, bourgeois, Western, heterosexual women, but it also had a strong following amongst gay men and more limited appeal (relative to its occasional representations) to lesbians and women of colour (see below). If *SatC* empowers heterosexual women, it may proportionately have disempowered heterosexual men, many having found it unsettling.[9] But, if the point of the challenge is to make visible on television, in Astrid Henry's summary, 'the impact that gay, lesbian and queer cultures and sexualities have had on heterosexuality' (2004: 80) and thus 'by treating heterosexuality itself as problematic – that is, as something to examine and discuss' (Henry, 2004: 78), the progression or liberation afforded by *SatC* may ultimately be of benefit to all. I will return to the overall political impact of the series through a range of readings below but first, following a short summary of its key provocations, a look at the form and content of the show, and how they relate to each other, will illuminate how *SatC* functions as a television drama and how it might have appealed differently to different viewers. In the account which follows, I am indebted to the range of writings on the series and, particularly to the contributors in Akass and McCabe's edited collection of essays *Reading Sex and the City* (2004).

Challenges

The primary challenge posed by *SatC* is its presentation of a group of women who enjoy an affluent and independent New York lifestyle and are sexually active in ways which depend little, if at all, on men, other than as objects from which mainly sexual pleasures are taken. Thus a hegemonic cultural praxis of patriarchy in which women defer to – or in various ways are required to be submissive and subordinate to men – is simply shattered. As Deborah Jermyn reports from her audience research, female fans took 'sheer delight in a programme where the primary focus and core narrative lies in a set of female friendships' (2004: 208). The radical impact of such delight is, of course, apparent only to those who recognise that culture – and television as an aspect of culture – is typically shot through with patriarchal discourse. To such women, and men, *SatC* is rendered fresh and challenging in its very format. A *donné* of the situation affording the protagonists' independence is that each of the women has a successful career to fund an expensive Manhattan lifestyle. Little of their professional lives figures in the series, however, since the focus is on their romantic and sexual liaisons and leisure pursuits. Their affluence thus demands simply to be taken as a given of the situation, but the emphasis upon high lifestyle invites discussion of the economic implications of *SatC* below.

Samantha, in particular, has a voracious sexual appetite and is famously interested in 'having sex like a man' (i.e. supposedly without any emotional commitment), but all the women regard sexual pleasure as their right and are disposed towards sexual experimentation. If standard sexual practice under patriarchy implies heterosex in the missionary position, this second *donné* of the series opens up the opportunity to explore the unspoken – at least in public by women – details of sexual practices 'ranging from anal sex, and female ejaculation to vibrators, cunnilingus, abortion, infertility and sexually transmitted diseases' (Akass and McCabe, 2004: 3). Some of these have been aired previously in TV dramas, but it is the knowledge about, disposition towards and casual discussion of such topics and practices by women that is designed to shock. It is the public articulation, verbally and graphically, by women which makes *SatC* avant-garde in the sense noted above.

For example, the 'c' word is used and a joke is even made about it: when the overtly prim, Charlotte, speaks of 'his big beautiful cock' and Carrie querulously interjects, 'We are using the "c" word now?' ('The Awful Truth', 2:2). The joke in this scene of a typical conversation over brunch is that it is precisely the romantic and outwardly conservative Charlotte who turns out to know how to 'talk dirty' in bed. But in an earlier episode, it is also Charlotte who is involved in a more shocking scene in which the even less acceptable 'c' word is aired, along with the visual image of female genitalia.[10] In connection with her work as an art gallery director, Charlotte visits the studio of an established artist, Neville Morgan, whose latest work has been inspired by, 'The most powerful force in the universe. The source of all life and pleasure and beauty ... "The Cunt"' ('The power of female sex', 1:5). But here the word is dislocated from its usage on the street and in some movies as an expletive with derogatory connotations to a denotative usage affirmed when, alluding to Morgan's invitation to Charlotte to pose for him, the elderly and genteel Mrs Morgan matter-of-factly remarks, 'I bet you have a beautiful cunt dear' ('The power of female sex', 1:5). Given *SatC*'s disposition to be shocking in respect of sexual taboos, it is perhaps inevitable that the 'c' word would figure, even though it is perhaps the least acceptable of four-letter words, taking the series to the edge of audience toleration. But when it is spoken, the impact is greater than the simple breach of a taboo. Rather than have the word dropped casually by one of the four protagonists over brunch (though it is used again as a term of endearment in this context when Carrie departs for Paris in 'An American girl in Paris (Part Deux)', 6: 20), the writers contrive to draw attention not just to the taboo nature of the word itself but to the sexual politics which make it taboo, namely the appropriation of a word in patriarchal discourse to be derogatory about women. The denotative significance of the 'c' word re-emerges through its being spoken by an elderly woman in the context described which naturalises not only the word but also the old myth of the artist–seducer inviting attractive women to sit for him. Though there are occasions when *SatC* shocks for the sake of being shocking; at its best, as in the above example, a modernist–formalist use of shock invites a reconfiguration, a fresh seeing.

Though, in my view, there are critical questions to be asked of the allegedly post-feminist attitudes informing the series (see below), its positive political impact in the context of everyday television lay in its legitimisation of women's interests, and particularly women's pleasures. As Anna König remarks of the protagonists' preoccupation with fashion, and particularly shoes, 'the characters are seen to enjoy the clothes they wear … dressing up equals fun, and fun equals empowerment' (2004: 140). The excess of the New York lifestyle in which the four friends luxuriate is seen in such readings in itself to challenge the oppressions of bourgeois restraint or "victim feminism". The guilt experienced in buying a pair of very expensive shoes is turned not only into pleasure but ultimately into a "third-wave" feminist strategy (see Henry, 2004: 75 ff.).

Overall, in Akass and McCabe's summary:

> *Sex and the City* challenges prohibitions and breaks the silence, so that women can begin to tell their stories and speak about sex differently. Through finding 'spaces of deferral' that allow access into discourse, and for the camaraderie created by shared laughter, mechanisms of humour lift the veil to offer new revelatory truths about the female sex. (2004: 196)

TV categories and dramatic form and content

First, to address its categorisation, *SatC* has been variously dubbed a comedy series a TV sitcom and a drama. To judge by the awards it won (see Akass and McCabe, 2004: 5), 'comedy series' would appear to be the industry's categorisation, whilst the episodic format, with each episode notionally based on a topic for the regular column written by Carrie Bradshaw's (Sarah Jessica Parker) for the *New Yorker* focusing on an aspect of social–sexual life in Manhattan suggests an overtly sitcom form. The staple form of sitcoms has traditionally afforded a space for the negotiation of cultural change with its capacity to pit a type, embodying one social position or set of attitudes, against other types. Though the balance of forces – which viewers are invited to laugh *at*, as opposed to *with* – has with hindsight frequently been perceived to be politically incorrect, it perhaps indicates the TV sitcom form's use as a vehicle for the cultural address and assimilation of social change. The sitcom form, then, might well be used to negotiate the changing role of women in modern societies and, as commentators have pointed out (see Dow, 1996 and Akass and McCabe, 2004), there have been several American sitcoms involving feminist characters over the past thirty years (e.g. *The Mary Tyler Moore Show, One Day at a Time, Roseanne, Murphy Brown*) frequently focusing on one woman character. Though they extended the range of what was presentable on (particularly American) television and dealt with issues such as having a child outside marriage (*Murphy Brown*), the central figure might appear isolated and, at worst, the butt of humour. The centrality and dynamism of the four women protagonists in *SatC*, in contrast, not only increases the range of women's perspectives and experiences but also affords, through their commitment to each other, a sense of the irresistible centrality and solidity of a cultural trend.

In terms of dramatic form, sitcoms are episodic rather than serial in their narratives. Each episode, that is to say, tells a story complete in itself, placing the central character (or characters) with a given and known disposition in a situation likely to aggravate that disposition and give rise to humour. The characters are thus types who do not learn from their experiences and develop in consequence but sustain the same disposition in subsequent episodes and have no power to alter or break free from the situation in which they find themselves. The characters in *SatC* are initially drawn as types. In Akass and McCabe's formulation, the protagonists are:

> Carrie Bradshaw, a thirtysomething New York-based journalist … [who engages in] her pseudo-anthropological quest to make sense of modern socio-sexual mores … [and] her three close friends – PR executive and sexual libertine Samantha Jones (Kim Cattrall), corporate lawyer and relationship cynic Miranda Hobbes (Cynthia Nixon) and art gallery manager and romantic optimist Charlotte York (Kristin Davies). (2004: 3)

Many of the men in the series are known only by type names such as 'Mr Big' and the four women are primarily constructed to represent not so much individualised personalities but different attitudes.

In some sitcoms, the main aim is to create humour arising from extraordinary events, but the action of *SatC* is largely limited to the round of New York social functions, lunches and sexual encounters of the protagonists. Rather than playing out a situation, maximising laughs by way of gags or slapstick action, each episode foregrounds a theme – typically a sexual topic or taboo, as noted. Whilst, then, the treatment in *SatC* is light-hearted, comedic and by no means without wit (waspish one-liners being a feature of gay culture drawn into the series), it is the perspectival conflict between the four characters foregrounded in dialogue which is key to the humour, rather than dramatic conflict worked out for laughs in action. The main location for a four-handed conversation is Sunday brunch, but views are frequently exchanged between pairs, either directly or by phone. Though, as the series progresses, the characters to some extent develop (see below), in the first instance the types as characterised reiterate their typical response to situations they encounter and the thematic debate of each episode arises from their differing points of view. This may in itself mark a gender shift from the traditionally "masculine" resolution of difference through summary action to a more "feminine", dialogic exploration of a range of different options. Each episode, however, is designed to raise for consideration by contemporary women – within and beyond the series – an aspect of sex and romance.

As several commentators have remarked (see Bignell and König in Akass and McCabe, 2004), this aspect of the programme, besides conforming to a sitcom format, marks an overlap with the structure of women's magazines beyond the obvious link that Carrie Bradshaw writes a regular journal column. At the end of each episode Carrie's voice-over draws the episode's topic together in the draft for her column, articulating some kind of moral, or thought-provoking phrase, in the manner of a gnomic banner headline figured in the title of each episode (often seen typed on Carrie's lap-top screen). At worst, such magazine-style treatment based in conversation about lifestyle in *SatC* might be regarded, as in Angela McRobbie's (1998) view of fashion journalism, as little more than 'effusive babble' (König, 2004: 132). But, in Astrid Henry's much more positive view of *SatC*, 'the conversations between the four women are the central feature of the show' (2004: 68). Indeed, Akass and McCabe go further to make a sophisticated argument for a play between the content of the series and the mode of its narration such that a central and cumulative tension of *SatC* lies between the playing-out and repeated fracturing of dominant mythologies. As they formulate the narrative summaries, 'What Carrie does is to take the pleasures inspired by romantic fiction and use the language to write an alternative narrative about female accomplishment and personal happiness' (2004: 186). This reading would suggest a sophisticated development of both TV sitcom and magazine formats way beyond a situation designed around set pieces leading to punch lines.

In terms of form, sitcoms efface consequences as noted whilst serial narrative drama plays them out (though, in television narrative, forms often lack ultimate closure). The consequences of the action of early *SatC* episodes are followed through only insofar as narrative continuity demands (e.g. if one of the characters is having a relationship beyond a one-night stand) but each of the early episodes tends to move on to a new theme. Over the six seasons, however, the treatment, whilst singular, was not monolithic and, from a starting-point of a sitcom format and types, the characters and their lives developed considerably. From Season 4 when Miranda finds herself pregnant through into Season 5 when baby Brady is a few weeks' old, *SatC* has developed – or, in the judgement of Greven, undergone 'an inexorable descent' (2004: 42) – into a serial narrative drama. Thus, like many TV3 products, *SatC* developed into a new hybrid capable of functioning on different levels. This accounts in part for the various responses from viewers who watched it in different ways and saw in it something different. Casual viewing of an occasional episode might lead some viewers to a negative summary judgement about frivolous preoccupations, whilst long-term viewing might be deemed to amount to a cumulative consideration of sociosexual topics of considerable importance particularly to heterosexual women, but not to the exclusion of others. The viewing position of the observer emerges as another critical factor in the dialogic relationship between text and reader.

By the final season when reluctant mother Miranda finally marries Steve and moves to Brooklyn, Charlotte has been married and divorced and happily married again and even Samantha is in a reasonably enduring relationship with her young lover, Smith, an awareness of time passing is impacting more than usual. Miranda's motherhood serves initially to shift the relationship between the friends with visual images of breast-feeding and reference to 'the time before the baggage and break-ups and babies began to weigh us all down' ('Anchors away', 5: 1). Simultaneously, the quest for a long-term, romantic relationship which has rumbled through the series becomes more pressing as Carrie (deploying nautical metaphors for 'Sailors Week') questions whether the girls have 'missed the boat' ('Anchors away', 5: 1). Season 5 witnesses Charlotte's thirty-sixth birthday, celebrated by a trip to the casinos of Atlantic City but accompanied by the question, 'What happens after 36: I guess you fall off the table' ('Luck be an old lady', 5: 3). The winning number at roulette symbolically turns out to be twenty-nine. The series' characteristic romantic fantasy quest, based on the possibility of one (or at best two) great loves in a lifetime, takes on a tone of reflective hopelessness as Samantha is consumed by jealousy at competing younger women stealing her lover, Miranda sneaks off early to bed for the pleasures of pay-per-view TV, a chocolate bar and being free of her baby for a night, and Charlotte and Samantha find the men either of no interest to them or not interested in them. The group returns to New York, not on Samantha's rich lover's private jet as planned, but on the bus with old widows and maids.

As time moves on, the former easy-come, easy-go freedom of the group of friends is additionally constrained by concerns beyond 'shopping and fucking'. In Season 6, Samantha is diagnosed with breast cancer, Charlotte appears unable to conceive and Carrie becomes increasingly preoccupied with the ticking of her biological clock in 'Catch–38' (6: 16). Indeed, the drama has been extended into more complex characterisation with a serial narrative tracing its development. If not quite a dark shadow (there is still plenty of sex and fun to be had by Samantha), a more sombre mood nevertheless reflects back on the seasons before. For long-term viewers, the characters' former preoccupations – designer clothes, cocktails, being seen in the right Manhattan nightspots – are thrown somewhat into relief. It might be going too far to suggest that the lifestyle, so dynamically introduced in the early episodes and celebrated throughout the majority of the seasons, is called in question by evoking the consequences of age. But there is a telling moment towards the end of the very last episode when Miranda must anxiously comb the streets to find Steve's mother who, suffering from post-stroke dementia, has wandered from the house. Having found her and brought her home, Miranda bathes her to warm her up and the maid, Magda, glimpsing this act of kindness, remarks, 'What you did: that is love' ('An American girl in Paris (Part Deux)', 6: 20). Though this is juxtaposed with Big bringing Carrie home to New York from Paris to the accompaniment of 'You've got the love' ('An American girl in Paris (Part Deux)', 6:

20), there is perhaps an intimation not just of the fragility of romantic notions of love but of other kinds of love in a familial context. After all, both Sarah Jessica Parker and Cynthia Hobbs were by this time mothers in real life.

There is a parallel here with *QaF*, whose ending, though even more ambiguous than *SatC*'s in its overt emphasis on the longevity and value of unrequited love, is nevertheless addressing the same dilemma. Such serial narrative (in)conclusions importantly remain at odds, however, with the endings in marriage of the typical period drama (*Pride and Prejudice, Middlemarch*) which affirm the normativity of bourgeois monogamy. *SatC* and *QaF*, in contrast, merely mark the dilemma of those whose sexual preferences lie outside such norms in coping with a culture in which they still predominate, notwithstanding significant cultural shifts over the past thirty years.[11] Charlotte's accident-prone, Jewish wedding and Miranda's matter-of-fact nuptials distinguish *SatC* marriages and point up the contrast.

If, however, in terms of its dramatic and narrative form, *SatC* to some extent presented a challenge by constructing a new hybrid between sitcom and serial, its "edginess" consistently lay more in its content than in formal experimentation. Though the series deploys a few of the innovative formal presentational devices of TV3 (see Chapter 5) such as split screen, occasional freeze-frame and direct address to camera, it is not noted for its formal innovation. Indeed, in Tom Grochowski's analysis, interesting formal aspects such as the early use of vox-pop commentaries with ironic subtitles to give 'the feel of an ethnographic document, allowing for the fact that what we are watching is somewhat satirical' (2004: 156), diminished as the series progressed and faded out completely in Season 5. Though shot on film with high production values and a more "cinematic" than televisual feel, *SatC* increasingly relied on the fashion and the Upper East Side ambience for its visual style rather than a more self-reflexive camera treatment.

With regard to content, a culture of excess – particularly in respect of fashion, but in independent, "high-lifestyle" living more broadly – became by Season 3 the dominant presentational feature of *SatC*. In this respect, the series allies itself with the values of TV melodrama and, in the context of television, the legacy of expensive soaps (e.g. *Dallas* and *Dynasty*). Dramatic entrances made by the protagonists at Manhattan parties served as the modern equivalent of melodramatic tableaux, as the superbly coutured friends paused just inside the doors to afford time for the assembled company – and more particularly the viewers – to take in the designer costumes and lavish accessories. The appearance of guest stars (e.g. Alanis Morissette) served also to confirm the series' alliance with contemporary celebrity culture. It is here perhaps that a TV sitcom comes closest to fusing with magazine presentation but, even here, *SatC* pushes at boundaries between elite or "high" fashion and popular culture.

In respect of content, however, features cited by those commentators (in Akass and McCabe, 2004) who argue for its progressive representations include: a female friends family, a postfeminist sisterhood (with a small 's') (71) in which the arguments are over everything but men; 'dish' multivocal conversations between

the women airing differences of view which reflect 'a feminism that includes contradictions' (71); women's laughter 'worth noting for its rarity on TV and for its
implicit feminism'(69); and 'a forum about women's sexuality as it has been shaped
by the feminist movement of the last thirty years' (66). The women's economic
and emotional independence of men and their enjoyment of life which, though
allowing marriage as an option, critiques the (arguably still dominant) social assumption that marriage is a woman's destiny. Taking *SatC* overall as a forum for
debate of these issues, it includes the exposure to consideration, often through
graphic imagery, of 'a woman's right to pleasure' (75) particularly through a broadened heterosexuality in which women are active sexually, have sex like a man, use
sex toys (78) and experiment with a range of activities not customarily acknowledged, let alone shown, on television (e.g. cunnilingus). Contentious topics such
as abortion are addressed, with the protagonists controversially acknowledging
they have had them, though the limits of the American audience's tolerance is
perhaps reached on this topic since 'Miranda ultimately decides to have the baby,
and thus doesn't break the US taboo of depicting abortion' (72). In Astrid Henry's
measured summary of content:

> In its bold representation of women's pleasures, *Sex and the City* offers a refreshing
> alternative to most mass-media depictions of female sexuality. *Sex and the City* re-
> flects an important – if limited – vision of female empowerment, a feminism that
> mirrors contemporary, third wave attempts to celebrate both women's power and
> women's sexuality, to create a world where one can be both feminist and sexual.
> (2004: 82)

In respect of its "strong language" and "scenes of an adult nature", *SatC* perhaps pushed the envelope to the very limits of current audience tolerance and, for
many individual viewers, it went well beyond. In this respect the series is "edgy"
and, on occasion, this viewer had the impression that the wish to shock the audience overrode any attempt to embed the action in drama, even in the formula of
TV sitcom. But, overall, the location of challenges to viewers in a broader context
of contemporary issues marks *SatC* as distinctive television, if not quite perhaps
as distinctive drama.

Multiple readings

To judge by considered critical commentaries, many heterosexual women loved
the series and felt empowered and affirmed by it. As Raymond Williams (1997)
has noted, the trajectory of social realism in drama has extended over time to
embrace, and bring to centre stage, those social groups who have previously been
excluded. In the history of drama, the kings and queens of Renaissance theatre
displaced the gods and goddesses of the Graeco-Roman eras, and representations
of working-class life in the theatre of the 1950s and television of the 1960s displaced the bourgeoisie and petit-bourgeois representations which preceded them.
Placed in this generally liberationist trajectory, *SatC* builds upon the foregrounding
of women's experience in twentieth-century theatre and the television sitcoms,

noted above, featuring individual feminists. Seen through this optic of history, *SatC* might be adjudged progressive in its address of postfeminist, or third-wave feminist, praxis, despite its exclusions. But there were many takes on the series.

Lesbians, to judge by Mandy Merck's analysis, were at best disappointed in a lost opportunity and at worst appalled by the series' lesbophobia. Any series purporting to represent female sexuality in New York might well have included lesbianism in more than the token way that *SatC* does. But, as Merck remarks, 'Carrie's wide-eyed horror at the [same sex] kiss (from a hippie maiden played by Alanis Morissette) underlines the series' abjection of female homoeroticism' (2004: 54). Merck's sense, however, that, in respect of lesbianism, the series is a cop-out, using Samantha as 'the lightning rod for any unease the audience might feel about its sexual exploits' (2004: 57), is not shared by a lesbian respondent in Jermyn's focus group who identified 'with the women and the choices and compromises they faced' (Jermyn, 2004: 209).

Gay men generally loved the series because, like *QaF*, its representations challenge heterosexuality as the norm. The fashion, the 'dish', the 'clubbing', the lifestyle all affirm gay culture and much has been made of the creative contributions of the openly gay producers, Darren Star and Michael Patrick King in this respect. Just as Giddens (1992) has argued that the legalisation of homosexuality and consequent emergence to high visibility of gay culture has informed the "lifestyle" aesthetic generally, so it is assumed that Star and partner have informed *SatC*, despite the contributions of numerous women: the designer (Patricia Field), the writers (e.g. Jenny Bicks, Nicole Avril, Susan Kolinsky, Cindy Chupack) and the actors themselves. Though he acknowledges that *SatC* is 'steeped in queer approaches to gender and sexuality' (2004: 40), Greven takes exception to the narrow range of (mainly white) male bodies represented with its emphasis on 'uniform standards of physical perfection and male beauty' (2004: 37), arguing that 'most of the male freaks are outwardly desirable, inwardly monstrous' (2004: 36). Recognising that males as objects of the "gaze" invert Mulvey's seminal insight into women's "to-be-looked-at" function in early Hollywood cinema, Greven concludes that this aspect 'comes more and more to seem the inverse of its strengths: a misogynistic and homophobic approach' (2004: 40).

Straight men, by various reports, were either disturbed by the forthright talk and action of the four protagonists, feeling and fearing the power of women's talk generally, or they purported to be indifferent to the series, dismissing it (perhaps to avoid such a confrontation) as a frivolous, women's programme. It is an interesting statistic, however, that 40 per cent of the British audience for the series was male.[12] Some men appeared fascinated to learn how women really think and behave when not in the company of men and therefore beyond the constraints of patriarchy, and some even purported to enjoy the images of attractive women actively wanting sex and removing their clothes, 'more turn on than terrifying' in Billen's (2001) phrase, as if *SatC* were soft-core pornography.

Though audience research has long since informed us that variant readings are likely, even with factual programmes, and are contingent in part on where the reader is socially positioned, *SatC*, as noted, does appear to elicit strong views from all quarters, either positive or negative. In my argument, this arises from an "edginess" which makes it difficult to ignore and which, given its overt lifting of taboos and its fundamental challenge to social norms supported in many case by deeply held convictions about the world, is unsurprising. The critical commentary on its limitations, whilst forceful from broader cultural perspectives, sometimes overlooks not only that this is a television series but that it is ultimately a product of a market-place seeking an audience. It is to this aspect that I wish briefly to turn in conclusion.

HBO, *Sex and the City, Desperate Housewives* and the market

The target market for HBO is, as noted in Chapter 3, an affluent market niche. The four friends in *SatC* might themselves be taken as good examples of the desirable demographic and it is not perhaps surprising that Miranda opts to retire to watch pay-per-view TV in her hotel room in Atlantic City. However, in its broader dissemination – on Channel 4 in the UK, for example, and on other cable and subscription channels (though not as yet on American network television) – the series reached a broad, indeed global, audience and was patently watched by women beyond the primary demographic.

Within the series itself, economic questions are largely occluded, the independence of the four friends based on an affluence afforded by high-end careers, as noted, being taken as read. The single mention in the series of a serious lack of funds concerns Carrie's cash flow in respect of buying her apartment. Charlotte comes to the rescue and sells her Tiffany ring to lend Carrie the money, pointing out that Carrie could have funded the purchase from her income had she chosen not to spend it on shoes. Commentary upon this episode cites Charlotte's generous gesture to instance the depth of the women's friendships and, in the context of the series and positive responses to it, the notion that Manolo Blahniks are not a life priority is taken to be patently absurd (see 'A woman's right to shoes', 6: 13). Stepping back (rather than out) to take a critical view, however, it might be argued that the positive affirmations for women in the readings above rest upon an economic foundation from which very few benefit. As Bignell puts it, *SatC* 'can be argued to render invisible the questions of economic status, work and social power for women' (2004: 171). Bearing out this point, Carrie's lack of funds to buy her apartment, which in most people's lives would be a serious issue, is treated as no more than a temporary nuisance, readily to be overcome and certainly not inducing guilt about an over-indulgence in designer fashions.

It may seem inappropriate to ask critical questions of *SatC*: it is, after all, a comedic television programme. But I propose here merely to mobilise a train of thought in respect of the series which I will follow through in Chapter 7 in respect of contemporary "quality TV" more broadly. The empowerment of viewers in watching *SatC* noted above rests largely on psychology, on a feel-good pleasure derived from the series. But the strong foregrounding of fashion and a high-leisure lifestyle as a means of mobilising those pleasures does invite critical questions. A critique from an economic base, however, might equally be made of "third-wave" feminism itself which depends on women being able to adopt their preferred lifestyle, or, indeed, being able to have it all. It would appear that such a stance also implies a level of economic independence, since choice depends, in the everyday realities of most women's lives, on a basis of economics, on whether or not they have sufficient income to take advantage of lifestyle choices.

Widening the angle of vision a little, "third-wave" feminism might itself be located in the wider shift amongst advanced industrial nations to economic postmodernity with its emphasis on services over hard industrial products and its attendant cultural implications in respect of conspicuous consumption, so well brought out in David Harvey's (1989) seminal analysis. As Harvey summarises, 'The relatively stable aesthetic of Fordist modernism has given way to all the ferment, instablity, and fleeting qualities of a postmodernist aesthetic that celebrates difference, ephemerality, spectacle, fashion and commodification of cultural forms' (1989: 156). *SatC*'s celebration of spectacle and fashion and its licensing of the pleasures of consumption by viewers, albeit in the high-street store rather than the designer fashion house (see Niblock, 2004: 144–148), is, from this perspective at least, double-edged. Samantha's makes a telling observation when instructing Smith to put on some cool shades for a television interview: 'If you're not wearing something the kids can't afford, how do they know to look up to you?' ('A woman's right to shoes', 6: 9). Though this witty remark might be taken to instance *SatC*'s self-awareness, the series also bears it out in its fashion imagery and in the discursive position sustained throughout by the 'gals' that to wear anything without a designer label puts you beyond the pale. Thus the series may well afford pleasure and psychological empowerment on the level of the politics of the personal, but, refracted through another lens, it might also be seen as both a product and a tool of an individualist consumer capitalism which does not serve well the many women who are condemned by their low economic status to be excluded from such pleasures and empowerments. In the context of a global television environment, the situation of women viewers beyond the affluent classes of rich nations might well demand consideration and I shall return to these issues.

In respect of cultural form, the noted playfulness of a postmodern aesthetic between subversion and affirmation leaves room for ambiguity or, as we have seen, very varied readings. The fact that playfulness is paramount, however, tends to militate against taking the form seriously. Television affords a leisure pursuit for most people who perhaps want to be entertained more than challenged in their non-working hours. Therefore, it is not only refreshing but also encouraging to those of us who do take television seriously as an object of study when a popular programme also has the potential to be radical. Some texts – and *SatC* serves as an example – invite serious attention more than others. The play between different aspects of the fluid hybrid mix which *SatC* represents opens up space for questions about its very 'instabilty and fleeting qualities' (Harvey, 1989: 156). Bignell insightfully suggests that the sitcom format 'focuses the audience's attention on the ability of Carrie and her friends to cope with emotional and social problems rather than their inability to analyse them or to change them' (2004: 171). Empathy, typically elicited for the plight of a character in a more realist drama, is deflected by the sitcom aspect of the hybrid form, effacing consequences. Thus, in the case of *SatC*, the friends effectively draw comfort from their socio-economic status which is neither explored nor explained but taken as a *donné* of the format as illustrated in the example above. In this respect, it is interesting, as argued, that when, in Seasons 5 and 6, the sitcom hybrid turns into a more dramatic form dealing with more rounded characters and consequences from episode to episode, shadows play across the upbeat energy of earlier seasons.

Carnivàle (HBO, 2003–5, two series)

When invited into the world of *Carnivàle* by the ironically named 'Samson' (Michael J. Anderson) speaking directly to camera in close-up, viewers familiar with *Twin Peaks* and the diminutive actor's role in its supernatural Red Room might anticipate that they are engaging with the extraordinary. And, indeed, there are many aspects of the 'carnies', over whom he is nominally boss, which in the first instance set them at the margins of society. Following a long tradition of travelling entertainments in the USA, the carnival troupe of *Carnivàle* has fallen upon hard times and is sustaining its enterprise with some difficulties. A group of itinerants at a time in the history of the USA, the Great Depression, when many migrants were on the move, the carnies find themselves as unwelcome in many towns as the refugees driven from their Midwest farms by the foreclosure of bank loans. The parallel is drawn visually by the juxtaposition of imagery in the opening sequences when the jaded vehicles of the carnival rumble past the temporary shacks erected by the 'Okies' as a makeshift shelter from the elements.

But beyond social marginalisation, the carnies are extraordinary in two other ways. A travelling funfair-cum-circus, the carnival includes elements of the freak shows which had featured in such entertainment since Victorian times. Besides Samson, their number includes a bearded lady, Lila (Debra Christofferson), a pair of dancing Siamese twins joined at the hip, Alexandria and Caledonia (Karyn and Sarah Steban), a blind seer steeped in absinthe, Professor Ernst Lodz (Patrick Bauchau) and a lizard-like figure with scales and a tail, Gecko (John Fleck). In addition, there is a pair of cootch dancers, Dora Mae and Libby Dreifuss (Amanda Aday and Carla Gallo), a female snake charmer, Ruthie (Adrienne Barbeau) and a young woman traveller, Sofie (Clea Du Vall), who is ostensibly a tarot card reader. But the readings are transmitted telepathically through her by her catatonic, bedridden mother, Apollonia (Diane Salinger), who has the power to sling objects across the trailer and slam its doors and windows without apparently moving a muscle. These various acts involve illusions and some magic powers, but the mysterious and, indeed, truly supernatural forces of *Carnivàle* lie elsewhere.

The two protagonists, overtly set in parallel in the intercutting of the main narrative trajectory, are Brother Justin Crowe (Clancy Brown) and Ben Hawkins

(Nick Stahl). At the outset, Hawkins has been a small-time farmer in Oklahoma trying to make a go of the dusty, barren plot of land belonging to his bedridden mother. His mother dies, having mysteriously refused his attempts physically to comfort her since she would not be touched by him. He is called upon to bury her and as he hacks at the unyielding ground to make a grave, a heavy demolition vehicle employed by the bank stands by to flatten the rickety wooden shack so that the land can be reclaimed. At this moment of tension, the carnival happens by and the carnies, having fended off the demolition just long enough to assist Hawkins with his mother's makeshift burial and funeral, propose that Hawkins at least travel with them. As the dangling chain of his leg-iron reveals him to be an escaped convict and since he has nothing left to lose, Hawkins is reluctantly persuaded to jump aboard a wagon, and the carnival rolls on with him in its company (Episode 1).

Crowe, in contrast, is comfortably settled at the outset as the Evangelical revivalist minister of the First Methodist church in Mintern, California, where he aims to re-instate that 'old-time religion'. In a sermon to his congregation he suggests that the sandstorms ravaging Oklahoma may be 'evidence of God's fury … harbingers of the Apocalypse'. And yet he reads the balmy breeze which accompanied him to church as evidence that California 'is truly the promised land' (Episode 1). A tension within him between malevolent and beneficial forces thus plays relatively mildly at this stage but both Crowe and Hawkins are destined – in the context of *Carnivàle* the word is used advisedly but not unambiguously – for more challenging tasks.

In town one day, pondering the possibly dubious activities within Chin's hotel, Crowe is approached by a courtesan who asks him if he is lonely. His angry reaction leads to a vision, extraordinary in its graphic presentation. First, snow abruptly falls on him and covers the now empty street in front of Chin's. Suddenly a torrent of rain falls from the heavens and turns into blood, drenching Crowe in crimson. The neon sign over Chin's explodes and transforms into a scarlet cross before which Crowe kneels. Legs pass him by and the scene is restored to a street bustling with people going about their business. The upshot is that Crowe believes that God has instructed him through this vision to take over Chin's building to create a chapel for the migrants who are not welcomed by the parishioners in his own First Methodist church. Beyond Crowe's visions, he appears to have supernatural powers. When Templeton, who owns Chin's, refuses to donate the building to Crowe in order for him to implement God's purposes, Crowe conjures up not quite a vision but a scenario in which Templeton not only takes a cash pay-off from Chin but receives gifts in kind, specifically the services of a young Chinese boy (Episode 3). Confronted with his shame, Dennison has no choice but to relent, and thus when the scene simply cuts back to Crowe's house, Crowe initially gets his way and the building of the chapel begins.

Hawkins, meanwhile, manifests his parallel supernatural powers through the laying-on of hands. As the carnival reaches Milfay, two young children are attracted to visit it, but the girl finds it hard to keep up with her brother as she is paralysed. Following an altercation with fortune-teller Sofie, with whom Hawkins has made friends, he runs into the fields where he encounters the girl. He lays hands on her legs and, as if an evil force is released into the environment, the surrounding rows of cultivated crops are embrowned, but the girl is able to walk. It is the first seen of Ben Hawkins's miracle cures, though, if his mother's reaction to him when on her death-bed is recalled, it may not be the first time that his powers have manifested themselves.

The publicity for *Carnivàle* suggests a Manichean struggle between good and evil, and the opening episodes of Season 1 set up the two powerful protagonists in parallel, though it is not clear which might be a force for good. The tag line for the series, 'Into each generation is born a creature of light and a creature of darkness', suggests that only one of these protagonists is benevolent. On the face of it, the established minister of the church, Brother Crowe, might seem better placed than the refugee roustie, but it is soon evident that in the world of *Carnivàle* things might not be as they seem, and it is too good a narrative tension to be resolved early or even, indeed, by the end of Season 1, on which this discussion will concentrate. No sooner has Crowe set up his chapel than it is consumed by fire and he disappears from Mintern. He attempts suicide and finds himself confined in a lunatic asylum before, in Episode 10 (of twelve in Season 1), he is released and returns to the Mintern family home and his sister, Iris (Amy Madigan), who tells him that he has 'a destiny and now is the time to fulfil it' (Episode 10).

Though Season 1 intercuts Crowe's interim experience 'in the wilderness', specifically evoking Christ's journey of trial and introspection, with that of Ben with the carnival, it focuses more on the latter with its strong visual qualities. For, whilst the epic story arcs of Crowe and Hawkins are a central driving force in *Carnivàle*, it is the treatment which marks it as "high-end" and ultimately "edgy" TV drama. As one of the key directors of *Carnivàle*, Rodrigo Garcia, affirms, 'HBO encourages the people who make [the shows] to take many, many chances ... I've worked on, on *Six Feet*, on *Sopranos*, and on *Carnivàle*. And I would say they all share that HBO desire to push the envelope as far as possible.'[13]

The opening sequence of *Carnivàle*, whose visual effects were six months in the making by A52, manifests this extraordinary aspect and announces the distinction of this series in terms of both its content and its treatment.[14] Additional tarot cards fall into the vision of a tight crane shot over parched land on which other cards are strewn. The camera zooms in on a card named 'The World' and travels through the classical gods and goddesses depicted amongst clouds as if entering the space of a child's pop-up book with two-dimensional cut-outs. Still depicting a gargoyle-like figure in the down-left foreground, it reaches a tent in front of which poor men stand in line to receive hand-outs of food from other men whose better dress suggests the 1930s. What appears to be a still, sepia postcard suddenly animates and the first man in the line, having received his soup allocation, walks towards camera in what now appears to be a piece of documentary footage. A close-up of soup being ladled cuts to a denser queue of men in a city in the 1930s, which, in turn, cuts to images of science and technology (a dirigible floating past the Golden Gate Bridge being built and a 1930s motor car). The downside of scientific progress is suggested by a farmer sifting the dust of his land through his hand, and a family retreating to a wooden shack amidst parched fields. At this point, the camera zooms out of the historical montage back into 'Ace of Swords' card and pans across to the 'Death' card.

Zooming in and through this card, another still scene animates into a documentary of young people living in smelting ovens. A montage sequence cuts to documentary shots of Mussolini (fascism), Stalin (totalitarianism) and the Klu-Klux-clan (racism), setting the specific 1930s historical location of *Carnivàle* against the broader sweeps of early twentieth-century history before dissolving back to the 'Temperance' card. Another montage of documentary footage features positive aspects with people dancing and black sprinter Jesse Owens and the baseball hero Babe Ruth. An outward zoom returns to the cards only to zoom in again through 'The Tower' card to crowds approaching the White House and a make-shift sign pointing to City Hall juxtaposed with a truck overcrowded with men on their way to hear Roosevelt addressing the nation from a balcony.

In sum, the sequence evokes the specific trials of the Great Depression in the USA and Roosevelt as its potential saviour through the New Deal, juxtaposed with figures such as Lenin and Mussolini who wreaked havoc in twentieth-century history. The camera zooms out again on to the 'Judgement', 'Sun' (God) and 'Moon' (Devil) cards which blow away, the wind also dispelling the dust to reveal the title *Carnivàle* as it appears as the insignia of the travelling company.

Apart from its sheer visual impact and craft, this opening montage sets the tone as well as the "cinematic" approach to the series. It also sets out its distinctive and innovative mix of history, myth and the supernatural. On the one hand, it appears to be locating responsibility for human predicaments squarely with human beings such as Lenin or Roosevelt in specific historical moments whilst, on the other hand, it foregrounds fate and elemental forces which might themselves be associated with supernatural or mythic forces. Samson's opening words to camera are as follows:

> Before the beginning after the great war between heaven and hell, God created the earth and gave dominion over it to the crafty ape he called man. To each generation was born a creature of light and a creature of darkness and the great armies clashed by night in the ancient war between good and evil. There was magic then, nobility and unimaginable cruelty. And so it was until the day that a false sun exploded over trinity and man forever traded away wonder for reason. (Episode 1)

Prior to the opening of the story, situated precisely in Oklahoma in 1934 with the dying of Hawkins's mother, a dream sequence extends the enigma of the opening titles by rapidly intercutting a chase through high corn, shot darkly in close-up with a dynamic hand-held camera, featuring a well-dressed but dishevelled man, possibly a land-owner, being chased by a tattooed native American. Also in this sequence, images of death suggest the First World War trenches and other wars alongside hints of rape and pillage in civilian life. The face of a man with haunted eyes is shown in close-up against a gun and shootings in trench warfare. All this enigmatic material, for which no sense-making frame is initially offered, ultimately transpires to be aspects of Hawkins's dream, and indeed the dreams and visions of other characters with whom he appears mysteriously to be psychically connected. This extraordinary opening sequence informs viewers that *Carnivàle* is no ordinary television ('It's not TV, it's HBO') but an epic, elemental narrative of the Manichean struggle between good and evil. Furthermore, though the stories are materially grounded, like those in realist novels, in the circumstances of a specific place and time, they will also lead into other possible worlds of magic powers and the supernatural. Crowe and Hawkins, at least, have capacities beyond human norms.

As the series develops the world of the carnival setting up its encampments on its travels and showing its exhibits to more or less appreciative audiences (in Episode 5 Tipton is average, but in Episode 6 Babylon is a disaster), the daily-life business of pitching tents, cooking and eating food and preparing to perform in the evening lends a grounded ballast to the more imaginative and epic dimensions of *Carnivàle*. Though many of the characters have magic powers, there is an internal consistency in the carnival world in that they all believe in magic and the supernatural such that it comes to be part of that world, perhaps accepted as a given by characters and viewers alike. As in any powerful drama, the interrelationship of strong characters affords a centrifugal force. Contained within the epic narrative arcs of Hawkins and Crowe, smaller story arcs deal with such matters as the tensions between Samson and Clayton Jones, 'Jonesy' (Tim DeKay) over the company's deviation from its customary circuit. Samson insists that it is the will of 'Management' (of which more below) but Jonesy is increasingly unconvinced, particularly since he enters the forbidden trailer of Management only to find nothing there.

There are strong family frictions also between Felix 'Stumpy' Dreifuss (Toby Huss) and his wife Rita Sue (Cynthia Ettinger) and daughters Libby and Dora Mae, particularly after the latter is branded as a 'harlot' and hanged in Babylon. Stumpy enlists Jonesy as a customer ('trick') for highly sexed Rita Sue but their sexual lust becomes compulsive and ultimately ruins Jonesy's chance of a relationship with Sofie, to whom he has long been devoted. At the same time, Sofie's friendship with Libby is spoilt since she feels betrayed that Libby knows of the affair between Rita Sue and Jonesy and has said nothing. In this way, these and other subnarratives, such as may be found in soap opera, have the capacity to draw viewers in to more everyday human stories. But the characters themselves, as their backstories gradually unfold, are additionally interesting because so many of them are caught up in a weft of supernatural powers which curtail their free will. Sofie, for example, seemingly cannot leave her ageing and bedridden mother to start a new life with Jonesy, partly because she feels obliged to care for her but more because her mother telepathically conveys her thoughts, as noted. Moreovoer, in a dark dream which opens Episode 9, Apollonia reveals a glimpse of Sofie's unknown paternity when she conveys an image of herself being raped by a tattooed man who distinctly resembles the figure in the opening sequence. Thus Sofie's inability to escape her feeling of being trapped and pursue her desire to escape with Libby Dreifuss to a better life in the movies in Hollywood is motivated by both worldly and supernatural forces.

In the Crowe story towards the end of Season 1, the dynamics of the power relations between Justin and his sister Iris (Amy Madigan) and radio reporter Tommy Dolan (Robert Knepper) are increasingly fascinating as Iris comes to dominate both her would-be lover Dolan, in order to use his power over the airwaves, and her brother Justin, to push him to fulfil his destiny against his will. Fully to account for the threads informing a moment of high tension in Episode 12 when Crowe begs his mentor Rev. Norman Balthus (Ralph Waite) to kill him at the church altar requires backstory. Balthus cannot bring himself to do the deed – though he recognised the potential for evil in Crowe when the holy water of baptism turned to blood on his forehead – because he is Justin's and Iris's adoptive father. In a backstory vision in Episode 7 reminiscent of Poliakoff's dramatic strategy, it is revealed that Irina and Alexi Belyakov (Iris and Justin) were, in childhood, Russian refugees saved by Balthus from their captors. The revelation occurs after Crowe has tried to drown himself and in a semi-conscious vision sees a man (possibly himself) lying injured in the water (Episode 7). The man is found by two children who will not help him and he catches the girl and is hurting her when the boy (Alexi/Justin) breaks his neck through the sheer power of thought. Through this sequence of ambiguous and narrationally distorted imagery, the latent supernatural powers in Crowe are made manifest along with his true origins.

Genre and narrative

As illustrated, some aspects of *Carnivàle* follow traditional narrative and dramatic form in building strong stories, including revelatory backstories, around increasingly interesting characters. Set in times of adversity, the carnies have to struggle against the elements, such as the 'black blizzard' dust-storm in Episode 4, as well as against the poverty of the Great Depression and each other. But *Carnivàle* also mixes genres and forms in a manner typical of the contemporary drama under discussion in this book. The base level of specificity in Oklahoma and California in 1934 is reminiscent of Steinbeck's great novel of the period and, indeed, Garcia remarks that *Carnivàle* is 'part comic book, part *Grapes of Wrath*'.[15] But, in a slightly wider context than the history of the Great Depression in the USA, the series is located in an even broader historical frame between the two great wars of the first half of the twentieth century. The use of documentary footage in the opening sequence, as recounted above, establishes a documentary-history dimension which is sustained through the flashbacks to the trenches of World War 1 in which Hawkins sees himself covered in blood with his legs severed, or trampling over dead bodies to reach an enemy figure which emerges to be a bear. Though *Carnivàle* could scarcely be described as a documentary, it patently has a factual, historical dimension.

At the same time, *Carnivàle* functions on an epic scale. Visually the landscapes of the Midwest dustbowl are vast, with big skies and ravaging storms. The wide-angle shots of landscape or of the carnival at night are beautifully depicted to convey an elemental vastness, and special-effects dust-storms are powerfully realised in sound and vision (particularly in Episode 4). The epic forces in nature are conscious tropes for the battles between good and evil both within and between the characters, as outlined in Samson's opening words. Furthermore, in some specific incidents, *Carnivàle* draws upon other epic genres such as the western. When, after Dora Mae's murder, the carney men go into Babylon town to wreak revenge, the empty streets evoke a high- noon atmosphere before it transpires that there is literally nobody about (Episode 6).

There are strong mystery and thriller elements to the series which crank up in Season 1 and become even more complicated in Season 2. Though some concessions to a demand for narrative resolution are made – HBO noted that 'the main question fans wanted answered by the end of the season was who was good and who was evil' – no ultimate answers are given, even by the end of Season 2.[16] This is partly accounted for by the plan of Daniel Knauf, the creator of *Carnivàle*, to run to three books, with two seasons per book, over six years. The termination of the project after two series, owing to fluctuating, but generally diminishing, viewing figures, left a raft of intriguing but unanswered questions, It also left devoted fans petitioning HBO for the show's retention and much speculation on the *Carnivàle* website of possible narrative resolutions and ultimate meanings. This speculation reinforces the level on which the series functioned as a mystery or thriller, since fans continue to take what Umberto Eco calls 'inferential walks' to make sense of narrative forms

Above all, however, *Carnivàle* falls under the heading of "telefantasy" taken as an open category used by fans and as discussed by Hills (2002) and Johnson (2005). As Johnson summarises:

> Hills convincingly argues that fantasy texts have a particular propensity to become media cults because the representation enables the maintenance of two textual attributes that are central to the cult text. These attributes he terms 'perpetuated hermeneutic' (a central mystery that repeats familiar characteristics but whose resolution is endlessly deferred) and 'hyper-diegesis' (an internally logical, stable, yet unfinished fictional world). (2005: 2)

The world of *Carnivàle* has, as noted, an internally consistent logic fusing everyday life with magic powers which all accept, and, as the termination of the series ultimately dictated, an endless series of unanswered questions, both narrative and ideological. But even without the untimely halt in production, *Carnivàle* has, like *Star Trek* in Hills's account (see 2002), mobilised a number of possible worlds, in the reality of 1934 Oklahoma and California, in the past and future of the evils of war, and in supernatural spaces to keep 'creative speculation' going, even if the narrative loose ends had been more securely tied. This 'creative speculation', when located in historical context, contributes to the sense in which *Carnivàle* is "edgy" television. But before considering "edginess" in conclusion, a little more needs to be written about production values.

Production values

The opening sequence of *Carnivàle*, as recounted above, heralds an HBO "American Quality TV" product in the density of construction of its imagery. Beyond this, the *mise-en-scène* is painstakingly constructed and beautifully shot. Much attention was paid to the base level of realism. As historical adviser Mary Corey relates, 'in terms of what the carnival was like, and what their lives were like, and what they wore, and how they slept and their cars and all the material culture, it's impeccable'.[17] Besides the wide-angle establishing and framing shots, noted above, long-lens close-ups sharply foreground the carnies going about their daily business and smudge the background to lend the imagery a glossy, brash, dramatic beauty. Particularly given the magic powers and supernatural dimension of the series, special effects were restrained and used sparingly, but to great effect. Primary director, Garcia, believed in 'not going to the magic world with big effects. But just to let the magic happen as if it were just another dramatic element in the scene.'[18] Nevertheless, even a plate whizzing past Sofie's ear across Apollonia's trailer could be very powerful and some of the grander effects such as the weather changes outside Chin's described above are visually arresting and shocking, in the Russian formalist sense of the shock of estrangement leading to new ways of seeing.

The soundtrack of *Carnivàle* is as dense as its visual imagery, involving specially composed mood music by Jeff Beal and a host of recorded sounds, ranging from popular musics of the pre–1934 period (including ethnic blues, folk and jazz) to European classical music (beloved by Prof. Lodz) and 1920s Rembetika music from Istanbul.[19] Beal distinguished the worlds of the two protagonists musically by scoring religious-sounding music on an orchestral scale with trumpet, organ and voices for Justin Crowe and a more fragmented track with strong mystical associations for Ben Hawkins. Such rich and eclectic use of music to delineate character, establish mood and thicken textual quality is a characteristic of the more experimental HBO series as distinct from the quality, but more mainstream, products of today's networks such as *West Wing* (NBC) (see Chapter 7). Extraordinarily redolent in itself, the subtle soundtrack, with refrains gently fading in and out, some diegetically motivated and some 'music over', serves as an additional marker of 'pushing the envelope' in production.

"Edgy" television

HBO primarily thinks of 'pushing the envelope' in terms of doing what the networks cannot do. On one level this is a matter of sex scenes, nudity and strong language, all of which feature in *Carnivàle*, though not in gratuitous ways. The cootch girls strip as part of their act. Rita Sue has passionate sex with Jonesy, and Sofie and Libby even dabble in a lesbian relationship, which makes sense in terms of their less than sensitive treatment by men. But neither strong and caustic language nor sexual exposure are main attractions in *Carnivàle* as they might be in *Sex and the City*. But HBO also affords freedom to be imaginative to its creative teams. *Carnivàle* is a "high-concept" product, strong in both its imaginative constructs and its production values. And it is ultimately its conceptual ambition which affords moments of Todorovian 'hesitation' (see Chapter 1) and invites complex seeing. First, the blurring of boundaries between forms and genres, particularly those of documentary and the supernatural at the outset, creates moments of productive 'hesitation' in posing a challenge to viewers about what they are watching. These moments are extended throughout when disturbing sequences appear to be actuality. There is frequently ambiguity about whether a person is present or is merely a vision available only to the one who evoked it. Though many visions are subsequently revealed to be dreams, the dreams of *Carnivàle* are not clearly distinguishable from the psychically shared forces in play. But it is the broader frame of epic struggle between quasi-religious forces which, in my view, ultimately opens up the possibility of "edgy" impact by raising many questions about moral fervour and religious fundamentalism in the USA.

Particularly following the 9/11 attacks on the World Trade Centre in New York and in Washington, President George Bush has constructed what he calls the 'fight against terrorism' as a battle between the values of the allegedly free world of Western democracies and the closed world of Islam. Thus a TV drama which evokes wars in the first half of the twentieth century and sets up in its internal narrative a primal conflict between good and evil cannot help but resonate in today's cultural circumstances. Furthermore, in *Carnivàle*, perhaps as in contemporary political actuality, there can be little clarity about which side is which. President Bush and Prime Minister Blair are convinced in their Messianic fervour that they are in the right and, indeed, have a moral obligation to act as they have. The Taliban in Afghanistan and Al-Qaeda see it differently. Indeed, there are also many ordinary citizens, in the USA as well as in the UK, who find Bush and Blair culpable of instigating – some would say contriving – a war in Iraq which has had particularly disastrous consequences in its aftermath. In this context, a TV drama with strong religious overtones, Manichean conflicts and journeys of self-discovery in respect of the moral righteousness and ethical obligations of power may well be read metaphorically. The first season concludes with what sounds like a 'State of the Nation' address in voice-over:

> The clock is ticking, brothers and sisters, counting down to Armageddon. The worm reveals itself in many guises across this once great land. From the intellectual elite cruelly indoctrinating our children with the savage blasphemy of Darwin, to the craven Hollywood pagans, corrupting them in the darkness of the local bijou. (Episode 12)

But the voice is that of Brother Justin the Evangelist, now himself tainted. Furthermore, the mysterious Management of the carnival invites speculation about who is in control, which resonates with questions about the benign or diabolic forces motivating Crowe and Hawkins. Even when, in Season 2, Management is revealed actually to be a man named Lucius Belyakov, Ben Hawkins's predecessor and the previous creature of light, the mystery is less explained than deepened. Belyakov shows Ben a vision of the first atomic test near Alamogordo, New Mexico, and tells him that the devastating explosion he's just witnessed is 'the final link in a chain of events that is unfolding even now. You must break that chain' (Episode 13). The only way to do that, Belyakov tells him, is by destroying the preacher whom Ben sees in his visions. Thus the mysteries of *Carnivàle* remain inextricably bound up with the devastating events of world history.

Earlier telefantasy dramas such as *The X-Files* resonated with a post-Watergate sense that no one, perhaps especially not politicians, might be trusted (See Nelson, 1997 and Johnson, 2005). *Carnivàle* sustains this tradition of TV dramas operating on several levels, a prime level of entertainment through strong mystery narratives and appealing characters but leaving open, through a densely layered textual composition without closure, the possibility of metaphorical readings.[20] HBO targets the wealthier, better- educated demographics through its high production values and "must-see" approach to television and, in its encouragement of creatives to push the envelope, it is partly mindful of offering something with a greater intellectual challenge than LOP output. The advantage of long-form serial texts which are not closed in either narrative or ideology is that they keep audiences watching (to find out what happens), sustain subscriptions, and afford culturally critical readings without laying themselves open to the charge of political bias, since the implications are oblique and are constructed largely in a dialogic relationship between readers and texts. One strain of the complex narrative associates its mysteries with the Knights Templar and thus with the Crusades (see sequence analysis in Chapter 5).[21] Thus, though it would not be possible to justify a claim that *Carnivàle* was "about" the current conflict between Islam and the West, it is plausible to claim that *Carnivàle*, intentionally or otherwise, resonates, through its epic frame and the historical specificity of its location in respect of world events (before World War I) and the historical moment of its showing (after 9/11), with a contemporary power struggle between two powerful global forces, neither of which can be seen as unambiguously good or evil.

Chapter summary

The first of my three chosen examples of "edgy" television, *QaF*, comes out of a small independent company in the UK, whilst *SatC* and *Carnivale* are produced by a substantial, and even more independent (in the sense of free from regulation), subscription channel in the USA. Provisionally, then, I am suggesting that TV drama which challenges its audience might emerge from the commercial sector in contemporary circumstances in ways which were not possible in the past because the industry structure (in the influential American context particularly) was very different. Where, in the past, commercial companies were thought to be chasing large audiences to please advertisers in a context where a disposition to bland product to achieve ratings held sway, niche marketing opportunities today allow – indeed encourage – bold companies to aim to attract primary audiences with distinctive product and only subsequently to seek to build bigger audiences by new means of secondary distribution, some of which may increasingly be through platforms beyond the traditional networks and domestic television monitor. Given the nature of the younger, more affluent target-market demographic, there is room furthermore for product which sets out to shock, though it must be recognised that some questions – those about the basis and distribution of wealth, for example – may be off limits. And, as my examples suggest, creative treatments can render the material such as to elicit a shock of new insight rather than merely shock for the sake of shock.

Over the years since the pronouncements of Adorno (see Chapter 7), there has been a residual tendency in the academy to regard the culture industries with some suspicion. Even where negative attitudes have softened in respect of the alleged ideological dangers of commercial television, challenging programmes might (in the UK particularly) be expected to emanate from those institutions with a public service remit (such as the BBC). Thus the proposal I am making, that the output of a highly commercialised sector of contemporary television production might be counter-cultural, is itself somewhat radical. However, not to over-emphasise the radical in contemporary "quality TV", I set down a marker in my summary above of the economic implications of *SatC* on the possible limitations on the kinds of challenge such output might make. My provisional suggestion – further to be explored in Chapter 7 – is that aspects of the contemporary production circumstances imbricated within contemporary culture may well constrain those challenges within specific, and perhaps relatively narrow, notions of the political which not only do not address but also effectively preclude serious constraints on people's meanings and pleasures in a global context. The next chapter, meanwhile, takes a general look at the techniques of contemporary television and its related cultural forms.

Notes

1 The experimental television work of Stan Vanderbeek in the late 1960s and early 1970s, for example, amply evidences the social potential of the medium beyond the broadcast strictures into which it fell, as well as the potential for a range of principles of composition beyond linear narrative forms. Vanderbeek's New York archive is currently being researched by independent scholar Mark Bartlett who presented preliminary findings to the Screen Conference, University of Glasgow, July 2006, and whose book-length study is forthcoming.

2 As Lez Cooke has recently brought again to our attention, some early experiments in and around the Langham Group at the BBC in the early 1960s aimed to be innovative in form. At the Screen Conference, University of Glasgow, July 2006, for example, Cooke presented on the montage approach of *Three Ring Circus* (written by Jack Gerson and produced by James McTaggart for BBC Scotland in 1961). The drama-documentary interventions of Loach and Garnett in the mid–1960s illustrate another kind of experiment in form and content.

3 Jim Allen authored the controversial *Days of Hope*, produced by Tony Garnett and directed by Ken Loach for BBC in 1975

4 In a discussion of *QaF*, Creeber recounts previous television treatments of gay issues and the controversy caused by Davies's fresh depiction (2004a: 128 ff.).

5 Russell T. Davies is, of course, well known to be a *Dr Who* addict, the writer of *Dr Who* novels and ultimately the screenwriter for the series revived in 2005.

6 For an overview of Chekhovian dramatic technique, see Styan, 1981.

7 Davies himself acknowledges that the series had a mixed reception amongst the gay community in the booklet accompanying the 'Definitive Collector's Edition' of the series published on DVD in June 2003.

8 http://abc.go.com/primetime/desperate/about.html.

9 This claim was affirmed in seminars in my TV Drama Studies groups at Manchester Metropolitan University in 2003–5 and by some small-scale qualitative audience research conducted by members of the groups. Some men claimed to watch *SatC* to ogle the talent and learn things about women's sexual preferences but there may have been some bravado in such expressed dispositions. The majority seemed at least to feel the impact of being treated as sex objects and some found the series more profoundly dislocating in respect of sexual politics. I acknowledge the students in those groups and thank them for sharing their insights.

10 As Akass and McCabe report (see 2004: 191), many viewers were offended by the use of a word which is 'rated as one of the strongest terms of abuse and capable of causing great offence' (Channel 4 1999).

11 Ashley Nelson reports that, ' In 2000, 43 million American women were single – making up more than 40 percent of all adult females, up from about 30 percent in 1960. Moreover, while 83 percent of women between 25 and 55 were married in 1963, only 65 percent were in 1997 (Edwards 2000)' (2004: 87).

12 Figure cited in Merck, 2004: 59.

13 Website interview, www.hbo.com/carnivale/behind/rodrigo_garcia.shtml.

14 For an insider account of the imagery and the sources in classical art for the card images, see www.hbo.com/carnivale/behind/index.shtml.

15 In an interview, www.hbo.com/carnivale/behind/rodrigo_garcia.shtml: 7 July 2006: 3.

16 See interview with Daniel Knauf, www.hbo.com/carnivale/behind/danile_knauf2.shtml, 7 July 2006: 2.

17 www.hbo.com/carnivale/behind/mary_corey.sthml, 7 July 2006: 3.

18 Cited in an interview, www.hbo.com/carnivale/behind/rodrigo_garcia.shtml: 7 July 2006: 3.

19 For a discussion of source music for *Carnivàle* by Alexandra Patsavas and Kevin Edelman, see www.hbo.com/carnivale/behind/music_supervisors.shtml, 7 July 2006: 2.

20 Response to the invitation to be speculative is evidenced on a range of fan websites which led Daniel Knauf to publish The Gospel of Knauf (Avataric Rules), see http://en.wikipedia.org/wiki/Carniv%C3%A0le.

21 The ring which Hawkins steals from Phineas Buffo, his rival from Daley's freakshow, after it has triggered a powerful energy between them and visions of the Crusades, bears a red cross on a white background (Episode 8). Lodz conjures a vision 'by this sign' (Episode 9) and Phineas and the cross are seen by Sofie in a vision (Episode 10). Samson gives Ben a medal rumoured to belong to his father and bearing the insignia and, together, they visit the 'secret fraternal brotherhood' of the Templars in Loving, New Mexico (Episode 10).

5

Techniques, technologies and cultural form

The title of this chapter pays conscious homage to Raymond Williams's seminal work, *Television: Technology and Cultural Form* (1974), which established a way of locating the outputs of the television medium in the technological and cultural contexts of production and aimed to understand them in these terms. Though technology is not seen to determine cultural forms, it is one of the main forces in a field which shapes the programmes to appear on the small screen. In TV3, developments in technologies have played a significant part not just in distribution (see discussion of satellite technology, digital compression and encryption in Chapters 1 and 2) but also in approaches to making TV dramas and their textual forms. Developments influenced by technologies include an increased emphasis upon visual style, an aspiration to be as close to cinema as possible, increased dynamism of image and sound (and the two in relation to each other) and a new configuration of the tension between credible illusionism and textual playfulness.

Digital technologies afford not only a better quality of image and sound but a greater degree of manipulation of that image and sound. Furthermore, the capacity digitally to create imagery by computer generation (CGI) raises fundamental questions about the ontology of the image. In the past, there was an object external to the camera (in drama, typically, actors moving amongst physical sets or locations), the images being recorded by the apparatus (on film or on videotape). In television traditionally understood, as Lury puts it, 'The image produced is lifted from the real, an 'electronic trace' … images that are both live (so that the transmission and reception are truly seamless) and 'actual' (that is, taken directly from the real world') (2005: 11).

But this aspect of television's "realist disposition" is called in question by CGI and related factors in the digital environment. Some of the images of TV3 may well have been constructed or enhanced digitally and a wide range of soundtracks and sonic effects added in post-production. To take a recent example, the crowds in the hinterground of some scenes in *Rome* (HBO/BBC, 2005) were pasted in electronically and, as Lury (2005: 18ff.) has pointed out, entire environments in TV dramas such as *CSI* are increasingly computer-generated for convenience, when to shoot in the actual locations would be either logistically impossible or very expensive in terms of transporting personnel and equipment to locations. Reduced expenditure on extras or location work is not a frivolous consideration for producers who need, with today's demand for visual style in television, to make their budgets go a long way to make good-looking, distinctive product. Thinking about production, therefore, has undergone some significant changes in the light of digital capacities and related cultural shifts. This chapter draws freely on examples to illustrate the key impacts of technologies on cultural form in TV3.

Aspiration to cinema

Thus far in this book I have foregrounded the disposition in contemporary TV drama, particularly of the HBO Premium brand, to be taken as 'not TV', that is to say to be thought of as cinema, without fully exploring the technical distinctions between film and television. Technologically, even in its digital format, the television image remains undoubtedly distinct from the "cinematic" in being electronically configured rather than projected by light. The film image is physical and visible frame by frame in that the exposure of film stock to light chemically burns the image into specially treated material. In contrast, the magnetic configuration of videotape or the zeros and ones of digital recording are intangible and invisible until decoded. The visual qualities of an image projected by light on to a cinema screen are thus technologically different from the bursts of electrons sprayed at high speed on to a phosphor-coated television monitor.[1] Each medium has its own visual qualities in consequence and, historically, film has been taken to be a superior medium in terms of visual quality. Technically, the television image has been less stable since, beyond its configuration, the means of transmission were subject to interference over the airwaves. Furthermore, adjustments to the darkness–brightness balance and to colour could be made at both the transmission and reception ends of the broadcast process. To a considerable extent, however, digital signals, carried by either satellite or cable have overcome these alleged weaknesses. Though it must be acknowledged that many people still receive their television images through aerials on analogue monitors, the drift towards digital is inevitable and, in the UK at least, the analogue switch-off is already determined to be phased in over the next five years.

The recently introduced High Density or High Definition Television (HDTV) is just the latest refinement through high resolution in an increasingly improved image quality initiated by the digital revolution. HDTV can be simply defined as a television system that has more than the usual number of lines per frame such that its pictures show more detail.[2] Interestingly, in the current advertising jargon of major Japanese producer Hitachi, it is possible with HDTV to 'experience the beauty of true cinema with the new Hitachi UltraVision CineForm Series'.[3] It is clear that the traditional claim of film that its imagery is deeper and more rich in detail and thus more visually exciting and complex is being challenged by developments in television technology. Whilst purists may wish to sustain a binary (technological and aesthetic) distinction between cinema and television, many people have for years happily watched films on their television monitors and increasingly they watch them with the upgraded imagery on DVDs. Moreover, in respect of TV dramas shot on video as distinct from those shot on film, the vast majority of viewers do not perceive any difference. But there are aesthetic differences open to consideration.

The aspect ratio (the geometrical relation between the height and width of the image) has traditionally been different in cinema (typically 16:9 or 1.885:1) and television (14:9 or 1.33:1). In plain terms, that is to say, the cinema image has been wider than that of television. This difference potentially has significant aesthetic implications. Television, because of its relatively small monitor screens and narrower aspect ratio, has been seen as the close-up medium, where film has had the scale and width of vision to be able to locate subjects in their broad environments. Where a dialogue on television will typically cut from one talking head to another, for example, film has the option for a two-shot or indeed a wider angle of vision.

When films made for the cinema are shown on television, they are typically shrunk into letter-box format.[4] Where films are made for television, or where television is to be a secondary distribution platform (as is now typical under horizontal integration), directors are often required to bear alternative aspect ratios in mind. As Lury recounts:

> The BBC instructs that programmes (intentionally) shot in 16:9 must 'protect' their image so that it can be seen in 14:9. This means that although they are shooting in a wider format, the most 'significant' elements (particularly for instance, when characters or objects come in or out of shot) must make sense in 14:9 ratio. (2005: 23)

Whilst, then, there are both aesthetic and practical implications in differing aspect ratios, any sharp difference between film and television is rapidly being eroded in TV3. Many people already have widescreen television monitors. As the apparatus becomes less expensive, more and more people will in the medium term upgrade to widescreen, HDTV and the larger screens of "home cinema", the more affluent buying large, flat, wall-mounted plasma screens. Thus, even though the experience of a TV drama on digital television will perhaps never be the exact equivalent of a visit to the cinema, it is becoming a much closer approximation, close enough for TV drama producers increasingly to think cinematically and for established film directors increasingly to be prepared to work in television (if only perhaps as a guest director). Quentin Tarantino, for example, directed a double episode of *CSI*, 'Grave Danger', Parts 1 and 2, (Series 5, Episodes 24 and 25) in 2000. Indeed, David Lynch, with *Twin Peaks*, opened up a liminal territory between film and television in more ways than one.

Indeed, writers and directors have been encouraged to be aspirational. More importantly, they have been supported with substantial budgets. Thus it is in a force-field that the circumstances for visual style in television production have arisen, with technological developments playing a very significant part. Where, in the past, the industry hierarchy kept film directors away from television, today personnel move freely between the two mediums (see Bianculli, 1994). Very differently from in the "network era", directors construct "high-end" television drama as cinema in respect of both working conditions and practices.

Writer–producers David Chase (*The Sopranos*) and Darren Star (*Sex and the City*) both speak disparagingly about the constraints of network television, under which they have formerly been obliged to work. After an unhappy experience working on *Central Park* for CBS, Star reflected, 'The network brought me in to attract younger demographics, then changed its mind, making me retool the show. That experience taught me a great lesson. I'd rather not work for 10 years than write to serve network dictates' (cited in Sikes, 1998: 37). Chase's disdain for network television goes even further: 'I loathe and despise almost every second of it' (the Rucker interview cited in Lavery and Thompson, 2002: 19). Chase has a long-standing antipathy to network television's imbrication within American corporate capitalism, believing that it stifles creativity. As a young man, Chase 'hated everything that corporate America had to offer… [he] considered network TV to be propaganda for the corporate state – the programming not only the commercials' (the Rucker interview cited in Lavery and Thompson, 2002: 19). Though now, ironically, he works in one of the most commercially driven of sectors, his disposition to make films in the European art-cinema tradition has finally found an outlet with *The Sopranos*. Indeed, this signature series has contributed much to the discourse of the Home Box Office tag line pronouncing, 'It's not TV, it's HBO.'[5] The very idea of a box office evokes a cinema visit rather than a domestic experience of the "goggle box" and, even allowing for the hype of HBO, there can be little doubt that visual style in television has become something to be appreciated in itself.

Visual style

The most evident impact, particularly in "high-end" contemporary TV drama, is in visual style. This is not, of course, a single style but a tendency towards production values which aspire to the depth, complexity and visual interest of those traditionally associated with cinema. There are many and varied visual treatments of different TV drama vehicles, as exemplified in the examples in this book. The digital effects in *CSI* differ in purpose from those used in *Ally McBeal* (see below). Likewise the visual iconography of Manhattan in *Sex and the City* has a different function from the location shots of the New Jersey environment in *The Sopranos* (see Chapter 2). But digital technologies have, directly or indirectly, contributed new colours and new angles to all these programmes. The dynamic use of close-ups of still photographs to bring the past into the present in Poliakoff's *Shooting the Past* is very different from the techniques of textual density deployed in *Carnivàle* for dreams and visions in almost subliminal flashback (see Illustrations 1 and 2).

Shooting the Past sequence

Committed as he is to slow television, Poliakoff makes good use of still photographs in StP to create dynamic thought and memory processes which have a similar density of visual texture to Carnivàle but which are much more lingering and reflective. In the sequence illustrated overleaf, the trail leading to Anderson's discovery about his family reaches its end. Anderson is hooked by the narrative of his mysterious and wayward grandmother, but retains a grain of scepticism about whether the woman in the many photographs really is related to him. The final frame is the clincher. In a sequence of 53 seconds Marilyn reveals the photograph of Anderson as a young boy on his mother's knee visiting his grandmother at the Gadarene Club in Paris. Having seen all the images which make up the story, culminating in this one, Anderson must finally digest its implications as he reflects on this crucial photograph. The dynamic of panning shots across the scene which relates them and the repetitions convey something of the dizzying in his brain as he tries to digest what he has just heard. In the edit, his own startled eyes in close-up are juxtaposed with those of Marilyn and his mother and grandmother as a younger woman, bringing them all on to the same visual plane and apparently collapsing time. The soundtrack picks up the haunting strings – and piano refrain which runs throughout the series, building to a climax and underscoring the emotional impact of this sequence on Anderson and, vicariously, on viewers.

Carnivàle sequence

The frames overleaf are selected to illustrate the density of a sequence in Episode 9 which is only a minute in length when Phineas Buffo, having cheated Ben Hawkins over the new carnival act, approaches him to shake his hand. He gets more than he bargained for, since the handshake triggers a kind of electric reaction through Phineas's signet ring which bears the sign of a red cross on a white background. Intercut almost subliminally – the editing is so fast – are some thirty shots which evoke the Crusades. These images resonate with other visions experienced by Hawkins of past wars, and other images of a red cross, overtly associated in Episode 10 with the Knights Templar. Though not all sequences in Carnivàle are quite so visually rich and suggestive, this sequence is not entirely untypical. Whereas many films would cover a handshake in a single shot, seven shots from different angles are used in this sequence to set up the action of the handshake alone. The first illustration overleaf (shot 5 of 30 in the sequence) shows the fifth of these handshake shots, the one where the violent reaction kicks in. Some twenty shots in a montage sequence then intervene before actuality is restored with Phineas, minus his ring, nursing his hand, (shot 30 of 30, the final shot illustrated). Illustrated in between overleaf is a selection of the fast-cut images featuring crossed swords, severed heads and limbs and a succession of Crusaders in chain mail,

Illustrations: 1 Compilation of shots from Shooting the Past, Part 3, written and directed by Stephen Poliakoff (p. 114); 2 Compilation of shots from Carnivàle, Episode 9, created by Daniel Knauf (p. 115)

revealed to be wearing the red cross. The bell tower shown appears again in Episode 10 when Samson and Phineas seek out the Knights Templar.

Most "high-end" output today is shot on film or HDTV on location, with variations on the traditional processes of "cinematic" – as opposed to television studio or outside broadcast – approaches. Constructing and lighting individual shots, as distinct from two-to-three-minute studio takes, affords what is generally regarded as the higher-quality visual product. In particular, lighting is more focused in respect of the specific visual style aimed at, in contrast with general studio lighting which tends to flatten out features of faces and environments. More time and care can be taken over production than is possible under the industrial process demanded by, say, the rapaciousness of a thrice-weekly soap. The opportunity for a number of takes in the "cinematic" approach facilitates greater freedom in post-production editing, contributing also to a more refined outcome.

Film is not, of course, new at the "high end" of TV drama where prestigious projects have been shot on 16mm or even 35mm film for many years. The difference in the digital era is first that domestic television monitors are capable of reproducing a better-quality image than their analogue predecessors. Thus paying attention to the aesthetics of visual style is worthwhile. But there are other innovations and advantages. Digital technologies afford some short-cutting in the time-consuming, and thus expensive, cinematic process. Fewer takes are needed when a digital video camera, running alongside a film camera, can give instant playback approximating sufficiently closely to the cinematic image that unnecessary retakes, "just in case", can be avoided. With wider aspect ratios, the detailed work on shooting shot-reverse-shot "singles" might be avoided by the use of a group shot, saving expensive location time.

The manipulative capacity of digital technologies is deployed in different ways to adjust in the editing process the images viewed on the domestic television monitor. Some usage is intended to be invisible (e.g. the crowds in the background in *Rome*) but other usage aims to acknowledge the capacity for manipulation by visibly playful distortions. In *Ally McBeal*, for example, a range of digitally generated visual effects contribute to the viewing pleasures the show affords. In a celebrated example, Ally's tongue extends ridiculously in cartoon fashion, poking out across the room, when she dislikes someone. Similarly, on advice from her therapist to 'think lips' when she needs to feel romantically confident, Ally puckers her lips until they expand (by digital effect) with a pink lipgloss. Whilst such devices may be dismissed as visual gimmicks, the disposition to be visually playful contributes to *Ally McBeal*'s parodic and, at times, subversively challenging tone. The court cases which figure in each episode frequently turn established social norms on their heads. In the episode, 'Silver Bells' (Season 1, Episode 11, 1997), for example, the judge finds in favour of a *ménage à trois* over the traditional heterosexual couple. Digital treatment does not invert social values but, in *Ally McBeal*, it invites a playfulness in both form and content which, at best, is both visually and culturally innovative and challenging.

The use of strong colour, disregarding naturalism, is another feature of digital treatments. *Clocking Off* (Red Production Company for BBC1, Series 1, 2000) affords an interesting example since its location, a factory in the North of England might suggest gritty social realism. But executive producer Nicola Shindler wanted to get away from the dour and dark look of traditional British northern drama and instructed cinematographer Peter Greenhalgh to 'make it look "beautiful" not, grimy and industrial as one would expect' (cited in Cooke, 2005: 191). Accordingly, the design not only foregrounded colour in the locations but used enhanced primary colours (see Cooke, 2005: 191–193). Besides making the final product more visually arresting, the use of colour in *Clocking Off* reflects a broader treatment, as digital effects do with *Ally McBeal*. Working in the British tradition of social realism, *Clocking Off* moves the tradition on. As Cooke summarises, 'It was the stylistic inventiveness of the series – faster cutting, mobile camerawork, a creative use of colour in the mise-en-scène, together with a lively music track … which had distinguished *Clocking Off* on its debut' (2005: 196).

A snappy editing rhythm yielding a strong visual dynamic is perhaps a cultural feature of contemporary TV drama as much as a technological one, but digital editing does afford an ease of creativity which in turns feeds back into the narration. A recently overused feature, for example, is the dynamic 'crash zoom' accompanied by a whooshing sound which serves to cover an edit such as a change of location. The device has even been deployed to drive the pace of the complex multistrand narrative in the otherwise traditional genre of period drama in the recent BBC production of *Bleak House* (BBC1, October, 2005), shot experimentally on HDTV. This serialisation was also constructed (by writer Andrew Davies) in the manner of a soap and, whilst this treatment is not digitally driven, it again illustrates a disposition to do things a bit differently in a new technological environment. The treatment has sought global interest in the production. As the BBC's website reports, 'BBC Worldwide – the BBC's commercial arm – said there had been a "huge amount" of international interest [in *Bleak House*]. About 20 countries are said to be keen on showing the period drama, which has been aired on BBC One in half-hour episodes with soap-style cliff-hangers.'[6]

Another feature to emerge from digital editing is the advanced use of a split screen. Split screen in drama is not in itself original since there are cinema precursors, but *Trial and Retribution* in the UK and *24* in the USA appear to be the first substantial usages in prime-time television.[7] Since this device marks a significant change in how the screen space might be perceived, the split screen will be more fully discussed below. The point to be made here is that it is encouraged by the 'Trim Edit' function in Avid digital editing which juxtaposes two images and by Timecode which allows several images to be set side by side. In sum, digital editing, besides the technological advantages of greater flexibility, special effects and avoiding degeneration as images are rerecorded, lends itself to a creative practice.

Technology alone has not, however, determined the disposition in contemporary TV drama to create a stronger visual interest through dynamics, structural complexity and special effects. The influence of production companies such as Fox Television in identifying and targeting the 18–24 demographic (see Chapter

3) has disposed television to seek to appeal to the youth market. Younger people, brought up on a range of new media technologies (cellphones, walkmans, PCs, playstations, iPods, palmcorders), inhabit a visually and aurally dynamic world. Thus industrial and cultural aspects function with technologies in the force-field which shapes product. The examples above illustrate some of the visual contributions of technology in the digital television environment and we shall return to the implications of breaking the frame with a split screen, after a brief consideration of sound.

Soundtrack

Contemporary television drama invariably uses a music soundtrack and/or sonic effects but, as Negus and Street have recently noted, 'Television has been conspicuously neglected in studies of popular music, and music has been notably absent from most accounts of television' (2002: 245). This may in part be accounted for by the fact that the extensive use of music, particularly in TV drama, is a relatively recent phenomenon, in part triggered by the desire to appeal to the youth market noted above. Early television naturalism, following its theatrical precursors, required everything in the diegesis to be motivated and hence, beyond the dialogue which was central, any audible sound had to be either ambient (the sound naturally occurring in that location) or diegetic, visibly sourced within the frame (e.g. a radio would be seen to be the source of 'music over'). Early television dramas had a signature tune played at the outset, to hail viewers to watch, and at the end, to mark the episode's closure. As TV drama developed, variations on the signature theme were used to cover breaks in narrative continuity and, for prestigious projects, specially composed music was used, as in cinema, typically to underscore emotion or to signal mood (e.g. romance or impending danger).

Contemporary popular music was little used – *Up the Junction* (1965) being a notable exception in its use of 1960s pop music – until Dennis Potter used popular music extensively. Potter did not use music soundtrack merely to underscore mood; indeed, he developed a complex set of relations between songs and the characters or narrative moments to which they related. He famously had characters mime to a well-known recording of a popular song, frequently transgressing gender with a male actor miming to the voice dub of a female singer. Unlike Loach and Garnett in *Up the Junction*, he did not use pop music of the time of writing as ambient soundtrack but popular music contemporaneous with the setting of each series. In a variety of interesting ways in his seminal series he used 1930s music in *Pennies from Heaven* (1978), 1940s music in *The Singing Detective* (1986) and 1950s music in *Lipstick on your Collar* (1993). Potter was thus innovative in his use of popular music, creating his own distinctive method which has been imitated, with arguable success, by Steve Bochco, in *Cop Rock* (ABC, 1990), and, more recently in the UK, by Peter Bowker, in *Blackpool* (BBC, 2004 – see Chapter 8).

Music, and particularly pop music, in contrast, is a dominant feature of television drama in TV3. British soaps such as *EastEnders*, which formerly avoided the use of ambient contemporary music (e.g. juke boxes in pubs) because the time lag between recording and transmission dated the soundtrack, have now followed the example of Australian soaps in incorporating popular music, though not for emotional underscore. Popular dramas such as *Heartbeat* draw on the nostalgia value as well as the postmodern retro appeal to a younger segment of the target audience (see Nelson, 1997). Undoubtedly influenced by MTV (first aired August 1981), much TV drama now draws upon popular music for its intrinsic appeal as well as, at times, complex interrelationships between sound and image. In the 1980s, *Miami Vice* was perhaps the first TV drama to use popular (in this instance, rock) music in this way. Buxton writes of 'the series' aesthetic affinity with the music videos shown on the all-clip channel MTV channel' (1990: 140), and Page points to Strinati's (1995) argument that '*Miami Vice* is "postmodern" because it drew attention to the aspects of popular culture of which it was composed' (in Creeber, 2001: 46).

The attractions of cutting dynamic images to a strong beat have since proved a phenomenon in Music Television. In Donnelly's account, 'The early 1980s simultaneously saw the proliferation of video technology, and the outlet of MTV inspired the gamut of video processing effects, as well as offering almost limitless possibilities for imagination' (in Creeber, 2001: 91). Initially designed to draw the much-prized demographic of young people, MTV has been very influential in contemporary TV drama, particularly where a younger demographic is the target market. Though the energy and visual style derived from cutting to the pace of a rock track is not the only factor in the tendency towards short narrative segments edited fast in contemporary drama, it has set a standard for dynamic visual storytelling.

Ally McBeal perhaps best illustrates a range of music uses in a prime-time drama, significantly for the pleasures popular music affords in itself but also in new ways in respect of television narrative and the treatment of character. Established singer, Vonda Shepherd, sings regularly "as if live" in the bar below the law offices from which Ally and her work-friends family operate. Episodes end with the characters congregating there to relax to the music over a drink. The lyrics and moods of the songs are chosen to reflect on the episode's narrative and, occasionally, key characters are themselves persuaded to take the microphone, particularly when the song has a special significance for them or their situation.

This whole approach resonates with the omnipresence of popular music as a soundtrack to contemporary life. Many people conduct their lives accompanied by popular music on the radio both at home and in the car, and, like the characters in *Ally McBeal*, are ready to take the microphone in karaoke bars. Young people in particular carry their music with them (on walkmans and iPods) such that everything they do is set to music and the sounds are inscribed within memories. *Ally McBeal* picks up on this contemporary phenomenon and adapts it to television. Another use of music quirkily relates the key characters to specific singers and songs in order to signify their sometimes fragile identities. Cage, for example, hears Barry White's 'You're my everything', whilst Ally is advised by her therapist to think Gladys Knight and the Pips when she needs a boost of confidence. Thus, besides the intrinsic pleasure to fans of the soundtracks, the music is used to articulate inner thoughts and feelings. At times it is unclear whether or not other characters hear the music which, although audible (and often visible in terms of the performing artists) to viewers, is assumed to be private to the character. This ambiguity is another dimension of the self-conscious playfulness of the series and even raises questions about the status of the television image to be explored below.

Narrative forms and devices

One of the keynotes of TV3, as noted in Chapter 1 is hybridity at every level. All the examples of TV drama discussed thus far evidence mixes of narrative form, genre or media mode. The horizontal integration of the media industries is disposed to a mind-set which crosses media borders not just in merchandising – though this is, of course, very important for profits – but also in respect of product. That *Sex and the City* is influenced by magazine formats should be no surprise when viewed from this perspective. In what follows, attention is paid to the tensions in narrative forms under new circumstances.

For some time, TV drama has relied on strong narrative drive with well-placed hooks to draw viewers in at the outset and a high temperature to bind them in. Though the environment has changed over two decades, the need to catch and hold viewers has become more pressing in a competitive, multichannel environment. Programme-makers have needed to be increasingly creative in forging hooks. New strategies developed to counter fears of losing audience include story updates at the beginning of each episode, and trailers shown across the intervening week. Where formats are structured to accommodate a commercial break, some dramas, mindful of short attention spans in a channel-hopping culture, have even included updates after the intermission. By these means, all the main, established drama formats are sustained in TV3 but the "flexi-narrative" tendency (see Nelson, 1997) to blur the distinction between serial and series forms with rapidly intercut, multiple narrative strands is accelerated. It is this tendency which Poliakoff's *Shooting the Past* calls in question by an advocacy of "slow" television, at least as part of the available diet.

In respect of series formats, the satisfaction of closure of a central narrative strand has been seen to be a pleasure anticipated by viewers, but, from a scheduler's point of view, the lack of a hook to draw viewers to watch the following week's episode places reliance on the pull of the vehicle overall.[8] In contrast, serial dramas moving to closure of the narrative over several weeks, whilst they have narrative impetus and can end each episode with a hook for the next, have posed problems of audience retention, since research has shown that viewers drop away if they miss an episode, fearing that they have lost the ability to follow the plot.

Television schedules in a 24/7 environment are more rapacious than ever but, as increasingly high production values are expected of TV drama, fewer programmes can be afforded. As Grant and Wood observe:

> Lavishly financed series like *West Wing*, *CSI* and *The Agency* have sharply raised the standard of production values by which audiences judge television drama. Broadcasters everywhere have reacted by scheduling fewer, albeit more expensive shows, and filling the air with cheap but popular 'reality TV' fare. (2004: 235)

Costed by hours of output, "high-end" TV drama budgets are not high by today's Hollywood blockbuster film standards, but they are significantly greater than those for even prestigious television projects hitherto. Strategies have been required to address this new situation.

The very idea of "Event TV", as expounded above, has helped to sustain some of television's most traditionally prized output with a strong serial-narrative dimension. In many instances (see, for example *The Sopranos* in Chapter 2 and *State of Play* in Chapter 8), long-form narrative with contemporary cultural resonances and featuring complex and developing protagonists are sustained by accommodating the narration and visual style to new circumstances.[9] Taking a specific approach to "Event TV", long-form serial dramas such as *Murder One* and *24* have created a sense of urgency and immediacy by the use of real time (see Chapter 6). Also, for shorter mini-series, particularly two-parters (e.g. *Trial and Retribution*), the showing of instalments on successive evenings is a strategy designed to reduce the period of time over which interest in a serial narrative must be sustained. Various commentators have recognised a distinct advantage of television drama over feature films to be TV serial drama's capacity to develop character in context over time. A scope of between eight and twenty-four hours' screen time allows for more complex storytelling and character-developing in relation to changing circumstances. It can in short, deal with shifts in fortune and the consequences of actions over time. Given the medium's sustained sense of paralleling everyday life (see Chapter 1), moreover, television is disposed to address contemporary issues. The diminution of long-form serial drama in the 1990s was thus a quality issue and its retention under the new circumstances of TV3 is significant.[10] The quality branded product is sustainable by achieving longevity on a range of platforms. Its rich visual style, along with its generic and narrative complexity, is designed to stand up to repeated viewings on subscription channels, in syndication, on DVD and even in the cinema.

In a contrast which illustrates the diversity of forms in TV3, some innovative, more playful and self-referential approaches to narrative have emerged. *Ally McBeal*, for example, has been dubbed a "dramedy" in the light of its mix of comedy and tragedy or, more precisely, its debt to sitcom, romance, courtroom drama and MTV.[11] The fictional world of the series in which viewers are invited to believe is the law firm, Fish & Cage, where Ally is employed. Like the other lawyers, Ally takes on cases and functions as an advocate in the courtroom. Though the cases are frequently unusual, not to say bizarre, the given of the series is that of a legal and courtroom drama, familiar in generic terms. This aspect is mixed with the romance genre since (pre-figuring the interest of 'the gals' in *SatC*) Ally (Calista Flockhart) is searching for 'Mr Right'. Her teenage sweetheart, Billy Thomas (Gil Bellows), who also comes to work at Fish & Cage, is married to another lawyer in the practice, Georgia Thomas (Courtney Thorne-Smith), affording opportunities for wistful reflections on lost love as well as the active pursuit of new love interests. Thus, in narrative terms alone, *Ally McBeal* is destined to attract several target audiences offering different pleasures to each, even before the music and digital effects come into play.

The notion of "dramedy" in TV3 deserves further exploration since many examples reveal a mix of challenging experiences in an overall comedy frame. To compare two seminal examples, each a "lifestyle" series based upon the lives of six friends, *Friends* (NBC, Season 1, 1994) undoubtedly started as a sitcom and retained that format, though it increasingly addressed social issues, whilst the British drama *Cold Feet* (ITV, Series 1, 1997) – sometimes dubbed the English *Friends* – consciously adopted a dramatic method which veered formally between comedy and scenes of considerable emotional intensity.

Though they may have begun as stereotypes, the characters in *Friends* develop to a limited extent as a result of their experiences in a manner untypical of traditional sit-coms. Joey, for example, in time addresses his unattached-macho-stud lifestyle to seek a sustained relationship with Kate involving, on his part at least, an emotional attachment. Rachel comes to recognise that her privileged background has meant that she has never had to feel her own weight and, having run out from her wedding, she cuts up her credit card and starts life as a waitress since she is unqualified for anything else. The apparently flaky Phoebe turns out to have had a troubled past, becoming homeless after her mother committed suicide. Though the characters' reversals and developments function within a relatively narrow frame of experience, mainly connected with their personal relationships, contemporary social issues such as homosexuality and lesbianism feature in ways unusual, particularly for series at that time (the distance between *Friends* and *Sex and the City* in this respect marks the distance television has travelled in TV3). Ultimately the comedy treatment, privileging gags and sharp one-liners with canned laughter, constrains *Friends* within a sitcom frame, but there are moments over the long-running series where deeper emotions begin to be engaged.

In *Cold Feet*, in contrast, the overall frame is that of a serial drama with roots in the British tradition of social realism. Set in Manchester, in the North of England where social realism has traditionally been located in an industrial context, *Cold Feet* differs in featuring the lives of couples ranging from working-class-turned-blue-collar Pete and Jenny to lower middle-class Adam and Rachel to firmly middle-class David and Karen. In featuring their everyday lives in relatively well-furbished homes, *Cold Feet* might be seen in part as a "lifestyle" drama. As in *Friends*, the main stories feature the interrelationships between the six friends in domestic, but affluent, settings, with some darker experiences to offset the comfort. The break-up of Pete and Jenny's relationship after they have had a child, for example, parallels Monica's situation after she realises that she must effectively bring up her child without the full commitment of his father Ross. But, rather than a mere recognition of the situation, the dramatic focus in *Cold Feet* is on the pain of Pete which is allowed to come through with full emotional force. When, in a later episode, Adam, feeling alienated from his newborn son, asks Pete's advice, he replies, 'the next months are the same, then your wife leaves you, taking your son with her'. Thus the real depth of Pete's emotional hurt is sustained and revealed over time in consequence of his separation from Jenny. In similarly dark territory, Rachel in *Cold Feet* elects to have an abortion (something still unacceptable on American television – see discussion of *SatC*). The final episode of *Cold Feet* features an horrific car crash in which Rachel is killed, the full anguish of her death being empathetically experienced from Adam's point of view as he learns of it at the hospital. Writer Mike Bullen acknowledges a dramatic method which refused established comedy or tragedy formats to create a hybrid which took viewers on a roller-coaster ride of emotional highs and lows. Though there were funny scenes and moments of comic action, the script was not written for one-liner gags and there was no canned laughter. Thus *Cold Feet* is perhaps a forerunner of the modal hybridity which informs much drama on television in TV3.

Thus there is no single narrative form of drama in TV3. If hybridity is too loose a concept to be accepted as a defining characteristic, the best which might be said is that a range of narrative forms is sustained in TV3 but most are inflected by the factors in the force-field charted in this book with a tendency towards "high-end" production values. From sustained serial narrative over a number of weeks (in the case of *24*, twenty-four weeks) to "flexi-narrative" forms which have a loose serial-narrative thread, but which foreground the serial or sitcom episodic narrative closure (for example *Sex and the City* or *Spooks*), traces of television's traditional narrative modes are evident. But, as pointed out in respect of the specific examples analysed in this book, most contemporary product is mixed-mode. Some narrative treatments aim to sustain belief in the fictional world and to draw viewers into it (*24* affords a good example), whilst the playfulness and self-consciousness of other vehicles such as *Ally McBeal*, comprising a multitrack bricolage (see Nelson in Creeber, 2001: 45) with each element affording a different appeal, tends to prevent viewers from believing too deeply in the fictional world. Though, being "regular" rather than "high-end" fare and not the subject of this book, the soap form (continuing serial-narrative drama) must be acknowledged as a sustained magnet for substantial audiences, either by carrying cultural specificity and thus local resonances (e.g. *Coronation Street* or *EastEnders* in the UK) or functioning across speech communities worldwide, as in the case of Spanish-language *telenovelas*. Exceptional continuing serial narratives with high production values such as *ER* illustrate the pull of "high-end" forces, even in this most everyday of TV drama forms.

New forms: new dispositions

The dominant codes and conventions in popular film and TV drama have historically sustained the illusion of a real (though fictional world), plausible in its geography and motivations. For the duration of the time of viewing, the audience suspends its disbelief and is drawn into the story. This contract has not perhaps been completely broken in TV3, but the hybridity, playfulness, irony and visual pleasures of contemporary fictions for the small screen suggests a greater complexity of engagement. Where the "realist disposition" may have predominated in popular forms with frame-breaking devices remaining the province of the avant-garde, an increasing knowledge of television awareness of the constructed nature of media products has perhaps seen a cultural shift to a 'both-and' mode of engagement. Yielding still to the seductions of narrative followability for the pleasures to be gained from vicariously identifying with character in context may not preclude awareness of the additional pleasures of excess in visual style and in the amusement of play. The generic hybrids spawned in TV3 suggest a capacity amongst viewers to deal in mixed modes.

A major historic tension between illusionism and aesthetic awareness has recently been revisited. Bolter and Grusin's concept of 'the double logic of *remediation*' (2000: 5) involves 'the twin preoccupations of contemporary media: the transparent presentation of the real [immediacy] and the enjoyment of the opacity of media themselves [hypermediacy]' (2000: 21). The television monitor has traditionally been perceived as immediate, indeed as a "window on the world". This disposition was captured in early discourse about television: 'People now look upon scenes never before within their range; they see politics as practiced [*sic*], sports as played, drama as enacted, history as it is made' (Dunlap, 1947, cited in Auslander 1999, 15).

Though television theory has long since unpacked this "naïve" view, there is a significant residual tendency to regard the medium as giving access to the external world beyond the scope of an individual's frame of reference (e.g. via news bulletins) and, in parallel in the case of fictions, to suspend disbelief and credit the fictional world of the diegesis. Indeed, even in respect of new technologies, Bolter and Grusin note that:

> the discourse of the immediate has been and remains crucially compelling … computer graphics experts, computer users, and the vast audiences for popular film and television continue to assume that unmediated presentation is the ultimate goal of visual representation and to believe that technological progress towards that goal is being made [in digital graphic imaging]. (2000: 30)

Immediacy, then, remains important but new circumstances have placed a new emphasis upon hypermediacy, initiating a changing habitus amongst viewers. The use of computers at work and domestically has increased rapidly and, indeed, many people have, over a short period of time, come to depend on PCs in their everyday lives. Increasingly, there is a symbiosis between the small screens in the domestic environment: the PC, the television and, most recently, the mobile phone. Some people already access their e-mail through their television monitor and the separate PC and TV monitors in most homes today may well become combined. Two common features derived primarily from computer technologies are digital interactivity and multiple screens within the monitor screen.

Though the notion of a fundamentally passive reception of television has been roundly called in question by the ethnographic study of television audiences, digital interactivity with the TV monitor involves a fundamentally different notion of viewer engagement. Though the options available in pressing the red button on the remote handset of a digital television apparatus are currently limited, the idea that viewers might be incorporated as agents in the media construction process shifts the perceived relationship between them and what appears on the screen. Even if it amounts at present to little more than selecting the player-cam to give another perspective on the game, the format of the screen, affording insert subscreens, fragments the single complete screen image. As with computers, windows carrying different kinds of information on a topic can be juxtaposed and, since the majority of people in technologically developed cultures are now accustomed to calling up information and manipulating it on their PCs, they might increasingly expect to do something similar with their televisions.[12] Digital technologies afford this possibility and, as the old analogue systems are replaced with digital, a new era of television may develop. As yet, experiments encouraging viewers to construct the narrative of a TV drama or offering choice of direction in a drama remain at a preliminary stage, though computer games suggest ways in which such interactivity might be developed. To explore a particular feature of the impact of PCs now spilling over into television, the split screen proves instructive.

Split screens

The limited use of split screens in both film and television historically is in part explained by the technological difficulties, involving time and expense, creating them prior to the emergence of digital technologies.[13] But an additional restraint is the disposition to illusionism, and the unwillingness visibly to break the frame for fear that it would break the illusion. But, in respect of split screens, the kinds of negotiation invited between one subscreen image and another in a split-screen or multiscreen mediation, depends upon how the windows are constructed, both individually and in relation to each other. The possibilities again reflect Bolter and Grusin's distinction between 'immediacy' and 'hypermediacy'.

As will be illustrated in Chapter 6, 24 uses multiscreens extensively to mediate the story of agent Jack Bauer's mission to save the life of Senator Palmer, potentially the first black president of the USA. The predominant usage, however, appears to be one of 'immediacy' since the images reinforce a compelling and complex narrative, the strands of which are periodically brought together in space and time through the use of multiple screens with the dominant impact of heightening the dramatic tension (see Illustration 3). In this instance, there is no 'hypermedial' attempt to bring a range of optics to bear on the situation such that viewers might be encouraged to disengage from the narrative and view it through a range of different perspectives. Similarly, Spooks – the example of a British political thriller to be compared with 24 in Chapter 6 – though bringing a range of optics to bear on the topics it raises, does so through narrative and character perspectives rather than through the multiscreen devices which it also deploys.

The potential of hypermediacy in multiscreen television treatment is visible

3 Split screens in *24*, Episodes 1 and 3, directed by Tim Iacofano and Rodney Charters for Fox Television

and audible, however, in the example of *A TV Dante: The Inferno Cantos I–VIII* (1989), the product of a collaboration between film-maker Peter Greenaway and writer–artist Tom Phillips to make a television version of Dante's *Inferno*. Their innovative approach to the narrative overlays one discourse upon another and sets them in play without harmonising them, thus leaving the sounds, words and images for the viewer to negotiate. The poetic narration initiated by a golden-masked John Gielgud is interrupted by the voice of David Attenborough's discourse of scientific natural history, with images of animals (leopards and zebras) running across the screen.

As is evident in Illustration 4, a range of images, some photographic, others

4 Split-screen montage in *A TV Dante*, created by Peter Greenaway and Tom Phillips

computer-generated, are overlaid in multiple windows, some with words superimposed. The eight cantos of the film are not conventionally dramatised rather they are illuminated with layered and juxtaposed imagery and a soundtrack which comments, counterpoints and clarifies. There are visual footnotes delivered by relevant expert authorities, and these often perform the function of narration as well as illustration. Tensions are set up between the screens and between word and image and, in sum, between the discourses. By drawing attention to the modes of mediation and to different discursive accounts of the situation which Dante describes, some of which (as in Attenborough's 'naturalist' account) are modern as opposed to ancient, this self-conscious text both affirms Dante's epic story and subverts it in the telling.

As yet, no TV drama to my knowledge has exploited the digital interface between computer and television to a greater extent, though the example of *A TV Dante* illustrates the technological potential. Since digital formats do not downgrade in editing in the way that magnetic videotape deteriorated through successive (de)generations, the scope to manipulate imagery is very much extended, but the audience for even "Event TV" is perhaps not yet perceived to be ready for such formal experimentation. The time may, however, have arrived for producers' residual disposition to immediacy, noted above, to be displaced through increasing familiarity with the potential of computer generation to do things other than reinforce the illusion of a coherently "real" (though fictional) world simply with more spectacular imagery.

Media-aware viewers, of course, enjoy special effects in such product, but the interface between television and computers has much greater potential for complex seeing, as illustrated. Presentational developments in TV3, though they are characterised by much-enhanced visual style, remain as yet within a relatively confined range of aesthetic possibilities. It is too soon clearly to see how the noted tension between immediacy and hypermediacy will play itself out. In TV3, television's historical disposition towards immediacy appears to have embraced the new visual capacities of the digital age rather than having been fundamentally altered by them. As van Vliet observes, however, 'next generation television strives towards interactivity and connectivity ... Both [television and the internet] "long for" what the other medium possesses'.[14] It may be, then, that television "viewing" will become increasingly hypermediate and interactive in the manner of engagements with computers but, at present, it appears that the television's historical disposition towards unmediated presentation as 'the ultimate goal of visual representation' may be sustained but with a higher-quality, more "cinematic" treatment of a wider range of visual images. New angles, that is to say, some of which are computer-generated in virtual environments, may ultimately be absorbed into the historical, enculturated disposition towards the immediate rather than the frame-breaking devices of the avant-garde.

Notes

1 For a detailed account of the technological differences between film and television, see Lury, 2005: 9–14).
2 There are currently three different systems with different resolutions in play (prior to HDTV): 425 lines with NTSC in North and South America; 625 lines with PAL in the UK, and SECAM in France and Eastern Europe.
3 www.thefreedictionary.com/high-density, accessed 6 November 2005.
4 For details of another adjustment process, 'panning and scanning', see Lury, 2005: 22.
5 Chase's interest in European art cinema is documented in Lavery and Thompson, 2002: 19ff.
6 http://news.bbc.co.uk/1/hi/entertainment/4534126.stm.
7 For an account of the history of the use of split screen, see Talen, 14 May 2002, www.salon.com/ent/tv/feature/2002/05/14/24_split/print.html.
8 There are many examples historically where executive producers have restrained adventurous creative teams from a more open-ended narrative structure, notwithstanding the popularity of soaps. A well-documented example is the experiment with form and style in *Hill Street Blues* (see Gitlin, 1994).
9 The values drawn upon in the praise of long-form drama in this way are closely related to those which value the nineteenth-century novel. Adaptations of classic novels directly fit this mould but television, both in Britain and in the USA, has a tradition of long-form dramas set in the contemporary and addressing contemporary issues (see Creeber, 2004a).
10 For a discussion of the distinctive capacities of TV drama , see Bianculli, 1994: 107–137.
11 To the best of my knowledge, this term was first coined as "dramedy" by Jane Feuer et al. (1984).
12 The "digital divide" means of course that such luxuries are not available in equal measure worldwide.
13 For a brief account of the optical printer and matte screen process involved, see Talen, 14 May 2002, www.salon.com/ent/tv/feature/2002/05/14/24_split/print.html.
14 See van Vliet, http://comcom.uvt.ni/e-view-OZ-1/vliet.htm, accessed in 2004.

6

Between global and national
24 and *Spooks*; *Buried* and *Oz*

Influences and resistances

This chapter opens with an outline of contemporary issues concerning the inter-play between forces which would transcend national boundaries and those which would resist them, not at the level of regulation and quotas but at the level of residual cultures which prefer texts which speak to them. Following a general in-troduction, the chapter focuses on two comparisons between American and Brit-ish product with the aim of bringing out both the textual influence of American television style and the resistances of British cultural product which, whilst it fre-quently absorbs developments in American industrial practice, nevertheless still refracts its approach through a prism of British television traditions and thus re-tains something of a cultural specificity.

In Chapter 3, the global outlook of the major media conglomerates was noted, along with their approach to extending audience reach – and making bigger prof-its – through transnational niche marketing and ancillary merchandising. At the same time, however, this book has pointed repeatedly to the sustained disposition of "home" audiences to prefer products that reflect their culture and way of life. Locally produced programmes with cultural specificity continue to draw substan-tial audiences, even though their production values may be less affluent than those for the "Event TV" products of key international players. Though *ER* (NBC), for example, is admired and has a significant following in the UK of 4–5 million view-ers, the less "cinematic", more static *Casualty* (BBC1) has sustained a substantial audience over two decades (1986–2006) and, even in today's fragmented market, regularly draws in the region of 15 million viewers. Though there are many fac-tors in play, such as scheduling, to account in part for this difference, the "local" feel of Holby City hospital and the British National Health context would appear to have a resonance with a majority of viewers not matched in the UK by Chicago's County General. The very titles of the programmes mark the cultural difference:

British hospitals have traditionally had Casualty Departments whilst American hospitals have Emergency Rooms.

Although there is an increasing industry disposition in the 'noughties' towards a global reach, therefore, it remains in tension with viewers' preference for the local. In selecting what to watch, viewers in large numbers still appear to go first to their "home" (regional or national) channels (which may still be terrestrial) before searching through the many other options possibly available to them by satellite or cable or by subscription and pay-per-view. Even where international programmes find viewers, their attractions are recognised to diminish with distance as the notion of "cultural discount" signifies (see Introduction). Thus the tendency for the major media conglomerates to make programmes which might build audiences transnationally leading to product without cultural specificity is at odds with the demand for the local. Though the energy, affluence and upbeat disposition of American programming appears to be attractive worldwide, there are also forces in play which resist its influence.

The television industry has found a number of ways to address the issue of local cultural specificity. The most dispersed means is the sale of formats which can be reproduced in each purchasing nation with a local inflection. The kinds of programming perhaps best suited to such format sales are game or quiz shows and the fast-growing "reality TV" sector. *The Weakest Link* and *Who Wants to be a Millionaire* instance very successful examples of the former, whilst *Big Brother* is perhaps the most globally influential of the latter. TV drama as a transnational product, however, has its drawbacks. Unlike quiz shows, it is not readily formatted and thus not easily adjusted to meet the preference for the local. With one or two notable exceptions, re-makes of British drama products abroad, for example, have not found great success. The American *Queer as Folk* managed three series but the remakes of *Cracker* and *Cold Feet* endured just one season, as did *Ballykissangel* (as *Hope Island*, September 1999–April 2000).[1] The failure of transposition is sometimes connected with cultural resonances in the original programme and context which simply do not translate to other cultures.[2]

Since formatting is not typically a viable solution for TV drama, then, products reflecting the apparent values of one culture continue to be exported to other cultures. The USA, as noted in Chapter 3, remains the biggest net exporter by far and the apparent dissemination of its ideologies and lifestyle worldwide has given rise to accusations of cultural imperialism (see Thussu, 1998: 2–4 ff.). On a more modest front, British product historically has had significant visibility in the international market-place with drama, notably period drama, taken to connote Britishness. It would be prohibitively expensive to remake costume drama and thus British adaptations of classic novels have sold abroad since they are not suitable for formatting and have not characteristically been produced elsewhere. The sense of British culture exported is, of course, a particular construction of Old England, and even that view is usually sanitised with what Andrew Davies has dubbed 'clean finger-nails for the American market' in defiance of the British television tradition of realism.

The market for British period drama, however, is at best limited. Besides the USA and Australia, only the anglophone communities in Europe, notably Sweden and Holland, are significant purchasers. Furthermore, this market is diminishing as greater emphasis is placed on home production of local fare, even on the American PSB channel, historically a major platform for such British exports. In respect of adaptations of classic novels, moreover, there are signs that the virtual British monopoly over production is diminishing. A pan-European approach to high-budget TV drama is becoming more common following the European 'Television without Frontiers' Directive 89/552 which encourages the breakdown of production and distribution barriers in Europe. Granada International's choice of *Dr Zhivago* for its first ever European co-production is significant in this light, as noted in Chapter 3. Thus, in respect of high-budget TV drama production, there are strong forces gravitating towards European or transnational co-production funding which have an influence on the cultural specificity of the product.

Particularly where there is co-production with American conglomerates, the latter tend to call the shots. Another Granada co-production *My Beautiful Son* (Granada International and Showtime, transmitted on ITV, 2001) illustrates the point. The idea of *My Beautiful Son*, an issue-based drama concerning a child with leukaemia, is not an obvious candidate for co-production. But set in American locations as well as in Liverpool, it starred Paul Riser (known from American sitcom, *Mad About You*) and Julie Walters and thus had star attraction on both sides of the Atlantic. However, it required further adjustments to suit the American audience of premium cable. Caroline Torrance, Head of International Drama at Granada International points out that:

> broadcasters like Showtime, HBO and Turner are absolutely one hundred per cent co-producers and they'll be very demanding editorially. You have to put American actors in, usually at least two well-known American actors. The story will have to have some American elements. It will have to open in America, because they reckon their audience will give them about twenty seconds before they flip channels and if the drama doesn't open in a familiar setting then the audience will flick onto another channel. If you notice, in *My Beautiful Son*, it opens in America. The first actor that you see has got to be an American actor. It can't open in Liverpool with Julie Walters, even though she's quite well known. (2001, cited in Steemers, 2004: 117)

As producers such as Granada, who have been major players in British TV drama in the past, are drawn into co-production in a transnational context, their programmes inevitably become less culturally specific. Indeed, the evidence suggests that many big "high-end" co-production projects (*The Gathering Storm, Shackleton, Skinwalkers*) have found funding precisely because they were *not* distinctively, or exclusively, British (see Steemers, 2004).

Television traditions: the case of Britain and the USA

In order to assess the impact of American television culture on British as an example of the global impacting upon the local, it would be helpful to establish the key features of each culture. Given, however, that the television output of each nation has been varied over a fifty-year history and given that the cultures are plural, this is no easy task.[3] In order to launch the debate, I propose to begin with an opening gambit, a kind of working hypothesis making broad characterising claims to distinguish American and British television cultures, claims to which counter-examples will immediately be evident. The following discussion will then serve to problematise the distinctions whilst evidencing that there is a grain of truth in the proposed characteristics:

US-produced TV drama tends to be:

- *shiny*: glossy and brightly lit with a filmic look, featuring conventionally attractive performers (good teeth, good hair, "star" quality) located in spacious, clean, well-furnished environments
- *action-led and fast-paced*: featuring dynamic action such as car chases and shoot-outs, with strong types rather than complex, individuated characters
- *entertainment-oriented*: up-beat, feel-good and lifestyle-centred

British-produced TV drama tends to be:

- *dark and gritty*: with a grainy documentary or inexpensive studio look
- *character-based and slower-paced*: foregrounding dialogue which, at best obliquely reveals character complexity and, at worst, overtly signals character inter-relationships
- *imbued with a public service ethos*: downbeat, reflective and engaged with social and political issues

For some quick comparative examples to establish this opening gambit, I invite readers to:

think *ER*	then	think *Casualty*
think *NYPD Blue*	then	think *The Bill*
think *Friends*	then	think *Cold Feet*

In the late 1990s and early noughties, critical discourse on "quality" TV drama has been dominated by the celebration of "American Quality TV". Even before film buff Peter Kramer remarked, as noted, that 'American fictional television is now better than the movies' (in Jancovich and Lyons, 2003: 1), a spate of publications has made visible and valorised current American television output in the academy.[4] In journalism, too, Andrew Billen, for example, wrote a substantial article for the *Observer* on 28 July 2002 entitled 'Why I love American TV' and subheaded 'British television could once boast the best writers, actors and directors in the world … but no longer. The greatest shows on earth now come from the United States' (2002: 5). Thus "American Quality TV" currently dominates the discourse. But this has not always been the case.

The American *TV Guide* of 1969 argued: 'We should envy the British their prime time program balance. It's what we need more than anything else' (9 August 1969). As Jeffrey Miller remarks furthermore, 'Already by 1956 a discourse in which

television programs "produced in England" were better than "standard fare …
produced in Hollywood" was being conducted in the single national publication
devoted to American television, [*TV Guide*]'(2000: 25). Throughout the 1960s,
The Saint (1962–69), *Secret Agent* (1964–67), *The Avengers* (ABC 1965–69), *The
Baron* (1966), *Court Martial* (1966), *The Prisoner* (1967) and *Man in a Suitcase*
(1968) were making a significant impact in the USA, even though, like so many
shows, many of the series were cancelled after a season. It is notable that these
dramas emerged in the newly established Independent Television sector and this
may indicate both a schism in British culture between the BBC and ITV and the
influence of American television upon popular television.[5]

The early- to mid-1960s in British television is marked by some historians as
the moment of radical experiment when Troy Kennedy Martin, McGrath and
McTaggart, Potter, Loach and Garnett were in different ways trying to break the
television mould (see Cooke, 2003). But while they were experimenting, Lew Grade
was looking to the USA and, though he was already operating at the more popular
end of the market (Pilkington in 1962 had alleged 'populism' in ITV), the great
ITV mogul was prepared to make further concessions to American taste in his
attempt to penetrate the America market. And this sets a marker for a more nuanced case in this discussion for reciprocal influences and resistances between the
two television cultures of Britain and the USA. It might be claimed that early
American television influenced ITV product, an influence returned, inflected
through British culture, to the USA but modified to ensure American industry
take-up. As noted above, American co-producers today call the shots but Grade,
as Miller delicately puts it, was 'willing to assist the American industry in its ab-
sorption and domestication' (2000: 27) of his product.

The concessions to American circumstances made by Grade involved the re-
titling of *Danger Man* (1960–67 in the UK) as *Secret Agent*, and extending the
original half-hour episodes to sixty minutes to suit American schedules. Where
co-production today demands an American star, *The Baron* similarly featured
American actor Steve Forrest as Texan rancher turned Fine Art dealer and undercover agent, and *The Persuaders* (1971–72) co-starred American Tony Curtis alongside the very British Roger Moore. In aiming for the American market, Grade had
already picked up on a taste for action-adventure but the American disposition to
reject anything without a recognisable location or American actor required adjustments. Unlike today, however, a 1960s British context was saleable in the USA
since Britain in the "swinging sixties" had a cachet based on the Bond and Beatles
factor. In 1964, Grade and ITC sold twenty-four episodes (the volume is significant) of *Secret Agent* to CBS, bringing ATV $1.25 million, but the most important
thing to Grade, as he observed was that, 'at least British product is getting a showing on an American network' (cited in Miller, 2000: 37).

If, in the 1960s, Grade leant towards American taste as characterised above, a
corresponding influence of gritty British realism on American product is evident
in the early 1980s in *Hill Street Blues*, reflecting, in the first instance perhaps, a
critical admiration of certain producers in the American industry rather than broad

American taste. In the early 1980s, the comfortable oligarchy of the 'big three' American networks, unsettled by the emergence of cable, satellite and video play-back, was desperate to stop the slide in ratings.[6] Executives were willing to give more creative control to producers with fresh ideas and Bochko and Kozoll cut a deal which led to *Hill Street Blues* (see Feuer et al., 1984, Gitlin, 1994). Affording a counter-example to the characterisation of American television above, the pilot for *Hill Street Blues* was initially shot on 16mm film in black and white and, even when director Butler resorted to 35mm in colour, he shot everything hand-held. Seeking a sense of constant movement, he had the extras walking through the scene, 'bumping into the principals, reaching across their desks to pick up forms, nobody honouring anybody's privacy' (Butler, cited in Gitlin, 1994, 293–4). The visual strategy of *verité* messiness was extended to sound, with overlapping dia-logue and ambient sound. The construction of character differed from established norms, revealing the self-doubts and peccadilloes of the key male cops and thus undermining the heroic male image of previous television copshows. Also, for the first time in American network television, female characters could combine pro-fessional competence and sexuality. *Hill Street Blues* owes a debt, acknowledged by Bochco, to the tradition of British social realism and perhaps even the Loach–Garnett documentary drama. Though it remains marginal in American television culture, a strain of more gritty realism runs from *Hill Street* through *Homicide: Life on the Streets* (NBC 1993–99) to *Oz*, as we shall see.

Jump-cutting to the 'noughties' and the dominant strain of American televi-sion today, John T. Caldwell has emphasised its extended visual qualities, its "televisuality" (1995), broadly subdivided into videographic and cinematic quali-ties. TV fictions may draw on both visual dimensions, as Karen Lury has demon-strated in respect of *CSI: Crime Scene Investigation*, (see 2005) but the dominant emphasis is perhaps on the cinematic disposition which informs HBO and other "high-end" producers, as noted. So "American Quality TV" today would appear to exemplify a more sophisticated version of shininess but with some products, *The Sopranos* for example (see Chapter 2), also picking up on other marked fea-tures of the British tradition such as character development.

British TV drama, in contrast, is perceived by international buyers to remain, 'too dark, too slow, unattractive, too gritty or socio-political … with "distasteful characters", "storylines" and downmarket lifestyles' (Steemers, 2004: 53). Where once "Britishness" was marketable in the "swinging sixties", Prime Minister Blair's efforts to mobilise "Cool Britannia" in the late 1990s and early 'noughties' have had limited success in respect of television. Hence the regulatory adjustments, noted in Chapter 3, aimed at improving the export situation. So it would appear that the characteristics sketched at the outset for British television – at least until very recently when to some extent it has responded to the production values of "American Quality TV" – still apply. Furthermore, British TV drama remains too low in volume, which is an issue since the American market needs at least 22 episodes for syndication purposes whilst British TV mini-series tend to be 10–11 episodes at the most. Perhaps the current trend, as in *Spooks*, for example, to have several seasons is part of an American industrial influence.

That British product remains distinct from that of the USA may be a good thing in terms of sustaining the "local" resonances of television culture in the UK. Beyond the brief historical overview above, the purpose of this chapter is to look at how the market conditions of TV3 influence product both globally and in more modest, but nevertheless "high-end", national contexts. In a competitive environment where the stakes are very high in terms of the cost of drama, there is an inevitable tendency for the pleasures of visual style to take precedence over an "edginess" or critical reflection which might dislocate social orthodoxies to the point where some viewers might literally switch off. This tendency is likely to be stronger where broader, rather than specific niche, markets are sought. Even in a situation where American product dominates the global market, however, the pull of local needs and traditions might nevertheless refract the outcome through a prism of cultural specificity. To consider the sustained specificity of British traditions in a genre where American output has recently been highly influential, this chapter first makes a comparison between *24* (RealTime and Imagine Television for Twentieth Century Fox Home Entertainment) and *Spooks* (Kudos for BBC1). Finally, a comparison is made of the treatments of prison experience at the grittier, more socially conscious end of the spectrum in *Buried* (World Productions for BBC3, January 2003) and *Oz* (Levinson Fontana Company for HBO Premium, 1997–2006).

24 and *Spooks*

Both *24* and *Spooks* might be located in the genre of political thriller but both have familial dimensions reminiscent of soaps. Thus they serve as additional examples of that hybridity of form which distinguishes most drama in TV3. Both series foreground new technologies within the narrative frame and in the visual presentation and they thus have a "state-of-the-art" feel. The thriller element of both, however, demands a level of credibility in the *mise-en-scène* since they aim through narrative conviction to keep viewers on the edge of their seats (and glued to the channel). Indeed, *24* is notionally a real-time drama documenting minute by minute, second by second, the intense events of a challenging day.

24

In the first series of *24*, to be used as the example here, Special Agent Jack Bauer (Kiefer Sutherland) is charged to prevent an assassination attempt on David Palmer, a black senator standing in the presidential primary in California to be held that day. The clock, shown prominently on screen in brightly lit, digital form, starts at midnight on the day of the primary when the Counter-Terrorist Unit of Los Angeles, for which Bauer works, receives strongly credible intelligence that an attempt on Palmer's life will be made in the course of the day by a hired killer from outside the USA. However, the series opens in a domestic situation in the Bauer household with Jack playing chess with, and talking to, his daughter, Kimberley, just before she goes to bed. From the oblique dialogue it emerges that Jack and his wife Teri have had marital problems and that, partly for Kim's sake, they are trying to reconstruct their relationship. However, shortly before Jack is called by phone into the office for an urgent briefing, he and his wife realise that Kim has not actually gone to bed but has 'snuck out' to meet some boys. Initially they are annoyed at their daughter's unruly behaviour though they are not unduly alarmed. But there is a sense of domestic pressure on Jack because when he determines he must go immediately to the urgent briefing at the office Teri implies that Kim's whereabouts should be a priority. The backstory of their marital problems, and the impact they might have had on their daughter who appears to have played them off against each other, sets up feelings of guilt to crank up the pressures on Jack particularly. A key point in hybrid-genre terms, however, is that what might seem to be an action-adventure political thriller in the James Bond tradition – and indeed to a considerable extent is – opens on soap territory. The pressures Jack Bauer feels are both personal and professional and, furthermore, they are interrelated.

At the end of the briefing at the office, confirming the threat to the Senator's life, Bauer is told in confidence by his boss, Richard Walsh, that there may be 'an element inside the agency involved in a hit on Palmer'. Since there is no indication of who the mole might be, Bauer is placed in the emblematic position of protagonists in American political thrillers in which he is isolated under the pressure of sole responsibility. To take on the challenge of defending Senator Palmer, with which he is told he alone can be trusted, he needs to have absolute confidence in his team but, in the circumstances, he can trust no one. Thus, Bauer is located in a mythic American cultural position where an individual pursuing a just cause in defence of democracy in his country is pitted against the explicitly malevolent "other". The fact that Senator Palmer is black adds a particular political dimension to Bauer's crusade because attention is drawn by Richard Walsh to the fallout should 'the first African-American with a real shot at the White House' be killed. There is a further frisson in the mix, moreover, since, as Walsh acknowledges, 'Palmer's no friend of the agency' and he is likely to close it down if he gets elected. If Bauer saves Palmer's life, therefore, he may find himself out of a job. But, true to the generic mould from which he is cast, Bauer may use dirty means to the end, but his goal is one of righteousness.

Bauer's integrity as well as his capacity to bend rules is focused in the opening episode when he needs source information in order to decode a disk and he is thwarted by District Director George Mason, who, knowing Palmer's view on the agency, suggests that Bauer should not put himself out to defend the senator's life. Bauer, suspecting Mason from a previous encounter, stuns him with a sedative dart and gets one of his team illicitly to access his bank account which, as Bauer expected, reveals an illegal diversion of funds. Bauer uses this insight to blackmail Mason into giving him the information he needs. Explaining his actions to a colleague, his commitment to the challenge of sustaining personal and professional integrity for people in his position is brought out when he does not condemn agents such as George, claiming that they are 'guys just like you and me, but they compromised once'. Thus, the opening hour of the twenty-four establishes Bauer in familiar generic terms as an outsider with ethical integrity but an agent who will go to any lengths to do a job in the service of his country, even when his self-interest is not served and his own life might be at risk. However, it also places him simultaneously in a domestic genre, associated with soap opera, as a man with family problems.

Tensions in Jack Bauer's relationship with his wife and daughter increase when it emerges that Kim has gone with a girlfriend, Janet York, to meet some men at a furniture store. Janet's insistence that they are dealing with 'men' rather than 'boys' seems initially to be borne out in respect of sex (Janet is soon in a storeroom bed with one of them) and drugs. That the girls are truly out of their depth in a dubious neighbourhood emerges, however, when they are effectively kidnapped by the young men and driven off through downtown Los Angeles in a customised van, the images being cut to a heavy rock soundtrack which customarily signifies danger. Cellphone calls are exchanged between Teri – who has joined Alan York, Janet's father, to go looking for the girls – and Jack in the office. Under pressure from the various revelations of the night, Jack is unable properly to give attention to his daughter's plight and the increasing worries about her augment the pressures on him in the work context. Thus a melodramatic-soap narrative compounds a political-thriller narrative to ratchet up the temperature of the drama. The sense of immediacy created by the real-time self-presentation of the series, figured in the onscreen digital clock accompanied by a strong, ticking soundtrack, marks the passing of each second and emphasises the range of tensions.

The episode concludes with the blowing up of a 747 by a young woman, Mandy, who steals the identity card of a fellow passenger before she ejects from the plane to parachute to her personal safety in the Mojave desert seconds before the bomb explodes.[7] Bauer, of course, only receives a report of the blowing-up of this flight from Berlin, whilst viewers are given access to the interior of the plane as events unfold. Given that the intelligence has suggested an outside hitman from Europe, Bauer wonders if there is a connection between the mid-air explosion and the assassination plot on Palmer. Viewers know more in their awareness of Mandy's exploits but are perhaps even less sure of how the events might connect. The broadly parallel ages of Mandy and Kim draw out an analogical relationship between the two plots set up in Episode 1 which are logically connected only by Jack's involvement in both. But the domestic-soap dimension and the political-thriller dimension seem by one o' clock in the morning somehow to be intertwined. A final multiscreen image – split four ways with a wide frame in the bottom half of the screen featuring Teri and Alan in their car still searching for the girls, and three square images juxtaposed in the top half of the screen which feature (from left to right) Senator Palmer, an LA city street, and Kim. An image of Jack Bauer, the protagonist and link between all aspects of the plot, drops into top centre before the credits roll.

As noted in Chapter 5, a distinctive feature of the televisual treatment of *24* is the repeated use of split screens paralleling their usage on PCs to carry different information simultaneously in juxtaposed windows. The view of Rob White, that the deployment of split screens in *24* was 'purely functional, subservient to the onward rush of the story' (2002: 7), underestimates, however, the contribution of this technique to narrative excitement. Though White is correct in implying that the split-screen device is not used here to break the frame and afford radically new perspectives on the situation presented (see Chapter 5), it is used quite precisely to enhance the impact of the series. Split screens are used in *24* particularly to present, simultaneously in time and space, events which, though contemporaneous, are spatially disparate. The traditional means in film and television of juxtaposing events happening at the same time but in different places is to cut from one full-screen image to another. Patently, this established method does not contemporaneously show the events happening but reveals them sequentially, leaving viewers to make the assumption of simultaneity from their knowledge of the narrative. An alternative convention is to use a vertically divided split screen which shows two separate locations in the same screen space at the same time. A basic use of this latter device, for example, is to show two people on the telephone to each other such that viewers can read the facial reactions in relation to the dialogue.

But *24* considerably extends both the device and its functions, using each subframe to evoke a strand of the narrative and bring its linear tensions into the present moment. In some respects, such usage brings the past into the present. For example, when Kim is in danger in the incident above – and subsequently when she gets caught up with her mother in Bauer's professional predicament – the reminder to viewers of the domestic backstory, with its cross-currents of guilt, informs and enriches the present narrative moment. The mixture of genres also feeds into the visual presentation of *24*. Action-adventure, with its demand for wide angles to accommodate big spaces in which dynamic movement can be located, have historically been better suited to the big screen of the cinema than the domestic television monitor. The latter, with its traditional disposition to the close-up has favoured the domestic interior and hence has been highly suitable for soaps and for the intensity of emotional interiors in human drama. Because, as noted in Chapters 1 and 5, the gap between television and cinema has narrowed on a number of fronts in TV3, a hybrid vehicle such as *24* is able to take advantage of both dispositions. Thus in *24* there are splendid shoot-out scenes, with actors running from cover to cover in open country amidst the small explosions of gunfire and the visually powerful exploding vehicle, alongside intensely emotional close-ups of family moments. Given the parallelism and intertwining of the narratives in *24*, the use of the split screen spatially and simultaneously to present images of different characters in different, but often equally challenging, predicaments serves even further to intensify an already high aggregate narrative and emotional temperature.

With regard to time, *24* purports, as noted, to be a real-time drama, the twenty-four hours of its title denoting twenty-four hours of both narrative and air time, one hour to be shown weekly over a six-month period.[8] In the context of remediation (see Chapter 5), interesting questions arise about a serial drama which takes to extreme the idea of the fictional spaces of television paralleling moment by moment the actual world inhabited by viewers. This 'as if live' access to parallel worlds perhaps indicates a mutually reciprocal influence of early television culture on computer culture. Though the fragmented presentation of the split screen may suggest hypermediacy, the emphasis placed upon the 'as if live' resonates with the immediate access which computers apparently afford to a range of parallel worlds.

In 24, the use of split screen serves not to fragment and dislocate narrative coherence but to reinforce it through spatial extension. In Bolter and Grusin's account, hypermediacy 'offers a heterogeneous space, in which representation is conceived of not as window on the world, but rather "windowed" itself with windows that open on to other representations of other media' (2000: 34). 24, in contrast, uses a structure of multiple windows within the screen space but primarily such that each window supports the others to confirm a 'looking-through' conviction in the diegesis. In evoking the virtual territory accessed through any single window of a PC, it serves to bind participants in to the experience of virtual space 'behind' the television screen in parallel with both the virtual world of the internet and with actuality. The juxtaposed frames typically invite viewers to take inferential walks in each of the intertwined narrative territories. As the temperature in the narrative strand being shown is cranked up, the multiframe interjections serve to remind viewers of a point of high tension in a parallel, and ultimately related, narrative strand. Furthermore, it is possible to infer the gap between the ignorance of one of the protagonists and the imagined threat to another protagonist, raising the level of anticipation in respect of the future discovery of the currently unknown.

For example, by 04.00 (Episode 5), Jack has worked out that Kim has been kidnapped and that there is likely to be a connection with his involvement in the Palmer case and that he is thus indirectly responsible. Since Teri is extremely anxious about her daughter and needs Jack to be with her, the backstories of both his personal and his professional life emotionally inform the situation. Much later than promised, Jack arrives at the hospital where Janet York is being treated. Hugging his tearful wife, he voices a line worthy of any good soap, 'Teri, I love you. I promise we're gonna get through this' (14.00, Episode 5). It is at this moment, however, that he receives a cellphone call from arch-villain Ira Gaines, who has apparently taken over the hospital internal security camera system in order to guide and watch Bauer out of the building. Thus Bauer, and the viewers, now know for sure that there is a connection between Kimberley's abduction and Bauer's mission, but Teri is left behind, both literally and in ignorance, since Jack has no opportunity to explain his sudden departure. The cliff-hanger of the episode suggests that Janet, the only lead to Kim as far as Teri is concerned, may be dying. In fact, at the beginning of Episode 6 she has pulled through, only to be suffocated, in a surprise reversal, by her father. Telling Teri that Janet is sleeping for a couple of hours, Alan York offers to drive her home. On the journey, however, she receives a cellphone message for Jack from his office which informs her that the mutilated body which Jack has discovered in a car trunk earlier in the evening is that of one Alan York. She thus realises that the man in the driving seat beside her is not who he pretends to be.

As in all good thrillers, it is demanded of viewers that they take inferential walks, based on their prior knowledge of the genre, down narrative pathways, with the aim of figuring out the direction of the drama. In the various obstacles to narrative progression encountered, a strong thriller aims to prevent viewers from seeing what is coming. As in the above example, *24* does this well and its intertwined domestic and thriller narratives intensify the drama. The function of the split-screen multiframes, then, is to bring into one moment a kind of real-time summary of the point which each narrative strand has reached and thus to aggregate the narrative and emotional investment. But, as Peacock observes, this is more than a recapitulation on the narrative, in one sense 'it is the story'; it is an advanced mode of televisual narration.[9]

For the most part, then, the distinctive device of *24*, over and above its real-time self-presentation, namely the elaborate use of multiple-screen interjections, would appear primarily to extend 'immediacy' rather than 'hypermediacy' in Bolter and Grusin's terms (see Chapter 5). They do not break the frame in the sense of Brechtian distanciation but rather increase involvement in the illusion of the world created within the diegesis. However, more than mere appendages – such as the rapidly edited recapitulations of key narrative moments which keep viewers abreast of the complex story – the interjected multiscreen frames serve the narrative function of heightening tension and emotional investment across the narrative strands. It may be, of course, that for some viewers disposed to hypermediacy, the multi-window means to an 'immediate' end elicits a 'looking-at' attention and affords an 'inside–outside' experience, but the principles of composition of *24* gravitate towards ultimate coherence and explication, even though there are narrative reversals and surprises in the process of the telling.

In my judgement, in sum, *24* is a very effective, but conventional, political thriller with strong elements of action-adventure combined with the familial dimension of soaps. Besides its generic hybridity, it is innovative in its use of multiple screening which lends the series a "state-of-the-art" feel. It is not, however, one of those products of a prime-time production stable such as HBO which consciously aligns itself with modernist, experimental cinema. As it is executively produced out of Fox Home Entertainment, it is not surprising perhaps that it is more mainstream than radical. The production values of *24* are equally as high as those of other media conglomerates in the TV3 context and it has distinctive features, aiming to compete at the high end of TV drama. However, it tends towards sense-making rather than a provocative openness.

In respect of politics, though it appears to be dealing with the radical, namely the possibility of the first black president of the USA, *24* is ultimately quite conservative. A domestic dimension of the Palmer household gets caught up in

Palmer's political aspirations in parallel with the personal–professional intertwinings in the Bauer household. A press tip-off reveals to Palmer that his son Keith has possibly murdered the white man Gibson who raped his sister Nicole and that his agent Carl and his wife Sherry have been involved in a cover-up, allegedly in his, and the family's, best interests. In a line equally as worthy of a soap as that cited above in the Bauer context, Sherry ripostes when confronted by her husband, 'I did what I thought was right for our family and your career' (05.00, Episode 6). Thus, at the height of a presidential campaign which has momentous implications for American politics and culture, Palmer too finds himself caught up in a domestic.

The long and tortuous trajectory of *24* with its many digressions, is well-handled in respect of sustaining thriller interest. But it does not break the mould with regard to politics. Jack, Teri and Kim all survive escape from Ira Gaines's fortified compound and many shoot-outs and car crashes, only for Teri to be murdered in the final episode by Nina, Jack's professional side-kick and former lover, who turns out to be the 'dirty agent' who has sold information to the villains. Palmer's life is almost lost in a bombing but is ultimately saved. His family life, however, like that of the Bauers, also ends in dysfunction. The open ends of the soap dimensions of *24* thus left loose threads to be taken up, as they were in subsequent series of *24* where the central action-adventure, political-thriller narrative had drawn to a conclusion. Though it had flirted with politics, *24* did not ultimately disturb on this front.

Spooks

Though it may owe a debt to *24*, and indeed programmes such as *CSI*, *Spooks* did not emulate its American predecessor in respect of politics. Whilst it is also a fast-paced, political thriller with powerful narrative reversals, its fair share of action-adventure tropes, and "state-of-the art" split-screen visual style, *Spooks* did manage to touch raw political nerves in Britain. It achieves its sense of immediacy in part because it engages with issues so contemporary that, on occasions, viewing feels almost like watching the news. Unlike *24*, *Spooks* is not a continuing serial narrative purporting to be in real time, but a series of episodes, each of which contains a story complete in itself, though on-going narrative threads concern the developing relationships of the characters. Indeed, Series 4, from which a key episode for discussion here will be drawn, involved domestic tension between one agent, Adam Carter (Rupert Penry-Jones), and another, his wife Fiona Carter (Olga Sosnovska). This particular episode, (Episode 7, transmitted on 20 November 2005, BBC1) paralleled the conclusion of *24* since it ended with the death of Carter's wife, like Bauer's, amidst political intrigue and a love triangle.

The episode opens with fast-cut fragments of the backstory of Adam and Fiona and a current narative, presenting new recruit Jo Portman (Miranda Raison) who, in the words of her boss Harry Pearce (Peter Firth), has been 'rescued from the jaws of journalism' to the intelligence outfit, with the tag line 'It's MI5 not 9 to

5.' The sequence functions as a very quick reminder of the situation of the series, but its brevity and pace, making the reader work hard to put together the fragments of information given, is indicative of the style of *Spooks*. Jo soon picks up on the reference to irregular hours in the tag line when, overnight, she must faultlessly assume a new identity in this episode as Vanessa, assistant to PR executive Emma (an alias of Fiona's), to infiltrate the Syrian Embassy.

A flashback, presented in soft focus and slightly slow motion, affords a glimpse of the chance encounter of Fiona with somebody she patently knows but initially wishes to avoid, in a London shopping street. The young woman of Arab appearance recognises Fiona but hails her as 'Amal'. On returning home, Fiona goes in distress to the bathroom where, leaning over the sink as if about to vomit, she recalls images of an evidently painful incident. Shot through a pallid green filter and a fish-eye lens to distort close-ups of faces, a group of men of Arabic appearance are fiercely beating up a white man who is just discernible as a very blood-spattered Adam, her husband. And thus the mystery of the episode is set up, not unlike *24* in outline, where the domestic history between a key agent and his wife gets caught up in their professional lives. In *Spooks*, however, the past really does inform the present both in terms of motivating the plot and, more tellingly for the texture of the drama, in terms of the main character's experiences.

A signature *Spooks* link – involving a fast-edited sequence of protagonists moving through stylish, hi-tech environments with digital cameras, expensive cars, cell-phones intercut with the multiscreen presentation of surveillance imagery (GPS maps, digital graphics, computer calculations), and all dubbed with a dynamic soundscape evoking eeriness and danger – leads to present-day Damascus. Here, another world is evoked with equal economy of information, with sound and a few well-chosen images. It is quickly established that, at a macrolevel, this episode concerns Britain's dealings with Syria and it is not long before Fiona is reporting to Harry that she has 'found a way into the regime's inner circle'. Fiona is more than usually keen to take on the risky assignment of trying to make contact with Riyad Barzali whom British Ambassador Wright has indicated wishes to talk with the Brits. In another scene of domestic tension between Adam and Fiona, with their little boy Wes in the background, it emerges that Fiona has been married before. She wants to take the assignment on, she says, because 'it's been hanging over us long enough, don't you think? I'm tired of continually living a lie' (Episode 7).

At this stage the mystery remains unexplained, serving, as its parallel does in *24*, to crank up the tension and temperature of the drama. That the domestic drama is entangled with major political events, however, is evident in Fiona's remark: 'Nobody wants another Iraq, and. if they're prepared to talk, it's worth a try' (Episode 7). That Fiona is engaging in a high-risk strategy is emphasised furthermore when Adam explains to Jo at a briefing that the Mukhabaraqh, the Syrian Secret Service, should be thought of as 'the KGB on steroids' (Episode 7).

Another flashback to the London street scene reveals that Fiona did not escape an encounter with Joumana, her Syrian former friend who tells Fiona that she and another young woman, Leena, had been raped by men who were looking for Fiona and that, unable to bear the shame, Leena had killed herself. The building impression of a violent and ruthless patriarchy in Syria is reaffirmed by repeated flashbacks, in Fiona's memory as it were, of the beating-up of Adam. The backstory is not fully revealed, however, until after an apparently successful meeting at the Syrian Embassy in which she establishes contact with Barzali, Fiona is obviously troubled. In response to Jo's questions, Fiona reveals that she was formerly married to a Syrian intelligence officer, Farook. Though she had converted to Islam and changed her given name, Amelia, to Amal, he abandoned her when she was unable to produce children. She then met Adam who was investigating Farook and fell in love with him. The beatings of her dark memories occurred when Farook found them out and, in Fiona's words, 'Adam almost died because of my stupidity' (Episode 7). Adam, however, had framed Farook as a Mossad agent and he had been hanged.

Though this conversation, in which Jo's function in *Spooks* – as the innocent who needs to be informed of things which others must already know about – is a little too evident, serves partly as sense-making, and explanatory of the flashbacks and memories revealed thus far, it also deepens the hold of the narrative hook as a deep personal revenge threatens to be intertwined with the intelligence and political threats. Both Adam and Fiona have appeared untypically nervous in this episode and, though viewers now understand why, the measured and time-shifting unfolding of the narrative has served to create a high level of tension and suspense. Viewers are invited to be deeply involved with characters as well as drawn into the events of the political-thriller action. Though intelligence and counter-intelligence is not the stuff of most viewers' everyday experiences, conflict in a domestic environment is, and thus viewers are afforded a more personal entry-point to the drama.

The next phase of the episode reverts to standard, though not unexciting, espionage by gadgetry. In order to separate Ambassador Barzali from his minder, Ali, so that he can have a political conversation, the Spooks' team injects the mint sauce at lunch with a gastric virus which knocks him out almost immediately. He is eating with 'Emma' and 'Vanessa' but his food and drink cannot be spiked directly since his minder habitually switches plates and glasses. Having rushed Barzali to hospital as part of a preset plan, it is necessary to drug the coffee which Ali is lured to extract from an automat (the Spooks have located a device in the machine to inject a sedative drug). The whole manoeuvre is directed by Adam from the control room of a mobile surveillance unit as if it were a teleplay within the play. Adam even uses stage directions, 'Rob, you're on' and 'Cue, Jenny' (Episode 7). The plot runs like clockwork and the Spooks appear to have everything under control. Indeed, this phase of the episode serves as relief from the building tension before things really begin to hot up. This sequence contains, however, some of the most overtly contemporary political dialogue of the episode. Revived on the operating table, with Adam masquerading as a doctor to cut a deal with him, Barzali explains:

> We don't want to see our country blown to bits like Iraq. The parallels between us and Iraq are frightening. But it doesn't seem to bother the Barthist hardliners who are running the country.

> I want you to help me get rid of the current regime … and replace it with a real government … a government for the people but one which can keep the Mullahs at bay. (Episode 7)

These views, with very strong political resonances for a contemporary British audience of the continuing conflict in Iraq (and further potential conflicts elsewhere in the Middle East), are spoken by a relatively sympathetic character at length at a moment of calm in the narrative when viewers are able to hear them clearly rather than lose them amidst the action. Much of the dialogue in *Spooks* is appropriately oblique, causing the audience to work hard to make sense of it, but the utterances above are clearly articulated.

This is not to suggest that Barzali is the mouthpiece of the episode or the series but to point out that *Spooks* goes way beyond *24* in immersing itself in contentious political issues very close to home. That there are differing ethical as well as political considerations in play is pointed up when Adam queries Harry Pearce's announcement that government consent has been given to go ahead with Barzali's request to try to take out the Head of the Syrian Secret Service. Harry proposes: 'in doing this we [the Brits] could help them [the Syrians] turn into a democracy without having to go through the mess like in Iraq.'

But Adam counters: 'This will end up just like Iraq. We [the Brits] keep doing this. We keep getting sucked up into these foreign nightmares and for what? Our job is to protect our country' (Episode 7).

A controversial view of the situation in Iraq is thus voiced by one of the central and most sympathetically presented characters in Series 4. Again, Adam's view may not be that of the series but a strong voice calling in question the British Government's policy is aired. The argument remains unresolved as the thriller action is resumed when, making a follow-up visit to the Syrian Embassy, Fiona is abducted. Her cover has been blown as Ruth Evershed (Nicola Walker) and Colin Wells (Roy Macgregor) at Thames House HQ have just discovered by painstaking and hi-tech analysis of the wired sound from the initial embassy party. The violent beating to death of Barzali by the very head of the Secret Service he has just been plotting against immediately prior to Fiona entering the room bodes ill for her future as the narrative thrusts forward again at high pace and temperature.

In the final sequence, *Spooks* gets as close as it comes to the action-adventure of *24*. The first plot reversal, as Fiona is required to change clothes and switch cars in an underground car park, is that her former husband, Farook, is still alive and indeed in the new car. Adam and his fellow operative Zafar Younis (Raza Jaffrey) are in pursuit, guided by a tracking device, which Fiona has secretly requested. But the device is lost in the change of clothes and Fiona's mobile phone smashed, so the trail goes cold. Adam and Zafar trace an associate of the Syrians and violently extort information from him. But the violence here is not the shoot-out and explosions of *24* but a physical tussle evidencing Adam's martial arts training.

The Metropolitan Police arrive on the scene but Zafar deflects them, allowing Adam to get away to continue the chase alone. In tracking Fiona, Adam is, of course, not merely trying to save a fellow agent from opposition agents but his wife from her former husband whom Adam himself has framed.

A security-alert delay at the small West London airport from which the Syrians plan to depart, taking Fiona with them back to a life of servitude, affords Adam a little more time and viewers some conviction that the forces of British intelligence are regaining control in the background. The techno-surveillance has been effective in locating the private airport and the intercutting between Fiona, who is locked in an empty portakabin, and Adam, who is racing in his car to the scene, strongly suggests a conventional ending of rescue at the eleventh hour. But this episode of *Spooks* has yet another tragic plot reversal. Fiona has managed to break the glass on the fire-warning notice in the portakabin and has cut her wrists. When Farook returns to find her in a pool of blood he approaches and she stabs him in the jugular with a shard of glass. Staggering towards Adam in the final sequence, however, she is shot in the back by Farook who, in turn, is shot dead by Adam. At a moment which viewers are invited to find genuinely touching through the emotion conveyed by the strained expression on Adam's face shown in close-up as he tries to rally his wife, Fiona makes him promise to 'keep Wes safe' as she lies prostrate, apparently dying, on the tarmac. As a major character in a popular series, she might be expected to survive this incident, but *Spooks*, taking risks with convention and its audience, has her die to a solo female song of lament on the soundtrack. Indeed *Spooks*, like *Oz* (see below), is noted for dispensing with major characters but, even to viewers who know this, the dramatic treatment of Fiona's death is powerful.

What might be made of the treatment of contemporary political issues amidst the action-adventure and domestics in *Spooks*? First, its riskiness in articulating contentious political viewpoints goes way beyond anything in *24* where an important political issue – the potential for a black person to become president of the USA – is a given of the plot but remains otherwise unexplored as an issue. Likewise, in *Spooks*, the political theme of conflict is used to raise the stakes and crank up the tension of the narrative, but here questions are articulated and left open in ways which invite thinking and, perhaps, debate amongst viewers. The representation of the Syrians is arguably a caricature which might in itself be questioned. The dominant impression given in this episode is of a highly patriarchal culture shot through with violent assault and rape. The beating to death of Barzali, the report of the rape and consequent suicide of Leena, the treatment of Amal/Fiona, all suggest a regime beyond the supposed civilisation of Western democracies. Thus far the old British adage of balance in political presentation does not appear to hold. However, the right of a foreign nation to intervene to impose Western-style democracy on an Arab culture is also called in question by Adam, as noted, even though British assistance to this end is directly sought by Barzali. Adam's insistence that 'our job is to protect our country' implicitly critiques unwarranted interference in another sovereign nation unless it is a demonstrable threat. This is the very issue which fundamentally divides British people over Iraq and might divide them further if other Arab nations (Iran, Syria) were also to be invaded on a pretext.

There can be no doubt, then, that *Spooks*, like *Carnivàle* rather than *24*, has the potential to touch raw contemporary political nerves. The episode analysed above is typical of a series which locates its narratives precisely in contentious social or political territory. The emotional pull of the finale of the episode above, however, is ultimately personal and domestic, a wife dying with her husband at her side, expressing concern that her little boy should be looked after. Since, however, the domestic issues in this episode of *Spooks* are so closely intertwined with the political and cultural through Fiona's former marriage and knowledge of Syria, much more so than in *24*, the emotional pull of character in context inextricably links the two dimensions in respect of the drama. A simplistic (one might say Bush-like), political conclusion, that countries such as Syria bring Anglo-American invasion upon themselves in their barbarism, is countered emotionally and politically in the final image since it is Adam (who, given the violent death of his wife, most has cause to take such a view) who has spoken strongly against unjustifiable foreign intervention. Despite narrative closure, the ideological debate is left open for viewers to take up should they wish.

Buried and *Oz*

Another illuminating comparison between American and British product is afforded by two prison dramas each of which reflects an identifiable but relatively rare TV drama genre, the prison drama. Both *Buried* and *Oz* are set almost entirely within the boundaries of prison walls, HM Prison Mandrake Hill and Oswald Penitentiary respectively. Thus their focus is relatively narrow, dealing with the lives of the inhabitants, the prisoners primarily but also the warders, and inhibited in respect of action and location by the confines in which they are set. Given the subject matter, each is at the dark, grim and gritty end of the spectrum of realisms depicted on television, *Oz* in this respect being particularly untypical of American output.

Buried

Buried, which aims to afford authentic insights into prison experience, was made by Tony Garnett's company World Productions which also made *This Life* and *The Cops*. Indeed, *Buried* lies in a long tradition of documentary-style dramas, many produced together or separately in Britain by Ken Loach and Tony Garnett, in which the 1977 'Play for Today' young offenders' institution drama, *Scum*, is a landmark.[10] The specific team of producers for *Buried*, however, is Robert Jones, Jimmy Gardner and Kath Maddock, the former two writing the majority of the scripts with Kath Maddock as producer and Tony Garnett as Executive Producer. The eight fifty-minute episodes, set on D Wing and its related Drug-Free Unit

(DFU) of a category B prison somewhere in the North of England, were transmitted on BBC3 in January 2003. The authenticity of its prison context was assured by adviser Professor David Wilson, an authority on criminology, who remarks that he 'wanted to work with World Productions ... because [he] knew that they would present prison as it really is, as opposed to comedic parodies of prison which give the public a totally false impression of what prison is like and who prisoners are'.[11]

The major serial story arc of *Buried* concerns Lee Kingley (Lennie James) who is a first-time prisoner sentenced to ten years for GBH and a firearms offence after pulling a gun on the man who raped his sister. Prior to this crime of passion, he had a clean record, unlike his brother Troy who has a reputation as a hardened criminal. Lee also believes himself to have been fitted up by the police who were mainly after the supplier of the firearm. Thus he commands some sympathy for his relative naivety in crime and because he feels aggrieved. From the outset, Lennie James convincingly conveys pent-up hurt and anger at his predicament. Once in prison, Lee Kingley gains respect from the other inmates, based on his crime and his brother's reputation in the prison pecking order, and, when Troy is admitted to D Wing in Episode 3, the Kingsley brothers rise to the top of the prisoner power hierarchy. But Troy's mental health is unstable and, in another betrayal by the authorities from Lee's point of view, he is finally removed to the maximum-security Belmarsh prison, leaving Lee in charge of a drug-and-money-lending business and supported by a sidekick, Kappa Kid (James Wells).

But a crushing blow for Lee comes in Episode 4, when he finally connects by telephone with his wife, Chloe, only to be told that she will not be visiting as he expected and that he can no longer see his daughter. Flashback images afford an insight into his feelings. The rumour, possibly spread by prison officers, that Kappa is a paedophile becomes rife. In male prisons particularly, any sexual molestation of children is considered beyond the pale and any prisoner with the record or reputation of being a 'nonce' is at risk of serious injury from his fellow prisoners. As prison top dog, Lee is actually asked by Steddon to sort out the Kappa problem but, when he is persuaded that Kappa has interfered with his own daughter Amelie, he beats Kappa violently to death with the support of his fellow inmates. Though the actual violence is only glimpsed in close-ups of parts of the action, the impact, through guided imagination and shots of Lee's face, is of a vicious beating. It is a metaphor of the release of all Lee's pent-up frustrations.

Now actually a murderer, Lee becomes haunted by his crime and is increasingly seen to be 'losing it'. He becomes preoccupied with a desire to hear the sound of the sea which inmate Anderson claims he can detect from his cell in the quiet of the night. Following his brother's delusions of being a Christ-figure, Lee begins to believe that he is 'the one who knows ... the swift sword'. Fellow prisoner Hector French marks the change by asking, 'What happened to the Lee Kingley who didn't want to get caught up in all this prison shit?' (Episode 5). From here on, Lee becomes increasingly introspective and sees visions of a battered and blood-smeared Kappa in his mind's eye. In one montage, an image of Lee battering a cockroach in the prison kitchen is intercut with memories of him beating Kappa to a pulp. Later it transpires that he has kept two cockroaches alive in a tin and he releases them back into the kitchen. When offered a possible way out of prison by the Police Complaints Investigation Bureau which is investigating DI Paul Brown who fitted him up, Lee is unable to trust anybody. He finally dies from a stab wound almost casually inflicted by his friend Hector French, whom he has offended simply with alleged disrespect. At the time, a major incident in the prison with an inmate about to commit suicide preoccupies the staff, and Lee is unable to push the panic button in his cell or to rouse his heroin-stoned cell-mate from a stupor. An added irony is that the young addict has been weaned on to hard drugs whilst in prison. Lee quietly bleeds to death with a half-smile on his lips as he hears the sound of the sea and a horse-racing commentary that he has earlier requested from a prisoner who, having been a former commentator, has a comprehensive memory of specific races.

Though this is the one story arc to span the eight episodes, it is by no means the central focus of *Buried*, which is much more concerned with the collective rather than the individual experience in the claustrophobic and tense atmosphere of the prison. Lee scarcely figures at all in Episode 6, for example, which foregrounds a sub-narrative involving prison officers. Indeed the 'screws', the prison governor, Chris Russo (Neil Fitzmaurice), and the psychologist running the DFU, Dr Nick Vaughan (Stephen Walters), figure throughout the mini-series, with many parallels being drawn between their lives and those of the prisoners. Prison Officer Dave Stour (Smug Roberts), in particular, appears to have no meaningful life beyond the prison. His marriage has failed and he lives alone and acknowledges that he has no friends. After his colleague, DD Burridge (Jane Hazlegrove), feels sorry for him and goes with him for a drink, he brags that he has slept with her even though the truth is that he has 'not had sex for over three years … even with [him]self' (Episode 6). Like some prisoners who have become so institutionalised that they cannot face life on the outside, Dave admits, that 'going home's no different to being here; just smaller' (Episode 4). His experience is juxtaposed particularly with that of Pele who, feeling betrayed by his former cell-mate Ronaldo with whom he has become close to the point that he has found a substitute wife, has become a recluse. Pele tells Dave that he is happier in the prison: 'Freer. Being an in-mate, it's liberating. For me, anyway' (Episode 4). Even though he is scheduled to be released, Pele is unable to leave his cell even to see his actual wife on a visit. As she remarks to Dr Vaughan, against the cries of children in the background: 'He's all-found here … twenty-two years married; fourteen he's been in prison. What's my life been? Waiting! This place is swallowing him up' (Episode 2).

Prisoner Blake, former accountant, advises Dave on his finances with a view to him finding a better life but tells him, 'You're strait-jacketed to a lifestyle you don't want – or even enjoy' (Episode 4). Prisoners, their families and prison officers alike are sucked into the institution.

Episode 6 (written by Stephen Brady) explores in depth the complex interrelationships and backstories of some of the prison officers. At its beginning, DD

Burridge, having spoken supportively on her rounds to one prisoner, Ronnie Keach (Mark Warnock), is suddenly punched in the face by Veeder (Ricci Harnett), the prisoner in the next cell. She reacts strongly, by hitting him hard several times with her truncheon, even though he is on the ground. She has to be restrained by other prisoners. Interviewed by her superior, Martin Steddon (Conor McIntyre), and under the threat of disciplinary action, even suspension, following Veeder's formal complaint, she is clearly upset. Meanwhile her colleagues are in the tea room exchanging sick jokes about prison. Referred to the young prison psychologist, Nick Vaughan, she remarks, 'This is worse than being punished.' She tells Vaughan she will not talk but she does open up and reveal that she has been married and 'wanted a normal life' but her husband abused her. She was hit by her mother as a child but adjudges, 'I got what I deserved: she always had a reason.' But the physical violence inflicted by her husband Eddie, was unwarranted and intolerable so she 'ended up in a refuge'. As she relates her story, she sees visions in her mind's eye of her husband intermingling sex and violence. She is deeply resentful that he is 'area manager now, young wife, two little boys'.

DD later regrets having opened up to Vaughan and perhaps touches a raw nerve of his when she alleges: 'I think you get off on this. People come here at their most vulnerable. All the little intimacies you attempt to share' (Episode 6).

In the next episode, Vaughan is revealed to have been under investigation himself for arson and to have allowed a friend to take the rap even though he had lit the fire. Thus his integrity in choosing to work with prisoners is called in question. Indeed, confronted by DD in this way he is sexually aroused and he kisses her with passion. Though initially she is angered and appalled, she is shortly shown having sex with Vaughan on the floor of his office. Their sexual activity is intercut with DD showing concern about and kindness to Ronnie Keach, whose mother dies without ever having visited him. DD and Vaughan together break the bad news to Keach and DD briefly gives Keach a cuddle, saying, 'You looked like you needed it.' Vaughan, apparently jealous, unprofessionally informs DD that Keach was violent towards his girlfriend. This information apparently intrigues DD and she asks Keach about it on his return from the funeral, winding him up eventually to a violent outburst in which he starts to ransack his cell. DD also, however, does him a favour, risking her job to bring him sleeping pills from outside. In her sexual relations with Vaughan, she seeks to be controlling and derides him. When he asks if she has come, she replies, 'Yes, twice: once in 1987 and once in 95.' After another unsuccessful sexual encounter in which, referring to Keach, Vaughan asks DD whether she is 'getting [herself] into another abusive situation, like Eddie', she questions the magic of his psychological cures by asking, 'What happened to your wand?'

This exposure of DD's past sets her complex motivation for being in prison in parallel with that of the inmates themselves. Keach presses the point when he tells DD, 'Go home, lock the door, climb in your bunk' (Episode 6). Many of the prisoners are obliquely revealed to be suffering from violence and abuse as children and from injustice, in short from psychological damage. By its strategy of appearing simply to show what is happening and intercutting between fragments of narratives, *Buried* avoids pointedly making any moral judgement on the characters it shows. Though it does not deploy a hand-held documentary camera, most of the scenes are in confined spaces and involve dialogue, which is often uttered in undertones or even whispers because there is good reason to avoid it being overheard. The camera thus appears to be a mere observer of events, occasionally cutting to close-up for moments of intimacy but avoiding an emotional prurience. It sustains a steady gaze which sees the strengths and weaknesses of the prison officers and inmates alike through a shadowy lighting. Key insights are often yielded by a face in darkness back-lit to a character in a shaft of bright light. When something important is being said, the camera often shows the back of a head rather than a full-face close-up. Ethical perspectives are brought into play by the predicament shared by all HM Mandrake Hill's residents and by oblique remarks unsensationally passed. For example, Steddon, when he discovers the outcome of sending DD to the prison psychologist for assistance, simply says to Vaughan, 'She came to you for help and you fucked her. You disgust me', and moves on.

Though the prison institution is critiqued and, at times, derided, it is presented as a culture in Raymond Williams's sense of 'a whole way of life' (see 1981: 87–93), involving a cynicism needed for survival in it but an apparent balance. As Steddon remarks, 'I laugh at anyone, Dr Vaughan: my mockery's democratic' (Episode 7). In contrast, Vaughan sardonically describes the 'pleasant establishment' as an environment of 'stabbings, slashings, piss-balls, gobbings and incessant obscenities 24/7'. But his own behaviour, as recounted, does not afford him an impartial position from which to judge. The prison institution is revealed to be brutalising and all-consuming, its tendencies to violence being precariously suppressed by drugs, both prescribed and illegal. Snorting 'puff', heroin or crack-cocaine is seen to be part of the culture. But the finger is not pointed at a single source of responsibility as the regular prison officers are seen by turn to be caring and casually brutal. The governor, Chris Russo, however, is shown to be distant, only mixing with the prisoners when a government initiative or an impending inspection warrants it. In Episode 4, he passes through the prison, talking up its achievements to a delegation of inspectors. However, this glimpse of educational aspirations and improvements is fleeting in comparison with the quotidian culture of survival in a tense, if not dangerous, environment. As Steddon remarks, 'He's always working for himself. You can be sure of that' (Episode 5).

The overarching story of Kingley, coupled with that of Carter who comes to the prison in Episode 8, leaves above all a sense of futility and waste since, 'There's not a con in here who fits with his charge sheet.' Carter is reputed to have killed four people, including children, in a car crash but he appears to be taking the rap for his wife who was actually driving. Ironically, it is Vaughan who finds the truth and tries hard to reveal it to a prison baying for Carter's blood, having extracted it at every possible opportunity in Carter's short stay on D Wing. As Kingley lies quietly bleeding to death in his cell, Carter is at the centre of the major incident noted above, about to throw himself from the top gallery to his death. Vaughan manages to grab Carter but the camera leaves us with a big close-up on Kingley's face and a big close-up on his cell-mate, Henry Curtis, snorting crack. The only prisoner apparently to avoid being sucked in by the institution is Rollie Man, a well-read drugs dealer, who is quietly released almost without notice in Episode 7. But he is represented as the exception rather than as a sign of hope. In the same episode, Steddon tries to persuade a cocksure young car thief just graduated from Young Offenders that the bravado of the prison top dogs is empty. He tells him, 'The smart ones know they are just passing through.' However, his words appear to be falling on deaf ears.

Buried is an exposé of prison life to that majority of television viewers with no direct experience of 'the inside'. It gains its power from the camera's steady, non-judgemental gaze and an apparent authenticity by taking full on those aspects of prison life which are almost as hard for a liberal, self-reflective society to face up to as they are for prisoners to experience. There is a constant sense of threat, even of one's life, in a microcosmic economy of petty competition and aggression. The use of drugs, some brought into the prison by officers themselves (see Episode 5), though occasionally challenged, is shown to be broadly accepted as part of the culture. As Vaughan remarks to Governor Russo, 'How am I supposed to run a drugs-free unit in a prison swimming in drugs?' (Episode 5). When a 'piss-test' is demanded of young Curtis, it is seen to be no more than a petty revenge by the officer concerned for losing out in a verbal exchange. Casual racism is evident. Grooming for sodomy, particularly of raw new recruits (see Episode 7), is shown to be rife. But, as Lee Kingley remarks, 'They're not gay most of them: they're just lonely' (Episode 4). None of the incidents is sensationalised in its depiction. The root problem, as Troy Kingley tells his brother, is that 'if you let your head get in the spin here, before you know it, you're fuckin' ga-ga' (Episode 3). Even the most hardened criminals are shown to be vulnerable and, in this sense, *Buried* clearly takes a liberal-left discursive position. Troy Kingley, the hard man, is shown to be fundamentally disturbed by the revelation that his father did not leave his family to emigrate to Vancouver, as purported, but has actually lived out his life in Coventry, married for eighteen years to another, probably white, woman. As Troy declares, he's 'lied to me all these years; kept on lying. That's worse than killing a man.' And, in a moment of unguarded self-reflection, he continues: 'It's behind your door, that's where you do your bird. 'Cos on the wing, we keep up a front, we are like men. But, alone, behind your door, you're just a boy. But if that boy ever shows outside your cell, you're a gonner' (Episode 3).

Oz

There are remarkable resonances between the content of *Buried* and *Oz*, largely accounted for by the fact that they are both dramas set in male high-security prisons dealing with similar experiences. Where *Buried* has its Drug-Free Unit, run by psychologist Nick Vaughan, Oswald State Penitentiary has Emerald City, an experimental unit dedicated to prisoner rehabilitation rather than retribution, and run by liberal therapist Tim McManus (Terry Kinney). But the televisual treatments of the two series are significantly different in ways which interestingly reflect British and American television cultures, as discussed above. Season 1 of *Oz*, made in 1997, was the first hour-long original drama to be commissioned by HBO. But, where *Buried* is a single mini-series of eight episodes, *Oz* has progressed over seven mini-series to more than fifty episodes, with writer Tom Fontana finally deciding in 2006 that the idea had run its course. Prior to *Oz*, Tom Fontana, with producer Barry Levinson, had a track record in hard-hitting American realism in the gritty police procedural, *Homicide: Life on the Streets*.[12] Using hand-held 8mm cameras, *Homicide* was filmed almost entirely on location in Baltimore, making the city environment more than a mere backdrop to the action. Thus the production team might be located in that strain of untypical American realism running from *Hill Street Blues* through *Homicide* to *Oz*, suggested above, a strain which has some resonance with the British tradition of documentary realism. Whilst, however, *Oz* is grimly realistic by American standards, when compared with *Buried* it reveals traces of those characteristics which distinguish the American television tradition from the British. To make the specific, illustrative comparison, I propose to look closely at the first few episodes of Season 1 of *Oz* in which it was establishing its conventions, referring forward only to address some general features of a long-running series in respect of such matters as story arcs.

From its opening titles, *Oz* looks much shinier and more cinematic than *Buried*. The titles comprise a montage of a number of images in close-up refusing to identify characters but offering teasers through selected parts of their bodies. One such recurring image is the tattooing of the 'O' of 'Oz' on a man's arm (the arm being reputed to be Levinson's). An envelope frame, as used to show films on 14:9 aspect ratio television monitors, is intermittently introduced to carry the opening credits above and below the images. Where *Buried* entirely eschews music soundtrack, this sequence is set to a strong beat with a cool jazz trumpet riff. Thus the feel of the series is cinematic from the outset, as has since become typical of HBO Premium product. The setting in Emerald City, the experimental unit of Oswald State Penitentiary is glass-walled, in a new version of Bentham's panopticon, allowing maximum visibility into the inhabitants' pods. The corridors and common areas are broad and spacious and the series overall is brightly lit and airy. Thus although the prisoners of 'Em City' are equally as confined as those in HM Mandrake Hill, *Buried* has a much more claustrophobic feel in its *mise en scène* alone.

The allusion to the world of Dorothy in the name of the experimental unit, Em City, carries an ironic contrast with *The Wizard of Oz*, inviting a metaphorical reading of the predicament of the inmates.[13] If the legendary film affords a metaphor of the road to success in the USA, *Oz* stands for the underside of American society. As actor Dean Winters remarks, *Oz* 'lets you know there's a part of society out there that you don't want any contact with', but Fontana goes further to observe:

> I'd like to think years from now that people will see past the surface shock of it and see hopefully the deeper truths we've been dealing with: the struggle to survive on a

day-to-day basis, whether you're in prison or facing Saddam. There is a faceless population in the US that deserves more recognition and attention than it gets by most of
us on the outside. (cited in Levin, 2003: 1)

Thus, on one level *Oz*, like *Buried*, takes an uncompromising look at the brutality
of prison life but on another level it seeks to be more abstract.

In terms of explicit devices, the most obvious difference between *Oz* and *Buried* in this respect is the use in *Oz* of a narrator. Although over the six seasons the
narrator changes from time to time, the first and enduring narrator is Augustus
Hill (Harold Perrineau), a former crack addict who operates from a wheelchair as
a result of having been pushed off a building by the police following a foot chase.
Keeping his distance from the other inmates, Hill occasionally offers helpful advice to newcomers but his key function is as commentator on the action. Spinning
disorientatingly in his wheelchair in a glass pod apparently suspended in space, he
comments on the action intermittently throughout but particularly at the beginning and end of episodes, making philosophical observations in the manner of a
Greek chorus. Though he frequently speaks in close-up intimately to camera, the
images of him are typically mobile, either gyroscoping, as noted, or shifting through
space by dissolving in one corner of the pod only to reappear in another. Early in
Episode 1, he dryly observes that: 'they call this the penal system but it's really the
penis system. It's about how big, it's about how long, it's about how hard. And
anybody who tells you different, ain't got one'. Thus he functions as a mercurial
commentator with a shifting insider–outsider perspective. He is a player in the
prison action, working in the dress factory and worrying about his beloved wife –
from whom he happily receives a conjugal visit in Episode 1, as well as being a
wise seer.

A second feature of *Oz* marking its different treatment from *Buried* is its use
of inserts of flashbacks of the characters' histories and other non-penitentiary
activities. Typically these are well filmed and sharply edited action montages of
the commission of the crimes for which the protagonists have been sentenced
and, since most of the crimes are violent homicides, the inserts afford fast-action
sequences typical of more mainstream American police dramas. These, of course,
add an element of entertainment which the less compromising *Buried* does not
afford but, by taking the action outside the confines of the penitentiary, they diminish the claustrophobic feel which *Buried* sustains. Both *Oz* and *Buried* use
occasional sequences imaging the interior thoughts or memories of individual
prisoners but, where in *Buried* these merely illustrate innermost tensions arising
from the frustrations of the environment, in *Oz* they link visually with the crime
action sequences to convey a vivid sense of life on the outside world. Thus when
Leon (Jefferson Keane), for example, sees images of his girlfriend (and, later, wife)
Mavis suggestively revealing aspects of her naked body from beneath a fur coat
outside the jail (Episode 2), the image is real (in the sense of actually being seen by
prearrangement from a staircase) on one occasion and imagined on others. These
scenes, together with those of sexual activity in conjugal visits (such as that of
Augustus Hill's wife noted above) and in flashbacks, afford attractions to hetero-

sexual male viewers now characteristic of HBO's freedom as a subscription channel from network constraints.[14] Above all, however, they detract from the claustrophobic and visually restricted environment of the prison interior and thus weaken the sense of action motivated by location which Levinson and Fontana achieved in *Homicide*.

Where *Oz* does breach the conventions of mainstream American television is in its willingness to kill off major characters with whom viewers have been drawn to identify. In Episode 1, Dino Ortolani (John Seda) is a charismatic, though dangerous, member of the Italian insider gang, his demotic drawl and arrogant but tense prowling in a white singlet being reminiscent of early Brando. His established position is to oversee the kitchen for the Italians but, following a fight in the showers in which he puts Leon's brother, Billy, in intensive care, Ortolani is denied the conjugal visit for which he has applied and is instead assigned to support Aids victims in the prison hospital. Here, having winningly but unsuccessfully tried it on with the attractive Dr Gloria Nathan (Lauren Velez), he reluctantly tends to the needs of Sanchez. A former heroin addict, Sanchez wants to die and asks Ortolani to assist him. Following a visit by Ortolani's wife and children during which they are separated by glass, Ortolani, who is clearly upset and has tears in his eyes, tells his wife to make a new life for herself and never to bring the children again. That night, he removes Sanchez's respirator and suffocates him. Dr Nathan sees it as murder, though, in the broader context, it is morally ambiguous and might be seen as a mercy-killing or an act born out of frustration and despair. Ortolani is beaten as he resists prison officers, and is 'banged up in the hole' and forcibly sedated. The door of the cell mysteriously opens, however, and a shadowy figure douses Ortolani's body with fluid. Caught by a camera from below offering Ortolani's point of view, a match is struck and dropped and a beautiful, flickering flame fills the screen to mark Ortolani being burned alive. Ortolani is the first of many significant characters to die in *Oz*. Indeed the bodycount of this rapaciously violent series exceeds fifty, with Ortolani's killer, Johnny Post, meeting a mutilated end in the second episode and seven significant characters being dead by the end of Season 1.

The flickering flame over Ortolani's dead body illustrates a cinematic visual use of metaphor in *Oz*. To take another example from Episode 3, Miguel Alvarez (Kirk Acevedo), whose father and grandfather are both incarcerated in Oz, looks to break the family legacy of crime with the birth of his son. Initially affecting a lack of interest, he is persuaded by Father Ray Mukada (B. D. Wong) to apply for leave to attend the birth and, once informed that his wife is in labour, he races to get there. The scene of the birth affords another 'beyond prison' sequence which is sensitively shot foregrounding the baby visually and with a soundtrack of religious choral music. Symbolically the innocence of the newborn is juxtaposed with the guilt of the majority of *Oz*'s protagonists, and the males of the Alvarez family in particular. The point is reinforced when, in a confessional conversation with Mukada when the baby is subsequently discovered to be suffering from a serious liver condition, Miguel confides that he 'thinks God is pissed off' (Episode 3) by his past arrogance. Thus, through a mix of symbolic sounds and visuals, *Oz* brings out the elemental forces which come into play in prison when the value of the freedom to live is starkly focused by the daunting prospect of a life wasted in confinement. Where *Buried* concentrates on character development in response to the events of prison life, allowing such moral conclusions as may arise to be drawn from structural comparisons between inmates and prison officers and oblique dialogue, *Oz* overtly highlights ethical dilemmas and offers philosophical speculation through its cinematic treatment and narrator commentary, with gnomic observations such as 'Oz is retro; Oz is retribution' and 'Hard times doing hard times' (Episode 1).

Each of the episodes of *Oz* focuses upon at least one narrative which is brought to resolution within the episode but, like *Buried*, it also has overarching story arcs. The main on-going arc features a middle-class white man, Tobias Beecher (Lee Tergeson), whose sole crime in an otherwise unremarkable life is to have killed a girl whilst driving under the influence of alcohol. Beecher affords an access point to *Oz* for white middle-class viewers. Similar to the relatively innocent Lee Kingley in *Buried* but without a hardened criminal brother to protect him, Beecher is an innocent in the lions' den. Unlike the vast majority of the Em City inmates, he has no experience of prison whatsoever and is completely out of his depth. Threatened first by his intimidating black pod-mate, he is befriended and apparently rescued by Vem Schillinger (J. K. Simmons), who arranges for Tobias to join him in his pod. But it very quickly becomes apparent that Schillinger is a redneck fascist who, by the power of his threatening personality as much as by physical violence, completely dominates Beecher. Leader of the Aryan brotherhood, Schillinger forcibly tattoos a swastika on Beecher's butt and rapes him.

By Episode 3, Beecher has been reduced literally to licking Schillinger's boots. His at once rapid and protracted degeneration from a regular middle American to a figure physically and emotionally broken ultimately involves a long and painful trajectory. On the outside, beyond his new world, his wife divorces him and later commits suicide and his son is kidnapped and murdered. Inside, he becomes a junkie in order to eke out a miserable survival and ultimately becomes sufficiently hardened to exact some revenge on Schillinger. Though he continues to suffer enforced indignities, he appears to have founded a good relationship, even love, with Keller, his next pod-mate. But Keller is in cahoots with Schillinger and, in a vicious attack in the gym at the end of Season 2, Beecher's arms and legs are broken.

The twists in Beecher's fate which continue throughout all the seasons and see him degenerate into a killer, whilst they may interest *Oz* devotees in terms of plot twists, emotional upheaval and violence, stretch plausibility beyond reasonable endurance in respect of realism. Indeed, compared with the overarching narrative of Lee Kingley in *Buried*, the extended story of Tobias Beecher's prison life becomes, at worst, a device of melodrama. Indeed, the rapacious demands of American network and syndication schedules and, latterly, subscription channels for more runs of a successful product ultimately militate against the very realism for which Fontana strove at the outset of *Oz*; although *Oz* drew a modest audience of some four million in comparison with the more popular *Sopranos*, it has a loyal fan-base and the potential for syndication, DVD sales and distribution in other markets, and thus HBO was keen for it to continue.[15] It is often difficult for producers to resist pressure to extend a series. Amongst British producers, Garnett is well-known for his capacity to recognise when to extend a good series may be to undermine its qualities, and the conviction of *Buried* might not have been sustained had it been extended beyond eight episodes.[16]

Where *Oz* does demonstrate the courage of its convictions, however, is in the sympathetic portrayal of groups not frequently represented, or merely negatively represented in news, on American mainstream television. Besides the familiar Italian–Americans, black homeboys and Irish and Latino groups in Em City is a Muslim group led by Kareem Said (Eamonn Walker). Not only is he depicted as a man of peace, overtly opposed to violence and able to resist provocation, he is shown to be a calming influence on his fellow Muslims, encouraging them to resist violence, drugs, obscenity, alcohol, cigarettes and unlawful sex, indeed all those things which most in-mates rely on to lighten their burden. Thus the Muslim group has a strength lacked by the other communities whose frailties stand in relief against Kareem's capacity for self-control. He calms the violent Leon whom he ultimately draws to the Muslim faith in Season 1, Episode 3 and he befriends Beecher in Season 3, reading the Koran with him. Though he has been convicted for blowing up a warehouse in a white area and believes violence in the Muslim cause may be justified, the representation of Kareem in Em City is largely positive, defying dominant contemporary opinion in the USA of people of his faith.

Oz is also not afraid to dabble critically in state politics. It presents the state governor, James Devlin (Zeliko Ivanek), as self-seeking and, not only uninterested in prisoner welfare but also actively callous if it serves his advantage with the electorate to be so. His hypocrisy is visually revealed when he visits the prison to complain about its management in the light of disturbances (Episode 3). Having casually imposed a smoking ban on the prison, he himself chain-smokes, with the smoke clouding into Tim McManus's face as he tries to explain to the Governor that the ban is contributing to the unrest. He demands the lifting of a lockdown recently imposed by Warden Leo Glynn (Ernie Hudson), not because it will ease the situation but because it will appear as a sign of state government weakness if sustained and will be exploited by his political opponents. In a staff–prisoner comparison, Devlin's redneck approach to prison echoes Vern Schillinger's aggressive self-assertion of rights when he proclaims: 'When I kill a man it's because he's standing in the way of my constitutional rights, I kill to protect what's mine. What God has given me' (Episode 3). Governor Devlin, argues with an equally blinkered self-righteousness in a television interview watched by Oz inmates that 'tax-payers shouldn't have to foot the bill for prison frills' (Episode 3). He proposes to eliminate conjugal visits and consequently causes a queue outside the welfare office of Sister Pete (Rita Mareno). Though there is evidently some humour in the treatment of this incident, a point is made about self-aggrandisement of people in power in a democracy at the casual expense of others. As Augustus Hill sums up the prisoners' predicament, 'What we were don't matter; what we are don't matter; and what we become don't matter (Episode 1).

The question is raised, however, as in *Buried*, as to whether the prisoners or the staff run the institution. Interviewed by Warden Glynn on his arrival at Em City, Kareem Said points out that 78 per cent of the inmates are men of colour, his brethren, and says, 'as of today, I run Oz' (Episode 1). From time to time, as noted, Said is indeed called upon by the warden to assist in keeping a lid on a troubled prison and, in Episode 3, Said is summoned, along with Nino Schibetta (Tony Musante) and Leon following a spate of murders and violent incidents and asked to stop the internecine feuding before there's a full-scale riot. So, although the warden can ultimately call upon physical resources from outside the prison in the shape of 'the Feds' to suppress trouble, he evidently relies on the goodwill of the prison gang-leaders to run the prison as some sort of self-regulating community. Fewer overt comparisons are drawn in *Oz* between the plight of the inmates and that of the 'hacks' (the guards). In slight echoes of *Buried*, Officer Diane Wittlesey (Edie Falco) relates to a colleague that she has a two-hour drive to and from work, so it's easier to stay over and work double shifts, and Warden Glynn is surprised when Tim McManus says that he has a date, since Glynn assumes that he has no outside life. But where *Buried* is at pains obliquely to draw comparisons between life inside and life outside, *Oz* focuses upon the destructive feuds between individuals, often representing their respective gangs on the inside, and draws any morals on the experience presented, either cinematically through symbolism or through the overt commentary of the narrator.

Since the use of action inserts of various kinds increases over the series, it would appear that the HBO environment requires some compromises with a grimmer realism such as *Buried* achieves and to which Fontana aspired. As he remarks, '[I] didn't want to entertain people. That's never been my goal in any of the shows I've ever done. If you're going to do a show about prison, you can't do a show that people will be comfortable watching. If I've made people uncomfortable, I've succeeded' (cited in Levin, 2003: 1). Fontana's aim to eschew entertainment is perhaps the antithesis of traditional, mainstream American television culture and he goes a long way to achieving it in *Oz*, given the "high-end" production circumstances of TV3.

My point in drawing the comparison with *Buried* is not to denigrate *Oz* but to bring out that, in the context of a British public service culture, the aim to make people feel uncomfortable, to make a society face up to its darker sides and be self-critical when confronted with it, can be less compromising. I applaud Levinson and Fontana for championing what is effectively a counter-cultural tradition in the USA with programmes such as *Homicide* and *Oz* since, although they may need to make accommodations in their production contexts, they nevertheless pose challenges to American audiences untypical of American television culture historically which has always privileged entertainment values. But, if gritty realism is the criterion, the codes and conventions of *Buried* are ultimately more persuasive that they have afforded insights into prison life as experienced by those who inhabit such institutions.

As illustrated above, any simple binary difference between American and British television cultures is ultimately unsustainable, but the two cultures do betray different tendencies. Where, even in the new circumstances of TV3, "high-end" American television can afford to be more experimental, a strong disposition to be primarily entertaining remains. British TV drama output, in contrast, retains traces of the legacy of British social realism even where, as in *Spooks*, it strives towards the production values of "American Quality TV". Ultimately, this is a mark of a disposition in British culture as much as a matter of television style. British culture, though influenced by that of the USA, is perhaps still less upbeat and feel-good, more prepared to be reflectively self-critical, but, in TV3, there have been shifts in television culture on both sides of the Atlantic.

Notes

1 Glyn Davies recently argued at the Reading TV Drama Symposium, 24 March 2006, that the American *QaF* may, ironically, be regarded as more progressive for developing along the lines of a soap. Since gay culture historically has been represented at the margins of culture, the regularisation of everyday living which constitutes soaps may have effected new ways of seeing gay culture more effectively than the more direct treatment in the first half of the UK *QaF* .

2 The American version of *The Office*, for example, found difficulty with the fact that the British version is based in part on a critique of American managerialism which Americans simply do not share.

3 American programming has, of course, been part of British television viewing culture since the 1950s.

4 David Lavery has edited collections of essays on *Twin Peaks* (1994), *The X-Files* (1996), *The Sopranos* (2002) and, with Rhonda Wilcox, *Fighting the Forces: What's at Stake in Buffy the Vampire Slayer* (2002). Kim Akass and Janet McCabe have contributed much since 2003 to the critical exposure of "American Quality TV" both in their Dublin conference on the subject in April 2004 and in their edited collections on *Reading Sex and the City* (2004) and forthcoming readers on *Six Feet Under*, *The L Word*, *Desperate Housewives* and more.

5 For further discussion of the intervention of Lew Grade and ITC in the American market, see Johnson, 2005: 43–45).

6 As Caldwell records, 'The networks had enjoyed complete dominance – an incredible 90 share – during the 1979–1980 season, but saw this figure plummet to a mere 64/65 share by 1989–1990' (1995: 11). This amounts to a loss of something like 150 million viewers.

7 In the light of the 9/11 bombings there was concern in the USA about the distribution of this footage.

8 Ironically, the advertisements (not included in its UK airing on the non-commercial BBC2 channel) reduced narrative airtime to approximately forty-five minutes per episode.

9 This argument was made in an unpublished paper presented at the 'American Quality Television' conference at Trinity College, Dublin, 1–3 April 2004.

10 *Scum*, written by Roy Minton and directed by Alan Clarke, was kept from the air for fifteen years for alleged sensationalism. The cast of this documentary-style tale of despair, violence, assault and power games in a young offenders' institute included Ray Winstone, David Threlfall, Phil Daniels and Danny John-Jules.

11 Professor Wilson's remark is recorded on www.uce.ac.uk/web2/newsline/archive/

people05.html, accessed on 27 March 2006.

12 Fontana also worked on the legendary series *St Elsewhere*

13 Although there is a gay section in the various groups which inhabit Oz and consensual homosexual activity as well as enforced buggery, the world of Dorothy reference resonates beyond the gay allusion more typically associated with the friends of Dorothy.

14 Compare the glimpses of naked dancers in the Bada Bing in *The Sopranos* (see Chapter 2).

15 Shown in Britain on Channel 4 and repeated on E4, *Oz* is currently available on DVD only in NTSC format which is playable in the UK on Region-1-compatible DVD players.

16 Despite strong pleas from Channel 4, Tony Garnett refused to make additional series of the successful *This Life* because he adjudge that the idea had run its course.

7
"Quality TV" in context

Contrary to discourses of the "dumbing down" of television, this book has thus far loosely constructed a narrative of improvement, suggesting that TV drama in TV3 may well be as good as, if not better than, drama on television in the past. To summarise, the argument is that, led by key subscription channels making expensive – and at times "edgy" – drama for selected target audiences, contemporary TV drama has both licence and aspirations. In some quarters, it aspires to the production values of cinema and is liberated from the LOP industrial context and regulatory constraints, to be creative in drama production. Where HBO Premium and Fox television have led, the American networks – and, in a slightly different context, the UK terrestrial channels – are bound in a competitive, global marketplace to follow. In the 'era of television plenty' (Ellis, 2000: 160), that is to say in a transnational, horizontally integrated, multichannel, digital, industry environment, television channels themselves, and their flagship programmes, must distinguish themselves through branding. The mediocre LOP which aimed to avoid offence with a diet of bland entertainment, can no longer sustain television companies. To reiterate Todreas's neat formulation, 'the great value shift from conduit to content' (1999: 7) has seen – and may well continue to see – significant industry resources invested in product. Though TV3 has its downsides, the climate is broadly one of opportunity for quality TV drama production.

This does not mean, of course, that all future television will be of high quality. The "high-end" drama with which this book is concerned sits at the apex of the television production chain in many respects. Forces in other areas of television pull in other directions and some cheap programming has to be made in some contexts to offset the costs of the expensive "high end". I would ultimately want to put the argument no more strongly than to say that today's production circumstances, highly commercialised as they are, ironically appear to have yielded a context facilitating creativity and distinctive product, indeed "quality television", at the "high end" of the industry, in TV drama. But such terms as "quality TV" and

"American Quality TV" must themselves be unpacked, and a range of caveats and finer distinctions made about quality for whom, and on what value bases TV drama might be adjudged to be of quality.

Any value judgement remains a contested site in open societies in which there is no strong consensus. Whilst this has always been the case in liberal democracies, it is worth noting at the outset of this discussion that Western, pluralist, postmodern societies are less consensual than ever. Economic strategies subdivide society into demographics and culturally personal choice is primary. Indeed, an extended political drift away from centrism and towards consumer individualism, initiated in the Thatcher–Reagan eras, has emerged to be discursively dominant. The world-wide success of American TV programmes in part reflects the cultural as well as the economic dominance of the USA. Broadly speaking, the political and economic hegemony of particular nations throughout history has been reflected in admiration and desire for that nation's cultural products.[1] Post-1989, young people particularly those from nations liberated from totalitarian regimes, have aspired to the American lifestyle, as refracted through the USA's cultural products, taken as a highly successful model of democracy and affluence.

The upbeat tempo of such discourses gives the appearance, however, that everything is a matter of "personal choice" and thus tends to efface the fact that not all individuals have equal social or economic power to make choices. Indeed, in a context of supposed pluralism, any sense of collective resistance through values mobilised to stand against an economically, as well as politically, driven consumer individualism is weakened. As noted, there has been a strong drift worldwide away from what in Britain was Pilkington's 1960s notion of public service and citizenship in television towards Peacock's 1980s commercial consumerist model.[2] Indeed, it now passes largely unacknowledged that the vested interests of powerful groups continue to inform social practices and judgements, in spite of the evidence that considerable parts of the world, notably the Muslim communities, directly resist Western hegemony on ideological grounds. The issues which arise here are patently beyond the scope of this study but, since I propose to maintain that cultural values, along with aesthetic values, lie beyond personal taste, I should bring out the ground on which I am standing to make the following analysis.

Whilst championing what I take to be TV3's quality output, I look to sustain a critique from a liberal-left, communitarian position of television institutions and cultures, if only by way of taking a standpoint outside the dominant individual consumerist trends. I consciously locate my standpoint in British television history and culture, again if only to emphasise modes of television equally worthwhile in my estimation as "American Quality TV", modes which might be increasingly under threat. Thus I aim to follow a 'both-and' line in at once celebrating and critiquing TV3 culture.

Many discursive forces are in play in the making of – and contesting – products of worth, and a value judgement in culture cannot simply equate with a reductive '*I* like it' appeal to personal taste. On one level, this is a matter of language usage.[3] To claim, as I do, that *Sopranos* and *StP* are exceptionally good TV dramas is to say more than that *I* like them (even though taste formation may inform my judgement). Values are posited in the analysis of programmes, as will be evident from the accounts of examples in this book. The challenge of the contemporary context is that the breakdown of traditional hierarchies which previously at least appeared to afford consensus opens up a force-field of estimations drawing upon a wide range of criteria whilst typically not being self-reflexive or acknowledging the institutional powers at work. Precisely because we cannot assume consensus, it is the role of the academic study of television, in my view, to undertake both textual analysis to bring out the qualities of television programmes and to engage in what John Corner calls 'expanded criticism'.[4] That is to say, the contingency of critical readings must be acknowledged through self-reflexion and both texts and judgements of them should be located in the force-field of influences upon them, as attempted in this book.

The major forces in the field impacting upon television fall into broad categories:

- economic (notably advanced capitalism)
- political (government policies, ideologies)
- institutional (corporations, companies, conglomerates, regulators)
- aesthetic (compositional traditions in the arts and media)
- technological (opportunities and constraints informing both product and its location in a media hierarchy)

They play out respectively in estimations of TV drama in such matters as:

- prizing the expensive simply because it costs a lot; modes of funding to mobilise product; profit or "not-for-profit"; ratings; advertising revenue; consumer choice
- legislating to promote institutions and dispositions; narrative forms – for example, foregrounding the individual not the collective
- regulatory bodies (e.g. Ofcom, FCC) steering the industry and overseeing standards; companies with missions, policies and remits
- the traditions of (particularly Western) art and literature: (in a liberal humanist tradition) celebrating multilayered imagery, narrative and moral complexity (in modernist terms) celebrating creativity and innovation and preferring, to different degrees, shock, surprise and even "edginess"; (in contemporary television) prizing visual richness and textual playfulness
- championing high-production values and the exploitation of the medium to the full (with digital apparatus affording significant advances in the television medium)

This chapter thus does not simply assume what is of worth but, in part by revisiting some examples discussed earlier and analysing some new ones, it locates and distinguishes dominant strains in what at worst can be a conflicting and multivocal babel on matters of worth. In what follows, I aim initially to bring out the qualities (as subtly distinct from "quality") of texts and locate them in different modes and traditions of TV drama. Though audience research suggests that people do not all see programmes in the same way, there is more of a consensus on qualities (the kind of drama any given example is, and its generic and singular features) than there is agreement on its worth (whether *Six Feet Under* is better than *The Bill*) for example. Because actual estimations are made in the context of the force-field sketched above, the discussion will touch on aspects of economics, politics, institutions and technology, even though these forces have been more specifically addressed in earlier chapters. The primary emphasis will, however, be on aesthetic matters, the kinds of textual qualities which ultimately inform judgements of "quality TV". My own passions and interests are no doubt evident to readers in my choice of emphasis in this book on "high-end" product, in the specific examples I have selected for inclusion and in my approach to the arguments. My aim in this chapter is to make the grounds for my judgements more explicit whilst also analysing judgements which are made by others on the basis of different criteria. First, since evaluation is a dialogic process between text and reader, we must briefly ask, 'Quality for whom?'

Quality for whom?

To a professional television scheduler working today for ITV Network in the UK, a quality programme might be one which attracts upwards of 15 million people to a prime-time slot. Its worth would be quantified in ratings against an ultimately economic measure of advertising revenue. In terms of the overall ITV brand, it will be 'TV to talk about' and the main ITV1 channel drama will, 'tell stories of optimism and emotion' to this end. In the past, the 'ratings discourse' (Ang, 1991: 50 ff.) informing such an industry sense of quality would have been paramount, but multi-channelling, as we have seen, has changed the rules of the game. Accordingly, substantial networks have subdivided their output and the smaller, more exclusive ITV 3 will be 'showcasing the very best in television drama', and trading in 'Quality drama that draws you in.'[5] Even this key British network, which typically aims for volume rather than niche audiences, recognises that viewers are more different than their classification mechanisms had hitherto imagined. As ITV's branding brochure declares, 'Mick Jagger and Michael Howard were both born in the 1940s and are both categorised as ABC1 men' but their tastes are likely to be very different. From an 'attitudes study', ITV deduces six categories of viewer: 'Ambitious fun-lovers', 'Home-loving TV addicts', 'Cultured connoisseurs', 'TV-loving trend followers', 'Middle-of-the-road traditionalists' and 'Plugged-in achievers'.

The point here of illustrating advanced viewer differentiation in a British commercial context is first to reiterate the impact of TV3 on established networks. Secondly, although the categories of ITV viewers are evidently constructed, it is to recognise with them that not all viewers are the same and that many will not value "high-end" TV drama which is targeted primarily at specific taste formations. Thus this chapter must pay some attention to the qualities of drama which appeal to other market segments and I propose shortly to consider a category of "quality popular drama" alongside other groupings based on "high-end" preferences. Even amongst audiences for "high-end" product, different taste formations may also be discerned, even though they may not yet be fully identified by publishers or schedulers. Thirdly, the account of ITV's market segmentation also highlights national characteristics and the preferences brought out in Chapter 6. To judge by the images selected by ITV to represent each market segment, these viewers, in spite of their diversity, are all recognisably British. In the light of the research cited above, some segments will tend to prefer nationally or regionally produced programming over foreign imports. The pleasures and meanings afforded British viewers in watching the popular *Casualty* (BBC) or *The Bill* (ITV), or indeed a favourite soap, are different from those offered by "high-end" TV3 products.[6] Thus the terms on which they might be evaluated are also significantly different, as we shall see. And, indeed, it is the failure subtly to differentiate programming by those who would denigrate the television medium entirely that has contributed much to the confusion in estimating its worth.

Commodification and critical aesthetics

Seminal accounts of "quality television" (Feuer et al., 1984, Gitlin, 1994, Thompson, 1996, Nelson, 1997) have been understandably preoccupied, in the context of a popular and significantly commercial medium, with tensions between art and commerce. Stemming from Adorno's seminal critique of the American Culture Industries, there has been a long-standing, though diminishing, sense that commercial product cannot be of aesthetic worth. Adorno took a modernist stance of critical negation, making a distinction, that is, between "authentic art" and the familiar, conventional, formulaic products of the Culture Industries, consonant with the purposes of capitalism. Adorno valorised high-modernist arts, difficult and inaccessible in their abstraction, because they appeared to defy the formulaic rationality of the Enlightenment and could not be commercially assimilated. Though he acknowledged variety in the products of the Culture Industries, Adorno seemed unable to accept that commercial product might be capable of that unassimilable difference which would afford it to be counter-cultural, to make a critique, that is, of the dominant – and in Adorno's view – oppressive bourgeois culture. Since his critique was primarily of instrumental rationalism, he sought creative spaces which lay outside, and could withstand 'being relentlessly hunted down by a schematic reason which compels everything to prove its significance and effect' (Adorno, 1979: 143). His fear, in short, was that human creativity might be dulled by assimilation into what might loosely be dubbed the mainstream of commodified culture.[7]

Acknowledging some limits to Adorno's critique but noting also that it has become not only unpopular but also a target of easy scorn in the past quarter-century, John Caughie has recently invited a reconsideration of 'Adorno's reproach' (2000: 226). At a time when postmodern relativism has both dislocated cultural bearings and inverted established hierarchies of estimation to leave no accepted

standpoint for critique, Caughie sees a visit again to Adorno as 'a way of identifying the issue of value' (2000: 227). In respect of television, Caughie sees a need for
'theoretical and critical debate [that] gives us a way of imagining a television and
a television drama which still has the possibilities of being other than it is' (2000:
233). Whilst I applaud Caughie's aims and agree that, in the academic study of
television, it is important to try to sustain a critical position, I doubt the perti-
nence of Adorno's reproach to TV3 in terms of a hard-line binary between high
art and popular culture. However, if difference within the culture industries might
be acknowledged and, as Caughie points out, there are unexplored hints within
Adorno which suggest that they might be ('the "tragic Garbo" is preferred to Mickey
Rooney, Betty Boop to Donald Duck', cited in Caughie, 2000: 229), then the reproach might lead us to draw meaningful differences.

The keynotes of TV drama at the "high end" in TV3 are difference and distinction. Where the LOP strategy of the network encouraged bland product, TV3
demands the exceptional. But the difference in these instances, as Johnson has
remarked:

> is that the aesthetic and commercial aims of such productions are co-dependent.
> The aesthetic signifiers of 'quality'... such as distinctiveness, single authorship, com-
> plex narratives and so on, function at the service of the commercial demands of the
> network, while the commercial networks demand programmes which can be read
> as aesthetically valuable. (2005: 118)

But this is only a critical problem if, following Adorno, a hard binary is driven
between the commercial and the aesthetically valuable. As I have remarked elsewhere, 'one of the contradictions in capitalism is that the drive for profit might
promote products which do not serve the system overall' (Nelson, 1997: 60). Thus,
though production cannot seemingly take place outside of commodification and
consumerism, the creative freedom afforded to practitioners to achieve distinction liberates them in some instances from the constraints of a crude approach to
profit-making which drives down the price and quality of goods and has tended
towards dull and formulaic television. Indeed, some TV dramas in TV3 seem to
me to illustrate the potential for resistances, though there can be no guarantee of
it. First, there are some television dramas in TV3 which aspire to align themselves
with modernist cinema (see below). The question is whether they have simply
appropriated devices from their predecessors, as has happened in advertising, and
thus assimilated them into a primarily commodified product in a process of the
'intellectualisation of amusement' (Adorno, 1972: 143), or whether they might
retain at least critical potential, if not quite a negative dialectic. Secondly, the creative practice in television of writer–directors such as Poliakoff evidently aim to
stand outside the formulaic repetitiveness of which popular culture stands accused, to sustain 'a difference which is not "indifferent" but in which something is
at stake' (Caughie, 2000: 231). Though works of the liberal imagination and modernist cinema texts may be rare on television, that they appear at all suggests that
Adorno's binary dismissal of the culture industries was too sweeping. Series such
as *Sex and the City* and *Ally McBeal*, though much more clearly imbricated within

commodification, particularly in terms of body image and fashion, may, nevertheless, mobilise an interruption of bourgeois norms – in their challenging content in the case of *Sex and the City* (see Chapter 4), and in their play with form in the case of *Ally McBeal* (see Chapter 5). Neither might be held up as unquestionably critical text in Adorno's terms, but a case may be made for both in respect of their critical potential.

Caughie is right in observing that, since the emphasis in 1980s ethnographic audience study on what people do with television rather than how it impacted upon them, there has been a tendency to celebrate the creativity of the reader in the act of consumption, at the expense of acknowledging the qualities of the text. Various accounts of the active reader (Eco, 1979; Barthes, 1997) have effected, in Caughie's words, 'a fundamental shift of attention – and of political faith – from the text to the audience … It is in consumption rather than in the text that originality and creativity are to be found' (2000: 232). As noted in Chapter 1, however, Bakhtin's concept of heteroglossia grounds polysemy in the actual political, economic, social and ideological statements that shape reception and meaning. If fine differentiations are required, it is appropriate also to distinguish variants of consumption. A viewer who watches *Sex and the City* only for the designer-fashion dimension and is mobilised only to visit the shopping mall might be distinguished from the viewer who feels psychologically empowered by the protagonists' assertiveness to resist the oppressive forces of patriarchy. A highly media-literate viewer might be prompted to call in question the very forms of mainstream film and television by the series' discursive play with popular genres. Thus, though it is in part dependent upon the disposition of readers, critical engagements cannot be ruled out where the production of meanings and pleasures is perceived as a dialogic process. The increase in media literacy since the 1940s when Adorno was writing does itself militate against the notion of cultural dupes. Moreover, academic criticism, in being self-reflexive and fully acknowledging the range of pleasures afforded, can work to think outside consumerism to foster critical judgement.

But textual forms themselves have an impact and in TV3, as illustrated, the texts demonstrate a greater visual richness and narrative-generic complexity such that complex seeing is textually promoted. As noted in the discussion of *The Sopranos*, though it is notionally possible, it would be difficult to feel empowered by the patriarchy of Tony's crew when so many other aspects of the text not only play against but also undermine its values. Indeed, it is the visual density and narrative-generic complexity of the texts of TV3 that are effecting a shift back to an analysis of textual quality in Television Studies. Since it is in the area which Caldwell dubs 'televisuality' (1995) that the greatest aesthetic advances have been made in TV3, it is worth revisiting visual pleasure which has been variously theorised.

In a critique of which Adorno might have approved, Neil Postman argues that the American television medium is:

> a beautiful spectacle, a visual delight, pouring forth thousands of images on any given day. The average shot is only 3.5 seconds, so that the eye never rests, always has something new to see. Moreover, television offers viewers a variety of subject matter,

requires minimal skills to comprehend it, and is largely aimed at emotional gratification ... American television, in other words, is devoted entirely to supplying its
audience with entertainment ... [and] has made entertainment itself the natural
format for all experience. (1987: 88–89)

Postman's emphasis upon entertainment (as opposed to information and education) and emotional gratification (as distinct from intellectual engagement) in
his dismissal of television suggests that the viewing experience comprises a numb-
ing mindlessness. Caldwell, in contrast, recognises that in recent years 'cinema
brought to television spectacle, high production values and feature-style cinema-
tography' (1995: 12) and 'points to the fundamental role that style plays in facilitating distinction' (1995: 20). He goes so far as to question the doxa of glance
theory (see 1995: 25–26) and posits that television viewers are knowledgeable
about the medium and that some watch with the intensity of the cinematic gaze,
perhaps with even greater intensity, since 'film is a one-shot experience that comes
and goes, whilst television spectatorship can be quite intense and ingrained over
time' (1995: 26).

In an era where style generally in culture is much more important than in the
past, there is of course a danger that the surface spectacle stands in for an effaced
content. However, the aesthetic worth of television fictions has not only enhanced
viewing pleasure but also afforded an arena for critical debate which would not
previously have made sense. Though there are circumstances in which surface
style masks a lack of substance, Caldwell's analysis reminds us that it is important
to make distinctions between different television products and engagements. If
certain forms of cinema might have critical potential, so too might certain modes
of television, particularly in TV3.

Underlying Postman's binary distinction between serious (educative and informing) television and mere entertainment is a range of implicit value judgements about pleasure. These circulate around an economy of the pleasure principle,
and social constraints upon it, which, in industrial societies, were located historically in a work ethic underpinning capitalism. The work ethic became a categori-
cal imperative, with indulgence in pleasures of all kinds in this tradition deemed a
frivolous distraction. A disposition towards excessive pleasure was itself contained
in marked periods of licensed holidays and festivals in which pent-up frustrations
might find a release. Over time, however, critical traditions such as the work of
Foucault (see, for example, 1979) developed to deconstruct dominant social forces
and bring out that power, rather than unquestionable ethical imperatives, was
operating to underpin these judgements and practices.

Power, in particular the forces of advanced capitalism, is also at work in contemporary culture but its strictures are less oppressive (in the Western world at
least).[8] Though industrial capitalism may have depended upon a dulled and regi-
mented workforce quietened by relatively mindless entertainment, the information age demands better-educated and more sophisticated employees aware of
the potential of new media and able to mobilise them, as well, perhaps, as to resist
being overly manipulated by them. But, at the same time in Western culture, the

increasing affluence of consumer individualism has, for good or ill, promoted immediate over deferred gratifications and the pleasures of excess. The basis for common adherence to any specific social ethic has accordingly become less secure. In its extreme formulation, postmodern relativism gives free rein to pleasure, since there can be no consensus on any constraining ethical imperative. In the long-running conflict between consumer individualism and public service, then, the former has gained the upper hand in Western contemporary culture. Where value cannot be separated from consumption, Caughie's concern and Adorno's reproach become most pressing for academic study. As Caughie complains, 'It gives criticism and critical theory, no way of knowing what it is for: no way, that is, of arguing for one kind of production against another, or of valuing some forms over others' (2000: 232).

It may be lamentable that there appears to be no outside to commodification, no clear highground from which critical judgements might be handed down. But this does not mean that differences cannot be drawn and values posited and argued for by practical example. It does mean that academics have been somewhat disempowered in the challenge to the culture of expert subjectivity, since they have no simple recourse to elevated territory such as that of elite art inhabited by Adorno. It does imply that critics have to work harder to make their voices heard amongst the many opinions voiced, particularly on popular culture. But capitulation to 'the more enthusiastically affirmative, apparently democratic, or outright populist approaches to popular culture' (Caughie, 2000: 228) is not unavoidable. The irony of TV3 is precisely that "quality" television – some of which might even have satisfied Adorno if he had more fully accepted difference within a popular medium – emerges in highly commercial circumstances. "High-end" production to meet the demands of niche market segments of relatively educated viewers suggests that there is some appreciation of a more demanding television inviting complex seeing. This is not the case across all television products and, as Ang remarks, 'evidence that audiences are "active" cannot simply be equated with the rather triumphalist liberal conclusion, often displayed by gratificationists, that media consumers are "free" or even "powerful"' (1996: 42). However, it opens up a space for questions of worth meaningfully to be probed.

Drawing loosely on modernist–formalist criteria (borrowed from Bakhtin, Brecht and Todorov) of "complex seeing" and "new ways of seeing" in what follows, I deal broadly with two textual strategies: social realist and formal complexity. In the first, the capacity to reveal the interconnectedness of things, to reveal sociocultural forces in play, to set agency in structure, can afford illuminating, sometimes shocking, insights into aspects of contemporary life. In respect of "complex seeing", television has not typically resonated with modernist art values but, in TV3, a multi-tracked complexity has emerged to function on a number of levels. Because the popular medium of television remains to some extent in tension with niche demographics, visual style, narrative layering and oblique writing leave space for viewers to engage in sophisticated dialogues whilst affording a generically recognisable track for those who prefer followability. Visually narrated

TV fictions might now be taken as valuable in themselves as well as located in the traditions of visual pleasure afforded by the high-culture traditions of the visual arts and cinema. The meanings and pleasures of television are being retheorised accordingly. The transgressive potential of the broad category of telefantasy, some of which texts are less "high end" than *Carnivàle*, has already been established by Johnson (2005). This chapter aims to contribute to the debate by differentiating four value traditions: British social realism; drama of the liberal imagination; quality popular drama; and "American quality tv" into "American Quality TV".

British social realism

In the relatively early years of drama written specifically for television, there was an impetus, along the lines of Raymond Williams's seminal concept of social extension in the development of social realism, for working-class life to be represented on television. Given the reach of television for the first time in the late 1950s and 1960s to a mass working-class audience as sets became more affordable, it is not surprising that there was a demand to replace plays in a middle-class, theatre tradition with plays which show "things as they are", in this instance, life depicted from the point of view of a working-class audience. The mid-sixties experiments of Loach and Garnett, taking lightweight 16 mm cameras out of the studio into actual environments and improvising with non-actors, increased a sense of television's capacity "to show things as they really are". When harnessed to a particular social issue, this capacity could seem revelatory. The seminal *Cathy Come Home* famously made the plight of the homeless visible to the nation and allegedly contributed to the inauguration of the housing organisation, Shelter.

Thus, in the British drama tradition, value has historically been placed on a strain of documentary drama whose power lies in its capacity to shock by showing not the surface of a society, the face it would prefer to wear, but "things as they really are", typically taken to indicate the less palatable facets of the social world. The consciences of those who had been ignorant of the particular social ill exposed in the drama might act to do something about it. The formation of Shelter has been taken in retrospect as an impact of this kind. Thus a drama of social conscience is, and remains, valued in a liberal-left tradition of allowing all voices to be heard and thus championing those writers and directors who articulate, in however disturbing a mode, the perspectives of the excluded and oppressed. At best the content is imbricated within the form. Though the documentary treatment is persuasive, the content – in terms of the social issues addressed – has a contemporary and relatively local resonance.

Though the programmes discussed have themselves developed considerably, there is a significant, though by no means exclusive, strain in this book advocating the value of social realism in this tradition as a mode of both providing engaging TV drama and social critique. The issue of representation in the political sense of standing on behalf of a community and making it visible remains in respect of sustained exclusion of some voices, or their relative "ghettoisation" in TV3 on specialist channels. The minimal representation of black perspectives in the predominantly white and up-market vehicles of "American Quality TV" is a case in point.[9] In respect of the British social realist tradition viewed from another perspective further to the left on the political spectrum, a drama that convinces an audience of the existence of formerly untold ills within a society might go further to raise awareness of the inequalities and injustices inherent in the very structure of society and, accordingly, promote fundamental social change. It might point up the contradictions inherent in the social fabric where it otherwise appeared smooth on the surface.

Amongst film and television theorists in the 1970s, there was considerable debate about the best formal means (social realism or naturalism, as distinct from Brechtian distanciation) to achieve the raising of social consciousness to the point of revolutionary action. But it was not at that time doubted – by the theorists at least – that television shared this potential fundamentally to change society for the better. Such a debate may sound irretrievably dated and today few people – particularly in the highly commercial context of "American Quality TV" – would pay any attention to such a social, let alone political, function of television, and would not place value upon it. The British television context with its strong public service ethos has historically held social-issues drama in high regard and, though such dramas may be less of a feature of British schedules today, they can still command critical and, at times, popular acclaim. *Shameless*, for example, though it departs considerably from the modes of historical social realism, nevertheless remains valued in the traces of that tradition as reviewers' comparisons with *Boys from the Blackstuff* suggest. Dramas such as *Cops* and *Buried* from legendary producer Tony Garnett continue to afford insights into a kind of experience inaccessible to most television viewers and to treat it seriously in a continuation of a socially critical British tradition.

Thus the advocacy of social realism informing this book is not just a matter of my preferences (though it may well be informed by them) but is made in terms of a historically valid mode of television reflecting the need for a society to be self-critical. Furthermore it stands in resistance to the dominant "feel-good-factor" drama which is ultimately allied to individualist consumerism in that, directly or indirectly, it promotes the sale of consumer goods. In sum, social realism is a function of TV drama which might well be effaced if current market trends continue and, if only in accord with the diversity principle, it deserves advocacy. Though – as this book, and this chapter in particular, is at pains to point out – the commercial sector produces work of quality, and even work inviting cultural critique, the concept of "market failure" recognises that it cannot serve all needs. It would patently be absurd if, in a multi-channel environment nobody chose to watch work in the social realist tradition, but what is proposed is not the reifying of an outmoded form since, as *Shameless* demonstrates, the form itself can adjust to new times.

Drama of the liberal imagination

Using the optics of history will also help unpack some key aspects of another conception of "quality". It will be evident in Thompson's formulations of "quality television" in the USA as well as implicitly in my own observations that creativity and innovation, the very avoidance of adhering to tried and tested formulae, are deemed to be aspects of worth. The contemporary television work of Stephen Poliakoff serves as an interesting example since his work as auteur writer-director fits closely with the conception of art arising from a distinctive perception of the liberal imagination.

Reviewing Poliakoff's *The Lost Prince*, Howard Jacobson rhetorically remarks:

> If there has been a greater work of the imagination for television ever, I challenge you to name it … Comedy of the highest level, too deep for mere mirth, but filled with a marvellous appreciation of the absurd, the cruel, the beautiful magniloquence of our natures … In their doomed endeavours to escape the mundane normalities of life, Poliakoff's crowned heads spoke to us from the very heart of humanity. (2003: 19)[10]

This is perhaps an unusually fulsome television review of an untypical TV drama but it serves to illustrate a set of values in a liberal humanist tradition which privilege artworks affording insights into the human condition. Like a dramatic poet, Poliakoff works through metaphor and thus his narratives are typically oblique, but his strong sense of place and environment, notably of London, grounds the metaphors in visual and material culture.[11] For example, environments such as Canary Wharf in East London's former dockland serve as metaphors for the monetarism of the Thatcher–Reagan years (in *Close My Eyes*, Film Four, 1980) and the Millennium Dome stands for the soullessness of a contemporary culture in which, as Poliakoff sees it, a weary irony has displaced conviction (in *Gideon's Daughter*, BBC, 2006).

More than most contemporary TV dramatists, Poliakoff is concerned about an apparent erosion of established European cultural values in postmodern times. As the elderly Viennese Frau Messner (Peggy Ashcroft), observes to Peter (Michael Kitchen) in *Caught on a Train* (1980): 'You don't care do you? You may think that you do, but you don't really care about anything.' Implicitly, the capacity to anatomise aspects of the human condition, and thus to open up questions of human value, through strongly visual metaphor is attributed by Jacobson to Poliakoff's distinctive vision and capacity to feel for the mediums of film and television. The conception also implies a common humanity from 'the very heart of' which the drama [speaks] to us'; that is, it implies a universality in human experiences.

Though in relativist times which emphasise cultural differences and an absence of shared values, it may be unfashionable to think and speak in this way, there appears to be a stubbornly residual sense of TV drama's potential in these terms. Poliakoff is, admittedly, a rare example of writer-directors who regard making films for television as a matter of both craft and art. He is also amongst the very few who are afforded the opportunity in the contemporary British television context to have substantial creative control over their work. Nevertheless, his output in TV3 is both broad and impressive (*StP*, 1999; *Perfect Strangers*, 2001; *The Lost Prince*, 2003; *Friends and Crocodiles*; *Gideon's Daughter* 2006), suggesting that there is still a space for work of this particular kind of distinction.[12] In a biographical TV feature, Poliakoff is located in the tradition of artist-observers who stand critically apart from their time but who are able to anatomise key social currents. As arts critic Mark Lawson observes, Poliakoff's work is preoccupied 'with two kinds of detail: historical detail from the past and historical detail from the present'.[13] Indeed, Poliakoff's very strong sense of history itself stands against the tide of postmodern times in which, as novelist Tim Lott puts it, 'people are disconnected from the past, living in a perpetual present' in a culture which manifests 'an extraordinarily horrifying amnesia', particularly in respect of the dark periods of the twentieth century'.[14]

Poliakoff sustains a belief, moreover, in the potential of TV drama to initiate a dialogue of cultural critique and a faith in the capacity of viewers to engage in such a dialogue. As he remarks, institutional forces, 'have underestimated people's power of imagination, of thought'. Indeed, Poliakoff leans towards the "dumbing-down" school when he attributes the malaise of our times to the displacement of thought by a fast-moving but contrived and mediatised culture, a trend which he aims in his drama to counter. Against all contemporary industry orthodoxy, he advocates "slow" television, a strategy which, in *StP* (see Chapter 2), consciously challenges the assumption of commissioning executives that unless the treatment grabs viewers in the first forty seconds, and hooks and holds them in with high temperature action at fast pace, they will be lost to another channel. Poliakoff celebrates imaginative, slightly quirky, original characters who, often in quiet ways, resist appropriation into the surface lifestyle and celebrity culture which inform other kinds of TV drama such as, for example, *Sex and the City*. That Poliakoff's characters are often revealed to have an informing history beyond surface appearances (see Chapter 2) is both a compositional principle of dramatic reversal and surprise and an affirmation of the importance of the past informing the present.

In many respects, Poliakoff might appropriately be located in the British single play tradition. He is first and foremost a playwright, having established his career in the theatre prior to moving into film and television.[15] As resident playwright at the National Theatre in the 1970s, he achieved very early a set of credentials which carry value in a literary–theatrical tradition, the kind of values, indeed, which informed early British TV drama. Traditionally, the playwright was accredited as the author – and seen as the mainspring – of drama on television. Poliakoff is avowedly 'proud that [he has] consistently done individual work in film, television and theatre ... work that has been unlike other work' (BBC, 2001).

In a broader context, the unconstrained individual voice has historically been valued in the liberal, political tradition as a sign of free expression in a free society both in Britain and the USA, even though the historic production circumstances of most television have frequently militated against it. Writers who conceive their function as being to reveal something distinctive about contemporary life, rather than being a cog in an industrial process of television production, are patently located in this tradition. In the historic tension between systems and the ability of the individual to affect change, Poliakoff champions the capacities of the human mind and creativity. Seen through this optic, Oswald Bates in *StP* represents more than a talented eccentric who gets one over on the bureaucrats, he stands for a cultural and political heritage under threat. Because, like Adorno, Poliakoff's family are exiles from a Europe under the threat of totalitarianism, it is not perhaps surprising to hear an echo of Frankfurt School critique in Poliakoff's express concern to resist the 'cynical manipulation of mass culture that's always with us' (BBC, 2001). Another interview insight reveals that Poliakoff believes that significant developments in history and culture are mobilised by exceptional individuals.[16]

To those who hold them in high esteem, works such as those of Poliakoff are culturally valuable because they expand human imagination and understanding. However, the distinctiveness of Poliakoff's oeuvre now renders it estimable in TV3 by other values: it is distinctive in terms of that aggressive, consumerist economy about which Poliakoff has reservations. Though it might be dubbed filmic, Poliakoff's "quality drama" in TV3 is, however, different from cinematic "American Quality TV". To take the most obvious differences, where Poliakoff advocates slow, contemplative television, American series might be characterised by their pace and narrative drive, though, as is evident in the discussion of a number of examples in this book, they are not without complexity and moments affording reflective thought. Where, then, the value posited for *Sopranos* lies in its capacity creatively to accommodate textual complexity to the drivers of contemporary television, the worth of *StP*, as I see it, paradoxically lies in its resistance to contemporary cultural and televisual trends. The key qualities both programmes share, however, lie in their capacities – different in specific ways, but similar in general – to compel with stories visually well told and to draw viewers in to be interested in fascinating characters located in situations which nevertheless resonate with – rather than directly reflect – broader perspectives on contemporary life. Though most of us are neither gangsters nor archivists, *Sopranos* and *StP* have something to offer beyond regular television fare.

Before turning to the aesthetic and cultural values of "American Quality TV", the middle range of British TV drama, fare for ITV's 'Middle-of-the-road traditionalists' deserves brief consideration.

Quality popular drama

Though the climate is changing, television remains significantly a domestic medium and accordingly serves needs which "the arts", including experimental cinema, on television do not aim to fulfil. In a recent reflective study of the medium, John Ellis (2000) places emphasis upon the 'witness' and 'working through' functions of television. As he sees it, 'Television imbues the present moment with meanings. It offers multiple stories and frameworks of explanation which enable understanding and, in the very multiplicity of those frameworks, it enables viewers to work through the major public and private concerns of their society.' 'Working through' is conceived as 'a collective process of making sense of the modern world that uses the linearity of the broadcast medium. It depends upon the universal availability of public service broadcast television services' (2000: 177). Ellis notes the television medium's familiar, direct address in presentation and the relative predictability of TV genres which are 'so explicit and so instantly recognisable' (2000: 102) that they 'provide stability in a system in which witnessed events of all kinds and their interpretation ceaselessly whirl around' (2000: 103). Where, then, high-culture or Adornoesque perspectives critique the very predictability of soaps and long-running series, many viewers find value precisely in the sense-making functions dismissed by critics as ideological palliatives.

Ellis is speaking of a more traditional television industry and viewing disposition than that foregrounded in the discourse of TV3, as indicated by his emphasis upon genre familiarity rather than generic hybridity. But, despite the fundamental changes in the contemporary television environment, Ellis is right to recognise the important residual use of the television medium to negotiate, and make sense of, the world beyond the living room.[17] 'Middle-of-the-road traditionalists' represent a substantial proportion of the UK audience, comprising '9 million of these heartland ITV1 viewers'; they are the residual group, as Ellis notes, of a broadcasting rather than a narrowcasting age. There is, then, a question of value in respect of this taste formation in comparison with that of the segment of "Event TV" viewers, who may be more valuable to corporations, a more lucrative target market, though representing a smaller number of people. Indeed, it might even be argued that 'middle-of-the-road traditionalists', in preferring a broadcast television which provides material for everyday social conversation, constitute a group resistant to the imperatives of contemporary commodification by niche marketing, audience fragmentation and profit maximisation in TV3. If it is a good thing on any terms that the middle-of-the-road traditionalists' needs should be met, however, the qualities of a "quality popular drama" demand consideration.

"Quality popular drama" is a tag long since used by ITV in the UK, and its archetype is perhaps *Inspector Morse* (1987–2000). This prestigious, long-running and much repeated series bears all the hallmarks of 'witness' and 'working through' as constructed by Ellis, in the form of a recognisable and popular TV genre, the detective series. In each episode of *Inspector Morse*, ageing and world-weary Chief Inspector Morse (John Thaw) supported by his younger sidekick Detective Sergeant Lewis (Kevin Whately) resolve a crime committed amongst, or in the rural environs of, the dreaming spires of Oxford. The architecture of the Oxford colleges and the countryside around the city afford visually splendid settings for Morse's vintage Jaguar (complete with walnut veneer dashboard and leather seating) to patrol.

Shot on film, *Inspector Morse* is equally as well crafted as Morse's car in terms of established popular-cinema production values. That is to say, there is nothing experimental about the camera angles or editing, but everything is well framed and well lit, and the continuity editing renders the settings deep and convincing, and the narratives plausible and followable. For those viewers seeking to make sense of the world through negotiating a story with some small surprises but no major ones, the mystery element of the detective genre and its ultimate resolution serves to reassure. In broader, thematic terms, Morse's conservatism and his respect for the residue of a craft tradition and its attendant values of community are evident in his car and his parallel loves of opera and real ale, the first expressing his romanticism and the pain of unrequited love whilst the latter associates him with the common man of "authentic" taste. Besides the snatches of Mozart, Puccini and Verdi, the original soundtrack composed by Barrington Pheloung affords a distinctive signature and punctuates the action and moods of each episode. *Inspector Morse* is thus emblematic of "quality popular drama" in that the protagonist's values, sceptical of the development trajectory of the contemporary world, resonate with the need to negotiate with it but not to open up fundamentally disturbing questions and, ultimately, to reassure through not only narrative but also ideological closure.

"Quality popular drama" represents just one of the many discourses in the overall flow of television's ceaseless whirl of events and interpretations but, because it is widely disseminated in a range of popular genres (hospital, police procedural, detective), it is an important one. Though I do not deny Ellis's point about the lack of ultimate, overall closure in contemporary television, it would be hard to make a case for the encouragement of critical negation since the frameworks of "quality popular drama" manifest a tendency towards making sense, and the affirmation of an explanatory paradigm. Thus, though no single meaning is offered, a reassuring notion that things can make sense is afforded.

However, as argued in Chapter 1, since meanings are a matter of dialogic negotiation, or, in Ellis's term, 'working through', the broad cultural disposition of viewers is as important a factor as the formal structures of the programmes themselves. Furthermore, it may be that, as product at the "high end" has become more sophisticated, "quality popular drama" has also developed into a vehicle capable of greater complexity. Though *Lewis* has emerged on ITV as a predictable spin-off from *Inspector Morse*, there are also new kinds of "quality popular drama" emerging which manifest the influence of more "high-end" drama in TV3. *Desperate Housewives* and *Life on Mars* are illustrative examples.

As indicated in Chapter 5, *Desperate Housewives* (Touchstone Television for NBC, 2004, two seasons to date) seems in many ways to be a network version of *SatC*. Four women feature centrally: Susan Mayer (Teri Hatcher), Lynette Scavo (Felicity Huffman), Bree Van der Kamp (Marcia Cross) and Gabrielle Solis (Eva Longoria) and, though they are technically not 'single gals' like their counterparts in *SatC*, their various relationships with men are equally foregrounded. Like the *SatC* 'gals', they are all physically attractive in conventional American terms. Indeed, they are exceptionally slim and thus look good in everyday jeans and T-shirts which the home-based environment requires, as well as the designer outfits to which they on occasion aspire. *Desperates* similarly foregrounds the lives, loves and aspirations of a group of thirtysomething women, and its setting, if not quite aspiring to the high fashion of New York's Upper East Side, is nevertheless affluent. Being independent through wealth (in this case of the husband) is vital at least to Gabrielle.

Indeed, the Manhattan context apart, there is almost as much focus upon fashion in *Desperates* as in *SatC*. An episode in Season 1 features a fashion-show catwalk similar to that in *SatC* and appropriate designer clothes are at issue in two consecutive episodes in Series 2 (Episodes 6 and 7; transmitted in the UK 22 February 2006 and 1 March 2006, C4). In the first, Lynette is ridiculed by her boss and business colleagues for supposedly wearing outmoded and shabby suits and she buys an excessively expensive white suit which, though she and her husband agree that they cannot afford to the point where she promises to return it, she feels pressured into wearing to make a business presentation. In the second, Gabrielle, though pregnant, tries to squeeze herself (and is eventually sewn) into a designer dress unsuited to her bulge. Though there is an undercutting humour in both instances – the label on Lynette's skirt betrays its newness and Gabrielle's gardeners are called upon to close the zip using pliers and grips – the dominant impression, like that in *SatC*, is that the female desire for fashion cannot be denied.

Desperates differs from *SatC*, however, in that it has more of a serial than a sitcom format, with a narrative thread of mystery established at the outset concerning the death of Mary Alice Young, a friend of the four protagonists. It is thus a hybrid form of comedy, murder mystery and lifestyle drama. Being a network programme, moreover, *Desperates* aims to appeal to a broader audience and includes teenagers (e.g. Susan's daughter) and older characters (e.g. Martha Huber, Lynette's neighbour). Constrained by the regulator, it cannot be "edgy" in the manner of *SatC* and arguably this prevents it from posing the kinds of potentially fundamental challenges outlined above in respect of that HBO series. Network derivatives of "edgy" successes in subscription channels, by not pushing any envelopes, may tend to affirm the pleasures of lifestyle consumption by being more followable in form and having titillating but acceptable content. Though they may not fundamentally challenge in the way that *SatC* patently has the potential to do, their wit and production values mark a step change in "quality popular television".

Life on Mars (Kudos Productions for BBC1, 2005) offers a variation on an even more tried and tested genre, the police series. Though each episode sees the investigation of a case, interest is focused not upon the resolution but on the means to the end by a comparison of twenty-first-century police methods with those of 1973. The "given" of *Life on Mars* is that Sam Tyler (John Simm) may have travelled through time and space. As he narrates it, 'I had an accident and I woke up in 1973. Whatever happened, it looks like I've landed on another planet. Now, maybe, if I can work out the reason, I can get home.' Thus this twenty-first-century policeman is seeking to resolve the mystery of his apparent time travel as well as the specific cases which confront his 1973 colleagues. In the Greater Manchester force, he is now DI Sam Tyler working to DCI Gene Hunt (Phil Glenister) who operates like somebody in *The Sweeney* (Euston films, 1975–78 for ITV). A vehicle is thus created which on one level follows a police procedural trajectory but on another makes comparisons between the ethics of today and those of another age, an era in the living memory of a considerable number of viewers. Another psychic or sci-fi layer is invoked in the mystery of how Tyler has apparently travelled back through time and his attempt to 'get home'. He hears messages on radio and TV shows and in snatches of popular music and has hallucinatory glimpses of a woman in a red dress running through a wood. The final episode of the first series comes close to unravelling this mystery and making sense of these images but no final closure was attempted, to allow for the second series, transmitted in February 2007.

Judging from viewer response on the BBC website, a range of pleasures in watching the series arises from the context of 1970s cars, fashions, pop music and action-adventure cop series themselves. But the comparison of living conditions and particularly police procedures between 2006 and 1973 affords food for thought in addition. As Jane Tranter, Head of BBC Drama commissioning summarises the 'unique and clever central clash of 2006 and 1973 sensibilities has totally captured the imagination of the audience and I am thrilled we have a new series of extraordinary performances, flares and 70s cars to look forward to.'[18]

To take a few illustrative examples from the penultimate episode (transmitted on 20 February 2006), which features DI Tyler investigating his colleagues after a young man has died in police custody from a drugs overdose, the script obliquely reflects the twenty-first century whilst affording a colourful 1970s discourse to DCI Hunt and an acquiescent compliance to the victim's relatives.

On learning of the victim's death, possibly at the hands of his cell-mate, Hunt concludes that, 'one scumbag offed another'. When Tyler is sceptical about the victim's alleged cocaine consumption, Hunt suggests that 'just because he wasn't playing the sitar and seeing purple elephants' does not mean that he was not using drugs. Hunt sees women as 'birds' and criminals as 'nutters'. This discourse, which, along with Hunt's shirts and his camel overcoat, might well have graced *The Sweeney* in the 1970s is now experienced at one remove. It might be nostalgically enjoyed by viewers but they are also invited by the 2006 perspective to see it from a critical distance. Having agreed with Tyler to be gentle when visiting the victim's sister, Hunt introduces himself by saying, 'Just come to talk to you to tell you how your brother copped it.' Her response to her brother's death, however, when later interviewed is equally shocking from a 2006 perspective in its compliance. She says 'I'm sure you've been very thorough. I'm sorry we've caused this much trouble … I'm sure you did what was right and I think that I can trust the police.' Even without the plot which, when investigated by Tyler, reveals that DS Ray Carling (Dean Andrews) had fed the victim cocaine in his cell, this subservient response invites a questioning of the distance between the 1970s and today's litigious culture. Moreover, it is not simply that things are better today. Many aspects of *Life on Mars* invite thought by way of comparative reflection upon both policing and culture more broadly, then and now.

Anachronistic references keep the 2006 perspective alive and contribute to the invitation to see how life has changed. For viewers with a local knowledge of Manchester, the absence of today's "curry mile" in Rusholme is striking when Hunt and Tyler visit the area in search of 'something different' and go for an Indian. To the perplexity of his colleagues back at the station, Tyler is alarmed that there is no police 'database' and would give much for a decent 'search engine'. In this episode he hears (and so de we) snatches of Britney Spears in his hallucinations, and the band Pulp is heard on the radio. More obliquely, when Tyler remarks, 'Let's make it a good day to bury bad news', the twenty-first-century reference to political underhandedness is there for viewers rather than his colleagues to apprehend.

The pragmatic ethics of 1970s policing ultimately win out in this episode when the Chief Constable destroys the audiotape evidence presented by Tyler which incriminates all his colleagues, and DS Ray Carter in particular. The Chief Constable is happy that the matter has been handled internally, with Hunt informally demoting Carter and threatening that; 'If you so much as belch out of line, I'll have your scrotum on a barbed-wire plate.' Tyler had hoped that, if he brought the whole world crashing down, he might have got home, but not in this episode.

Life on Mars is a "quality popular drama" in that it is a police series with a twist, but an original twist which opens up potential for it to be much more than a mere reworking of the ingredients in a formula. It offers the pleasures of the genre in resolving cases within the episodes but throwing out a serial hook in Tyler's quest to 'get home'. It even has potential love interest with Annie Cartright (Liz White) becoming a special friend to Tyler, the only one he feels he can trust. The ensemble is strong, with particularly powerful performances from Simm and Glenister, and the reconstruction of the 1970s is convincing. But *Life on Mars* is more than nostalgic "heritage" drama. In providing undoubted generic pleasures, it has the potential also to be thought-provoking and to invite complex seeing.

"American quality tv" into "American Quality TV"

To those aware of the history of American television, the qualities of a "work-friends" family drama convincingly played by an ensemble cast to create a realistic representation of the complexities of life in a specific sociocultural milieu might suggest not *Sopranos* but *Hill Street Blues, St Elsewhere* or even *thirtysomething*. Allied to such a recollection might be Robert Thompson's retrospective formulation of the bases for "quality TV" in TVII, the advent of cable, satellite and video rental which began to break up the network era's stranglehold.

With programmes such as *Hill Street Blues* and *St Elsewhere* in mind, Thompson posited that American 'quality TV is best defined by what it is not. It is not "regular" TV' (1996: 13). With regard to textual composition, furthermore, Thompson's criteria in his seminal account of Quality TV include:

- a large ensemble cast
- a memory
- a new genre by mixing old ones
- a tendency to be literary and writer-based

- textual self-consciousness
- subject matter tending towards the controversial
- aspiration toward "realism"
- a quality pedigree
- attracting an audience with blue-chip demographics (see 1996: 14–15)

In all these respects, *Sopranos* fits the bill as much as its illustrious predecessors but it manifests other qualities, as we shall see. But to deal first with those qualities which both fulfil and extend the features above, the trick worked by *Sopranos* is to combine high action delivered at narrative pace with moments of reflection through which depth of character may be revealed, and all done with wit and intelligence. It manifests a mix of the traditional American preference for high-gloss action-adventure with the British penchant for social realism. *Hill Street Blues* borrowed – and built upon – aspects of the British social realist tradition and was acknowledged for its 'visual strategy of *vérité* messiness' (Nelson in Creeber, 2004b: 101). *Sopranos*, as a "cinematic" product of TV3, has a glossy cinematic look and feel overall but it sustains oblique action, overlapping and multiple storylines, low-key delivery and a sense of neighbourhood community. A notable difference between *Hill Street Blues* and *Sopranos*, however, is that whilst the former meets the final criterion in Thompson's formulation that, 'quality shows must often undergo a noble struggle against profit-mongering networks', the production context of the latter in TV3 is different.

HBO is not a network but is located at the high end of the portfolio of media conglomerate Time-Warner. HBO accordingly distinguishes its brand and its output from typical network-era 'regular TV', but asserts its difference by implying through its tag-line, "Television? No this is HBO", not that it is televisually different but that it is not television at all. Indeed, HBO not only aligns itself with cinema but, as Jane Feuer has argued,[19] with the modernist, rather than popular, cinematic tradition, branding itself as a mode of art. Shot on film, *Sopranos* aspires to the quality of its mob-movie predecessors, and its production values are cinematically high. But with six seasons and eighty-three episodes, *Sopranos* is unmistakably a television product and its distinction lies ultimately in its ability successfully to combine dominant modes from the established film and TV media into a new hybrid television product, allowing, as suggested in Chapter 2, existential shadows to play across its surface gloss. It builds on the *Hill Street* tradition of American "quality", but TV drama in TV3 consciously aims to construct itself as a new mode of "American Quality Television".

To relate this sketch of its compositional principles to potential reader response *Sopranos* might be read from different historically and culturally situated angles. Despite its broad popularity and critical acclaim in the USA and worldwide, *Sopranos* is not without its critics. For example, feminist Camille Paglia objects not so much to the representation of women as to the construction of ethnicity when spearheading a vocal pocket of resistance to the series which sees *Sopranos*, in Paglia's words, as 'a buffoonish caricature of my people' (cited in Lavery, 2002: xiii). Other voices have testified to many other alleged depravities of the series, as

Lavery relates (see 2002: xiii ff.). Acknowledging, then, that some viewers in entrenched positions might take a very particular stance on *Sopranos*, I still maintain that its unusual hybrid mix of discourses (see Chapter 2) is disposed towards a mixed-mode television-viewer subjectivity. My aim in placing emphasis on the intermix of modes is to point out that it is difficult to take a very singular set of meanings and pleasures from the series because of its subtle intertwining within each episode of a range of treatments, constantly shifting perspective. Disturbing the ground on which any viewer at any angle might stand optimises the potential for calling into question any particular set of entrenched values. To pick up again on the notion of gendering, for example, though it is possible for a macho male viewer to have his values reaffirmed through watching *Sopranos*, it is equally likely – or even more likely – that the security of that position will be dislocated. Where women beyond the dichotomous angel/whore stereotype are effaced from the gangster genre, in *Sopranos* more regular women, and their historic televisual modes, are included. As related in Chapter 2, the play between modes is what makes the series textually distinctive and it may be that it promotes a more fluid subjectivity, appropriate to postindustrial culture. The undercutting of the traditionally masculine goal orientation of cause→effect→action→closure by a circular pattern of motivation ⌐reflection ⌐ dialogue ⌐ negotiation discourages traditional gender specificity.

Given that so much contemporary drama on television in TV3 is a hybrid of one kind or another, it may be that viewers socially constructed by tradition into gender and other social segments or microcultures by more monolithic constructs of the past might ultimately be reconstructed to be less reified and exclusive. The implicit values informing my assessment here include those in Thompson's seminal definition cited above, but extends the idea of the achievement of 'a new genre by mixing old ones' to suggest that the advanced hybrids of TV3, through establishing new modalities, have the potential to mobilise a more fluid and reflective subjectivity. In moving from description to make the evaluative claim that *Sopranos* exemplifies a new kind of "American Quality TV" drama, I extend the claim made above that textual richness makes for complex seeing and that seeing from more than one viewpoint is conducive to an engaged viewing experience and perhaps even conducive to a social good.

Though it remains slightly constrained, as noted in Chapter 5, by the size and shape of the domestic apparatus in most people's homes, "high-end" TV drama in TV3 aspires to cinema, and, in the case of HBO Premium particularly, to art cinema. To a considerable extent, the motive for such aspiration is a response to history. Since its inception, television has been seen as the poor relation of cinema. In its very early days, television production was confined to the studio and shot live in a multicamera set-up. Studio sets, based on a theatre-scenery model, were often flimsy and unconvincing. Lighting, in the studio context, was general from overhead rather than specifically motivated for each shot. The need for heavy cables to convey the television signal either to output on air or, subsequently – with the advent of magnetic videotape, to the recording apparatus, severely restricted camera mobility. At the reception end, the small, black-and-white domestic monitor afforded a very poor image for anything but close-ups. The scope and visual splendour of colour cinema in comparison undoubtedly afforded a richer visual experience at that time. But, even when the American television established itself in Los Angeles and colour and location shooting became prevalent, the cinema industry sought to sustain its distinction from the newcomer and sought further to exploit its advantages with even more glossy and glamorous production. Thus, if viewers can be persuaded to see "high-end" television fictions to be as good as, or in Kramer's formulation, 'better than' the movies, TV3 dramas achieve a status beyond the historic television medium.

Given that, with some small caveats, it might reasonably be claimed that the technological differences between film and television in contemporary production are insignificant, HBO Premium can plausibly claim that its output is "not TV", but "cinematic", as noted in Chapter 1. The first value factor is financial: films both historically and today command bigger budgets than even the most lavish TV drama production, but the gap has recently narrowed. In a capitalist culture in which all worth is ultimately reduced to financial values, the most expensive is ineluctably "the best". Thus, part of the prestige of the "high-end, Event TV" with which this book has been concerned, is estimated in terms of budget, just as the extraordinarily high budgets of blockbuster movies are advertised as part of their hype. But big budgets do make for higher production values. A key feature of "American Quality TV" output is the quality of the writing, often by teams but overseen with strong writer-producer steer. David Chase is accredited with *Sopranos*, Alan Ball with *Six Feet Under*, David Kelley with *Ally McBeal* and Chris Carter with *The X-Files*. Money buys writing teams with the time to draft and redraft. It also buys star actors, expensive locations, special effects, the time to set up and light each shot individually and afford a number of takes and, perhaps above all in the contemporary context, substantial publicity and promotion. Though it is not the case that 'narrative image', in Ellis's formulation (see 1994), can alone create a hit, success is unlikely in today's crowded market-place without a high degree of promotion. Branding is partly achieved in the making of a drama, but it is affirmed and distributed through product and channel promotion and further disseminated into related media through horizontal integration and merchandising.

In aesthetic terms, the "look" of a product is all-important in a contemporary Western culture preoccupied with style. In the economy of postmodernity, general commodity production and sales are typically marked by branding, displayed in visual style and logos. Furthermore, in an intellectual and social climate in which the fixity of personal identity has been called in question, individuals may refashion their identities by adopting new lifestyles. Commodities are designed to assist in this allegedly open process and the social hierarchy is reconstructed in terms of brands. A key part of the perceived distinction of HBO Premium product lies, then, in the cachet it has achieved in making a particular kind of "quality" product for the discerning. Not to commit to HBO is to mark yourself as inferior because you are unable to discern the qualitative difference between "television" (of the LOP era) and HBO. That HBO output looks expensive, however, does not preclude quality adjudged in other terms.

To make a broad generalisation, "American Quality TV" might nevertheless be characterised by an expensive, cinematic look, shiny in comparison with the British tradition of gritty realism. By this description, I mean to indicate not just the brightly lit colourfulness of typically American product but also the glamorous actors cast within a relatively narrow range of conventional good looks, and the presentation of them with strong, white teeth and immaculate hair, even in dynamic action. To pick up on one of the examples discussed in this book, Kiefer Sutherland and his co-stars in *24*, for all the pressure and action they experience, typically emerge looking good. The legacy of early Hollywood glamour is traceable in the visual sumptuousness and shininess of HBO Premium and other similar American "Quality TV" output. Though all "high-end" products have to be stylish, however, they are designed to have different looks. Important distinctions can and should be made between a generic "glossy" look and a range of "cinematic" visual styles. Products differ considerably in visual style and narration – the *mise-en-scène* of *Oz* is not that of *SatC*.

Within the contemporary American context itself, however, a difference in respect of quality might also be drawn between approaches which aim to be formally innovative in a manner evoking European avant-garde cinema and those which make no such claim but aspire to be more regular in form but distinctive from regular output by means of high production values. Jane Feuer has suggested, for example, that *West Wing* is basically a soap opera but with such smooth orchestration of its serial storylines that is has exceptional narrative rhythm and balance. The various story strands are carefully interwoven to exploit multiple plotting relations between them such that they add up to more than the sum of their parts. The soundtrack, though traditionally orchestrated rather than experimental, is finally crafted to underscore the resonances of the drama. Thus, for viewers who give the serial the more concentrated attention its construction demands, *West Wing* affords a mode of seriousness beyond "regular TV". In this respect, it extends the tradition of Thompson's formulation for earlier "quality TV" by being more sophisticated than, but not radically different from, the norm.

Six Feet Under, in contrast, particularly in the first season, set out to be radically different from regular TV, aspiring to evoke associations with modernist theatre or European art cinema in the manner of the HBO Premium portfolio. The orchestration of HBO's serial storylines, as Feuer argues, is bumpy rather than smooth and, in the case of *Six Feet Under*, more experimental in its eclectic mix of Western and non-Western musical forms and instrumentation. In the first season, furthermore, *Six Feet Under* created a deliberate confusion of both dream and reality and television modes. Ghosts, notably of the father, appeared without the use of established television codes to mark them as such. Advertisements for macabre, death-related products, were inserted, similarly without coding, to cause further, if momentary, dislocation of a kind favoured in the surrealist arts. The complexity of the characters emerged through an uncommonly slow unfolding of the narrative and with revelations conveyed in that oblique theatrical mode established by Chekhov. By means of self-referencing and intertextual referencing (alluding, as it does at times, to other HBO programmes) *Six Feet Under* consciously aligns itself with experimental arts practices. Its claim to value, then, lies not in distinguishing itself from regular TV fare but in not being television at all.

Where subscription channels are free to be "edgy", branding in the networks in contrast is constrained in its potential to be adventurous by its market position and the limits of regulation. But the FCC, whilst it proscribes high levels of nudity and violence, places no constraints on quirky or complex characters, slow narrative exposition or oblique modes of storytelling. Emerging network programming such as *Desperates* suggests that, over time in TV3, the networks are altering their disposition as the audience shifts on to new ground. Seen in this light, HBO has gained a market advantage by establishing its distinctive brand on territory comprised of a mix of popular and "high-culture" forms. It carries – and brands itself – with the cachet of modernist experimental arts, and art cinema in particular, whilst at the same time exploiting popular forms, such as the magazine format of *SatC* (see Chapter 5). At the same time it takes advantage of the less culturally aspirational draw of nudity and violence in *The Sopranos*, as afforded by freedom from FCC regulatory constraint.

Values in play

Overall, then, a number of sets of criteria for "quality" TV drama in Britain and America are now in play, with some subsets of criteria for "high-end" TV itself. Vestiges of the traditions of "high culture" in Western arts are evident primarily in drama of the liberal imagination but also, drawing on an alternative modernist tradition, in those experimental modes which inform some HBO Premium output. "American Quality TV" in contemporary commentary would seem to indicate, in the first instance, expensive output with (for television) high production values as typically exemplified by cinema. It remains shiny. But finer distinctions might be made within this broad category between exceptionally well-crafted, but not particularly innovative, product, and output which consciously aligns itself with – and, to a greater or lesser extent, achieves "complex seeing". The "quality TV" in Thompson's formulation of "not regular" continues, though, given the fundamental dislocation of the industry in the context of multichannelling and audience fragmentation, the benchmark of "regular TV" under the LOP disposition is itself increasingly eroded. Economic worth still underlies conceptions of quality but, where profit is to be made from content rather than distribution, the aesthetic quality of TV drama product, though unevenly and indirectly, is steadily being driven up.

But there are still medium-driven constraints. Television's rapacious demand for quantity of output continues to challenge series' producers who are perhaps too often ill-advised in being persuaded to make just one more run. Tony Garnett's famous refusal to make more runs of *This Life* is an exception to a trend which has seen *SatC* and perhaps *Shameless* and *Six Feet Under* extend themselves just a series too far. Such caveats apart, however, it is evident that a range of quality products has emerged in TV3. The range of those products illustrated in this book, wide though it is, marks just a part of interesting TV drama output. Though "American Quality TV" has had the higher profile, I would argue that UK output is equally wide-ranging and impressive without entirely abandoning elements of local/national/regional appeal in British television traditions.

Futures: upsides and downsides

Upsides

As the discussion above has intimated, there has been a complex interrelationship between economic values and aesthetic and cultural worth as advanced capitalism has developed. In the television industry – particularly in the UK, but with resonances worldwide – cultural value issues have typically been expressed in terms of a tension between public needs and commercial imperatives. In the substantially commercial world industry, the primary aim of commercial television companies remains that of making profits for shareholders. But, as argued and illustrated, this does not necessarily mean poor programming. Commercial forces can conspire to promote aesthetic values, and regulatory interventions may work to ensure provision where market failure might be insensitive to local cultural needs.

With HDTV, the image has significantly improved and, in a short time, the currently expensive apparatus for its reception will no doubt become widely affordable. Thus it would seem likely that visually arresting output will sustain its impact at the high end of TV drama. If market circumstances continue to privilege content in the competitive environment, an even broader range of more cinematic output would appear likely as creative people relish the production freedoms afforded. In the American context, world leader HBO Premium looks to consolidate its market position by producing shows with 'a strong, unique and creative vision'.[20] The American networks appear to be recognising that attractive niche audiences are drawn to quality product and, within regulatory constraints, they are following HBO's lead. In the UK context, a renewed BBC Charter and increased licence fee will ensure sustained public service and an effective digital changeover. Channel 4 may well become a second public service provider with free access to digital spectrum. ITV and a portion of Five will inevitably become increasingly commercial, though they will be drawn to improve quality in the competitive home context and possibly transnationally in the global market-place. To offset any tendency for the dominant terrestrials in the UK to foreclose on commissioning competition, the envisaged 25 per cent independent quota should serve to sustain at least the stronger independents and ensure a range of voices and visions are experienced on British television, assuming that they are on the right side of the digital divide in the first place. Many may be excluded from "high-end" access.

Downsides

In TV3, people's relationship with television and disposition to commerce is chang-ing rapidly. Subscription, or pay-per-view TV is increasingly accepted, particu-larly by the influential 18–34 age range – the audience of the future. Significant numbers of people already access television through broadband PC connections and the possibility of view-on-demand access through the internet to programmes, and libraries of past programmes, makes broadband the likely future distribution method for television. 'View-on-demand' capacities facilitated by broadband seem an attractive proposition to viewers whose leisure time is limited and who are increasingly confronted by an overwhelming choice of channels and programmes. Dominant computer and internet companies (e.g. Apple and Yahoo) have recently announced plans for content acquisition. Experiments in mobile television, viewed on cellphones, have demonstrated the potential for new, possibly additional, tele-vision markets. The big, open question for the industry concerns rights owner-ship of content in this context of media convergence and distribution proliferation. The big, open question for pundits of culture concerns the kinds of programming the context will yield. And the big, open question for viewers is will they be able to afford the increased cost of the cornucopia of television services.

In respect of industry funding, technologies (such as PVR and TIVO) which allow viewers completely to bypass advertisements threaten to destabilise a long-established relationship. In the short term, a diminution of income for television production is in tension with the disposition towards ever-more-expensive pro-duction values. Should advertisers ultimately decide that television is no longer a fruitful outlet for their purposes, revenues may dry up. By then, however, televi-sion distribution may have migrated to the other distribution platforms noted, to which advertisers will themselves turn. Where more direct subscriptions fund prod-uct, an increasing ambition may simply mean fewer, high-budget outcomes. Na-tional companies such as ITV may increasingly be drawn to product with transnational sales potential (such as *Dr Zhivago*) at the expense of the former commitment to regionality in the history of its component companies (notably Granada). By such means, local cultures are less well served. In a volatile commer-cial environment, it may well be advisable for countries such as the UK which have publicly funded provision not to abandon the PSB ethos and infrastructure. As noted in Chapter 3, however, the recent drift has been in the opposite direc-tion. As audiences have inevitably fragmented in a multichannel environment, the justifiability of a licence fee for PSB channels which many viewers no longer watch has increasingly been called in question. Thus what appears to be an envi-ronment of increased "personal choice" for the consumer of both platform and product may in fact constitute a significant diminution.

Whilst, in the current context, a wide range of services is available, there is a tendency to privilege the predominantly white, affluent segments of American society. The rise of Fox Television, as noted in Chapter 3, privileged youth culture by chasing the 18–24-year-old demographic. This had the contingent benefit of attracting black youth with its urban feel, but that segment was not its target. Showtime, and other cable–satellite suppliers, have filled a market niche in programming for the black communities but on effectively segregated channels. Diversity of programming may be currently assured but at the cost of any social exchange between cultures. The youth emphasis of Fox has been strongly influential in its use of popular music and the rapid pace of much contemporary television output. Though this impulse may be variously valued, from Poliakoff's point of view, a strong limbic pulse militates against reflective consideration of content. Similarly, the predisposition in the late 1990s towards the imagery of superficial lifestyles raises Postman's objection to pure spectacle in contrast with estimation elsewhere of a rich visual intensity. To judge by the 2006 Oscars, there is a current turn in cinema towards high concept, indeed social and political issues (in *Crash* and *Syriana*, for example) but fashions come and go. Since the money chases the taste formation of the attractive demographic, the breadth of a provision to meet the needs of all societies, groups and individuals cannot be assured.

Notes

1 This point was affirmed in a discussion on *Analysis: Yankee Doodle Dandy?* BBC Radio 4, at 21.30 on 16 July 2006.
2 For summary accounts of Pilkington and Peacock, see Hilmes, 2003 and Cooke, 2003.
3 The later Wittgenstein (1994, orig. 1953), on language usage, and Searle (1969), on 'speech acts' as performative utterances, established a basis for understanding, since much-developed, that we do things with words and that – since language is a shared, not a private, phenomenon – judgements are a matter of culture not simply of individual expression.
4 Corner outlined this idea in an unpublished keynote presentation to the *Screen* conference, University of Glasgow, July 2006.
5 Quotations are from ITV's booklet, *Your Pocket Guide to Our Brand*, distributed 2006.
6 It might be noted that *The Bill* is very popular in Australia, in part perhaps because of that country's historical connections with the UK. Thus audience "local" preferences may not always be contained within geographical boundaries.
7 The ratings discourse approach to television production in which series were commissioned in response to focus groups and appreciation indices defining market segments and desirable product perhaps bears out Adorno's worst fears in its suppression of innovation.
8 One of the downsides of a culture of individual consumerism is that it overlooks those without power. Much of the heavy industrial production which required a work ethic to sustain it has migrated to developing countries where cheap labour is available in highly oppressive working conditions.
9 As noted in Chapter 3, black perspectives and cultures have been aired on both Showtime and Fox Television but the first involves a dedicated channel and the latter addressed black issues somewhat by accident.
10 I am indebted to Sarah Cardwell for drawing my attention to this review in 'Patterns, layers and values: Poliakoff's *The Lost Prince*' (2006).
11 Poliakoff has lived all his life in London and his work is deeply embedded in the city. He frequently travels the city on public transport, partly as a means of gestating creative ideas

but he is also a very keen observer of change.

12 In respect of ratings, *The Lost Prince* achieved a significant audience, building to 8 million.

13 'Stephen Poliakoff – A Brief History of Now' (BBC4, 15 January 2006), shown prior to the first showing of *Friends and Crocodiles* (BBC1, 2006).

14 Poliakoff's Russian Jewish family escaped the aftermath of the Russian revolution, a historical landmark which Poliakoff's father witnessed in his pyjamas from an apartment near Red Square. Thus Poliakoff's personal and family history is deeply rooted in the great events of twentieth-century European history.

15 Poliakoff's first playscript, *Granny*, was produced when he was a pupil at Westminster School.

16 In an interview with Sarah Cardwell and Robin Nelson, 15 March 2005, Zilli Fish, Brewer Street, Soho, London.

17 Ellis acknowledges, of course, that there is nothing about the television medium to determine its predominant domestic use and also that much of the material shown on television is now prerecorded, as distinct from the early days when transmission was live. He is noting, rightly in my view, a residual disposition both on the part of viewers towards the medium and presentation within the medium which frequently uses a familiar, direct address. Ellis make the point that 'Transmission is live, even when the programmes are not' (2000: 31).

18 See www.bbc.co.uk/drama/lifeonmars/series2.shtml, accessed on 21 March 2006.

19 Jane Feuer in an unpublished keynote paper delivered at the American Quality Television Conference, Trinity College, Dublin, April 2005.

20 Simon Sutton, president of HBO International, gave this pledge at the Oxford Media Convention, 2006.

8

Singularity sustained
Blackpool, Casanova, State of Play

This final chapter considers three examples of recent British TV drama which reflect, notable strands in British television and develop them for new times. The first, *Blackpool* (BBC1, 2004), uses the device of popular songs both lip-synched and sung by the characters, as made famous by Dennis Potter. Like Potter, writer Peter Bowker uses pop music not only for its intrinsic attractions but also to add density to the drama, with lyrics commenting upon the action and inviting comparative reflection on the different characters' perspectives. The second example, *Casanova* (Red Productions with BBC Wales for BBC3), lies in the tradition of historical or period drama in that it evokes the life of a famous historical figure and a visually attractive Venetian setting. Though the production is rich in colour, the manner of the retelling of Casanova's life resists the period drama's typical inclination accurately to reconstruct historic costumes and locations in bourgeois, materialist sumptuousness. Instead it avoids the "heritage" or "bonnet" drama cachet by mixing a modern treatment with historic aspects. As Nicola Shindler remarked, 'We have never made a period drama before and intend to bring our key Red sensibilities – quality of script, cast, an innovative visual design and photography – to the project. As with all Red's work we hope to make *Casanova* provocative, funny and ground-breaking.'[1] Rather than foster illusionism, *Casanova* self-consciously winks at the audience (literally in the case of the young Casanova, David Tennant) and uses a range of contemporary music tracks to draw attention to modern perspectives on historical material.

The final example, *State of Play* (BBC1, 2003), is a political thriller taking forward the British tradition of drama which addresses contemporary issues and is not afraid to critique the current political milieu. The form of such TV drama historically has varied from hard-hitting documentary realism (*Cathy Come Home* and *Days of Hope* through to *Cops*) to more popular sociopolitical drama (*Boys from the Blackstuff*). Though it has a distinctly New Labour *mise-en-scène* to suit its topic, *State of Play*'s lineage might include *Between the Lines* and *Edge of Darkness* in its capacity to expose the dark intricacies of a political labyrinth in a compelling narrative.

Though each drama is distinctive, there are some links between them in terms of the personnel involved. David Morrissey is a central figure in *Blackpool* and *State of Play* whilst David Tennant figures centrally in both *Blackpool* and *Casanova*. Indeed, a new breed of outstanding British actors has emerged in the past decade, many retaining accents from the northern regions in which British realism is traditionally located. John Simm is central to *State of Play*, which also features Phil Glenister. Together they are the leads in *Life on Mars*, whilst both Morrissey and Simm feature in *Clocking Off*, both series being set in Manchester. The writers, Peter Bowker, Russell T. Davies and Paul Abbott (for *Blackpool*, *Casanova* and *State of Play* respectively), are also all associated with Manchester and with Nicola Shindler's Red Productions (see Chapter 3). Besides being a lead actor in *Blackpool*, Sarah Parish also stars in *Cutting It*, a series written by Debbie Horsfield and set in a Manchester hairdressers' whilst, before *Blackpool*, John Thomson was part of the ensemble in the earlier Manchester-based series, *Cold Feet*. Though, of my three examples, only *Blackpool* is fully located in the North-West – Manchester featuring just marginally in *State of Play* – the writers all convey non-mainstream and/or regional sensibilities and perspectives. Together they represent a loose repertory of writers, producers and performers who are responsible for a substantial body of recent British TV drama work which, though it refuses the clichés of the grimy industrial north, is concerned with the lives and experiences of ordinary people outside of London.[2] Though the heydays of BBC English Regions Drama at Pebble Mill and Granada's specific regional remit in the North-West had run their course by the early 1980s, a mode of British regional drama has sustained itself by drawing on its roots but moving on.[3]

Blackpool

Blackpool is an energetic hybrid, part romance, part murder mystery, part musical with shades of a western. In some respects it resembles a classic narrative of over-reaching enterprise turning to failure, since it traces the attempt of Ripley Holden (David Morrissey) to make it big by turning Blackpool into Las Vegas. It recounts his attempt to convert his amusement arcade on the sea front into a casino hotel. Ripley cuts a brash figure, part Elvis and part cowboy. His daywear is dark suits with waistcoats and bootlace ties. For celebratory events, such as the party announcing his business plans with which the first episode opens, he wears a white suit with black shirt and gold tie. The Holden family – wife Natalie (Sarah Parish), daughter Shyanne (Georgia Taylor) and son Danny (Thomas Morrison) are separately seen singing along with Ripley to the strains of Elvis's 'Viva Las Vegas' as they dress for the occasion.

The image of the family in harmony as together they descend the steps of the family home, 'Shangri-la', to take Holden's white American limousine to the Lucky Star Arcade, is destined to be tarnished as the series progresses. But, initially, the family stands for a collective upbeat energy. In a speech from the arcade balcony, Holden advocates 'abandonment to pleasure', characterising amusements arcades as 'the people's stock exchange' and making passing reference to popular television quiz shows with big money prizes such as *Who Wants to be a Millionaire* and *The Weakest Link*. Ripley tells his friends, 'We're living in a leisure economy: we gamble and we can't lose' (Episode 2). He speaks 'in praise of venture capital' and invites his guests to 'live the dream' with him. Following a choreographed dance to 'You can get it if you really want', Holden leads a rhythmic conga through the arcade to the strains of 'Win or lose you've got to get your share'. This opening sequence sets up a dialectic tension to be played out in *Blackpool* between its advocacy of a high-energy popular culture of an individualist, "get rich quick" self-assertion and a critique of that culture, an exposé of its colourful delusions.

Blackpool is itself noted as something of a fun-palace which attracted large numbers of working-class holiday-makers prior to the emergence of cheap package holidays to Spain and elsewhere. Indeed, as a boy, writer Pete Bowker was amongst them. As he relates, 'My first eleven holidays were spent in Blackpool. We'd go for a week in August and again for three days for the illuminations, so I felt that I knew Blackpool well. As anybody will tell you who has been there, it is unlike anywhere else in Britain.'[4] Always a site for carnivalesque masquerades and inversions, Blackpool has faded since its heyday but strives to sustain an ethos of unrestrained enjoyments.[5] Thus it is an ideal location for a colourful, comic-book *mise-en-scène* which *Blackpool* designer Grenville Horner exploits to the full. The Lucky Star Amusement Arcade is a blaze of red and yellow amongst the promenade's dynamic neon frontages. Inside, the lights on the multicoloured fruit machines flash incessantly and make a range of whooping noises against the clatter of coins falling into a lucky winner's hands. Ripley's office, raised above the games hall floor, is accessed by mock-Georgian stairs up to a balcony decorated with golden insignia. The door to the spacious office is padded gold. Though far removed in its colourfulness from gritty Northern realism, the seedier side of Blackpool is also contrastingly revealed in the large run-down Victorian houses converted into flats, one of which is owned by the Holden family and is a home to prostitutes and drug-dealers. When in need of ready cash, Ripley has no qualms about summarily evicting his tenants, throwing their few belongings on to the street. When questioned by his friends, he points out that he is 'driving the economic recovery round here' (Episode 1).

Indeed, Ripley Holden's discourse marks him as a conservative (if not a Thatcherite Conservative), full of prejudices, with a chip on his shoulder about being done down. He particularly despises gays and immigrants and has no time for losers and suggests 'This country's gone soft on criminals' (Episode 4). When advising his son how to escape from a brush with the law, he remarks that, if the worst comes to the worst, 'We can black you up, call you Ali and take you to the

European Court of Human Rights' (Episode 2). In Ripley, Bowker has constructed a character designed to elicit complex and conflicting responses from viewers. The upbeat Ripley Holden – in an all-singing, all-dancing, but superbly nuanced performance by Morissey – is quick-witted, with a ready answer for every situation and a sharp, if politically incorrect, turn of phrase. When his friend Terry has donned a new shirt for a date, Ripley remarks that he looks 'like a badly wrapped toffee apple' (Episode 2). But his favoured metaphors are sexual and, in explaining that he has no interest in Terry's girlfriend even after her 'boob job', Ripley observes that 'you don't want to drive an old transit just cos it's got new headlamps' (Episode 3). Thus, though his dynamism and self-confidence might draw viewers to him, they might equally be alienated by his casual racism and misogyny, his neglect of – and unfaithfulness to – his wife, and his violent abuse of even his friends. Ripley Holden's character is itself part of the dialectic that Bowker sets in tension. Bowker is aware that he created a character like Blackpool itself, as he puts it, a 'larger-than-life, slightly monstrous individual who the audience would end up liking'. Another dimension of Ripley Holden is revealed in glimpses of his harsh upbringing by a domineering, bible-bashing father, which accounts both for his ability to quote passages from scripture and his attempted suicide as a teenager. As he tells Danny who later makes a similar suicide attempt by lying down on the railway lines, 'When I was your age, I was the loneliest bastard on the planet' (Episode 1).

The major story arc of *Blackpool* follows the trajectory of Ripley Holden's rise and fall. Though more a Brechtian anti-hero than a Shakespearian tragic figure, Ripley, as we shall see, cuts a more likeable, though not unambiguously admirable, figure in his fall. But there are other popular story arcs in *Blackpool* involving romances, those of Holden's daughter, Shyanne, and of his wife, Natalie. Shyanne falls for theatre manager, Steve who, it turns out, went to school with Ripley and was unwarrantably bullied by him. Holden, who seems to ridicule all Shyanne's boyfriends, particularly resents her taking up with a man literally old enough to be her father. Shyanne holds her resolve, however, in spite of her family's attempts to dissuade her from Steve and Steve from her. Their union ultimately receives Ripley's blessing and he even pays for the wedding party on the pier with which the series ends in Episode 6. As Shyanne takes up with Steve, so her mother, also perhaps inappropriately, takes up with Peter Carlisle who, initially unbeknown to her, is the detective investigating her husband and son – the dead body of a young man has mysteriously been found early one morning dumped in the Lucky Star Amusement Arcade and some circumstantial evidence points to the involvement of both Ripley and Danny. DI Peter Carlisle (David Tennant) has been drafted in with his associate, DC Blythe (Bryan Dick), to investigate. Carlisle apparently falls in love on first meeting with Natalie. She soon appears to reciprocate and they have an affair. At a location noted for its front in every sense, it is fitting, however, that they both at times feel that they are being used by the other. First, when she discovers his police identity, Natalie believes that Carlisle has only seduced her to find out more about Ripley and Danny. Near the end, Natalie decides to stay with Ripley, and Carlisle accuses her of using him. The final outcome is part of a set of ultimate reversals of fortune in a series concerned more with luck than with destiny.

The character of Carlisle adds much to the offbeat humour of *Blackpool*. Paying homage to the quirks of *Columbo*, Tennant's DI Carlisle approaches the investigation indirectly with a casual disregard for police procedure or convention. He takes up with Natalie, for example, with no concern for the implications of the relationship for the case. In his scruffy mackintosh and open-neck shirt, he strolls along the promenade indulging his penchant for sweetmeats by eating candyfloss or an ice cream, doing apparently little. Eating appears to be a prime concern for Carlisle and, when trying to commiserate with him over the lack of progress in the investigation, Blythe appeases him by relating that he has got him 'a doughnut, pink icing, hundreds and thousands' (Episode 4). When he does interview suspects, the mates of the dead man or Blackpool's working girls, he chooses unconventional locations (e.g. Blackpool Tower's ballroom) and he orders plates of assorted fancy cakes with tea. He tells one of the prostitutes that she is a 'service industry worker, just like [him]' (Episode 2). Carlisle's disregard of establishment conventions runs to him dropping fish and chips' wrapping paper and plastic cups in the street when he has finished with them. However, like Ripley, Carlisle is more than his surface appearance. He speaks in florid terms not typically associated with television DIs, instructing Blythe, for example, to 'go and avail [him]self of the refreshments on offer' (Episode 6) and, gnomically advising ill-digested Ruth on giving her a packet of mints in the arcade, 'Never leave home without antacids: keep those, I'm taking kaolin and morphine on a trial basis' (Episode 1). On occasion he betrays literary leanings alongside his quirky everydayness, remarking, for example, 'a paradox that Wittgenstein would have a lot to say about' (Episode 3) and observing that 'if Proust had drunk McEwan's, he'd have written about moments like that' (Episode 4). He is also aware of American TV cops' conventions, remarking to Blythe that, 'to use the American vernacular, we're gonna nail Ripley Holden's sad ass' (Episode 4).

In the mock-western structure of *Blackpool*, Holden and Carlisle are pitted against each other as reflected in the windows of the slot machines which serve throughout as a motif showing the two antagonists in various conflictual guises. Carlisle purports to suspect Holden of the murder of the young man found in his arcade, though his belief in this theory is never absolute, and he uses an additional overt suspicion of Danny to get at Holden. Although Holden does not know it until late on in the series, Carlisle is also a rival to him for Natalie's affections. The self-conscious mix of Western and doppelganger cops'n'robbers conventions is brought out, beyond the plot and the slot machine imagery, in the soundtrack and the musical numbers. The soundtrack features a bass guitar twang redolent of spaghetti westerns. The song 'Walk tall' at the start of Episode 4, juxtaposes Danny, Ripley, Carlisle and Natalie in a collage of images which evoke their complex interrelationships. The line 'fell in with a bad crowd, laughed and drank with them' might apply equally to Danny and his father, whilst the conflict between

Holden and Carlisle is pointed up by Danny's remark to end the sequence, 'They're coming after you dad!', evoking a dramatically contrived head-to-head conflict. The trope is sustained with Carlisle unexpectedly appearing at significant moments in the Holdens' lives, and by long stares through café windows between Carlisle and both Ripley and Danny, as if from a saloon in a western.

The resolution to this central conflict comes only in the final episode and with a number of reversals in expectations and fortunes. Since Natalie and Peter Carlisle have found love in Episodes 4 and 5 and Carlisle has withdrawn from the murder investigation in the hope of living a utopian life elsewhere with her, one inferential walk through the narrative would see a happy romance ending and Ripley Holden bringing his Las-Vegas-style casino hotel dreams to fruition. But Holden's star is already on the wane. He has spent all he has borrowed on the Lucky Star Arcade, the tax man has finally caught up with him and the showdown is not with Carlisle but with accountant Adrian Marr (Steve Pemberton). When Marr informs Ripley that he has lost everything and should sell him the arcade for a token twenty pounds, Ripley retrieves twenty grand in cash from a false ceiling and, to the soundtrack of 'Having a Good Time' by Queen, he puts it all on green at the adjacent casino roulette wheel and loses. Returning home, he finds Natalie has packed an overnight bag ready to leave. He phones Natalie at the Samaritans, where ironically she works, and, in a speech which appears to be a moment of recognition in tragic reversal, he berates her for betraying him. She thinks he is talking of her affair with Carlisle but it turns out that he is speaking of the flats which she has put in trust for the children beyond his reach. Ripley returns to the arcade and throws everybody out, shouting 'We're shut: the dream's over' (Episode 5). He appears anguished that he cannot repeat the three bars on the fruit machine which at an earlier crisis moment in his life had caused him to trust in luck. To the soundtrack of 'Knock, knock, who's there?' and the now ironic refrain, 'It's Elvis calling', he evicts his tenants and burns down the block of flats entirely.

But Episode 6 opens a week later at Shyanne's wedding to the song, 'Hey little sister, nice day to start again' (from 'White Wedding'). Ripley appears to have recognised that you 'can't live on dreams' (Episode 6). The song, 'There goes my everything' with the lines, 'there goes the one of my dreams' and 'there goes my only possession' might read differently when related to the different characters but, to Ripley, it might with some irony connote both his wife and his casino. A big production number on the pier of 'Don't leave me this way' appears to bring the conflict over Natalie to a head as Ripley thinks that she is going, but Natalie has already told Carlisle that she cannot leave him.

Carlisle, reinstated to investigate alleged fraud at the Lucky Star, arrives with Blythe to arrest Ripley Holden on suspicion of murder. But Holden points out to Carlisle that the case won't stick when it comes out that the DI has seduced the accused's wife. To the disgust of Blythe, they shake hands on a deal. But Marr, the accountant, is arrested since he has been cooking Holden's books to his own advantage. In a somewhat sentimental denouement in a wedding speech, Ripley gives Shyanne and Steve his blessing, half accepts his son's recent revelation that he is gay and ultimately ends up by giving Danny the casino to pursue his vision of turning it into a modern dance venue with a café-bar. Further, Ripley tells Natalie that she should go with Carlisle since he has realised that she truly loves him. Though Ripley himself still cares for her, he finally puts her interests, like those of his children, above his own. The final sequence sees him walking alone along Blackpool's promenade but the end credits dissolve into a compound image of Blackpool–Las Vegas over which Ripley smilingly presides to the tune of Sandy Shaw's 'Always something there to remind me', as if it were better to have dreamed/loved and lost than never to have dreamed/loved at all.

In many ways, *Blackpool* is a moral tale of hubris in a poor man's aspirations. A moral–biblical strain runs throughout *Blackpool* from the Anti-Gambling Alliance representative, Hallworth (David Bradley), who stands watch outside the Lucky Star eighteen hours per day and with whom Ripley occasionally chats and exchanges bible quotations. There is a refrain through the series about doing the right or wrong thing which begins with Ripley illustrating to his son that 'the right decision is the one that makes you a winner' (Episode 2). It is echoed by Carlisle who suggests to Natalie in the supermarket that it is high time 'you and me should do the wrong thing' (Episode 2). In a conversation at the end of the episode, Hallworth suggests that Ripley should show a little 'humility'. Ripley responds by burning a £20 note. The refrain overtly concludes at the end of Episode 5 in the casino when, staking all, Ripley affirms that he does not 'believe in God any more, just luck', and he loses.

Just as some rock'n'roll songs feature the dangers of a rags-to-riches to rags narrative, so the main narrative arc of *Blackpool* gives full rein to Ripley Holden's energy and ambition, only to see it all fall apart in order for him apparently to recognise that love and family are more important than the perhaps-false glister of gold. The political theme evoking the 'loads of money' culture of the Thatcherite 1990s picks up on the moral debate above but is just lightly etched in the series, as noted above. When accountant Marr is arrested for fraud, Holden shouts after him, 'I suppose that's what Margaret Thatcher meant when she said entrepreneurs were special people' (Episode 6). This is the last of several such explicit references in the series to the monetarist prime minister who promoted a consumer individualism in Britain to match that of Reagan's America. Thus, though it is primarily a dynamic, colourful, musically driven entertainment, *Blackpool* gently provokes thought on aspects of contemporary culture.

The audience for *Blackpool* was a respectable 4–5 million in the UK and it was shown abroad on Australia's ABC and Television New Zealand's TV One and on the BBC America cable channel. In 2005, it won the 'Best Miniseries' at the British Academy Television Awards, having also been nominated for "Best Drama Serial" category, and it took the 'Grand Prize' award at the Banff Televison Festival in Canada. In December 2005 it was nominated (under its American title *Viva Blackpool*) for the 'Best Made for TV Mini-Series' category at the 2006 Golden Globe Awards. Viewer response on the BBC website strongly reflected respondents associating with the North-West of England. Harry Webb, who signs himself 'Exiled in Worthing', writes, ' The series has a special appeal to me being a Lancashire lad spending much of my youth in Blackpool, even living close by in my twenties. It evoked some strong emotions and revived some great memories.'

From a wealth of letters in praise of the writing, the characterisation, the acting, the use of song and the twists of the plot, Maria from Birmingham makes the case for the distinction of this kind of TV drama. She acclaims:

> What a piece of work. Bold and brilliant. Television's come of age – only that medium could have given us this work. Superb performances – can't think of one fault – excellent casting. And David Morrissey is an extraordinary actor, such range such depth. Visionary stuff from the writer, director, production team, and everyone else involved in getting this on air. Well done to those who commissioned it.
>
> Please let's have more of this artistically driven work instead of the predictable Holby and the rest. Too many good people and too much money [is] wasted on background noise/pictures pretending to be drama. Give us something which unsettles and provokes, makes us actively watch the TV screen.[6]

Casanova

Casanova begins as a picaresque romp, a rollercoaster ride tracing the rise and fall and rise again of the sex life of Giacomo Casanova de Seingalt but, not unlike writer Russell T. Davies's drama of gay life, *Queer as Folk*, it develops into a tale of unconsummated, enduring love. At the outset, it announces its intentions to be bathetic, to undercut, that is, the pomp of Venice with a comic earthiness, redolent of the carnivalesque. Grand music at the opening leads the camera towards a grand edifice on the Grand Canal, only for the glass doors to explode as young Casanova (David Tennant) makes a swift exit. He whistles for his horse and jumps from the balcony to ride away. But he misses the horse, mouths 'bollocks' (Episode 1) and makes a run for it. A comic chase ensues on foot across the small canal bridges and back. Eventually Casanova is cornered but leaps into a gondola, knocking the gondolier into the canal, and tries to blag his way out of the situation. Sheree Folkson's directorial treatment in *Casanova* employs a range of camera movements (whip-pans, crash-zooms and 360-degree rotations) which create a visual dynamic as developed in MTV and FOX television's youth programming. David Tennant's direct address to camera appears self-referentially to step out of the young Casanova role and knowingly to acknowledge, in a now-characteristic postmodern trope, the textuality of *Casanova*.

To offset this dynamic energy and afford some shade against a mock-eighteenth-century Venice's brightness, *Casanova* offers a retrospective view of the legendary seducer's life from the point of view of the Chevalier de Seingalt in old age (Peter O'Toole playing the old Casanova), confined as librarian in a benefactor's castle where his reputation is unknown or forgotten and he is largely ignored, even mistreated. However, Edith (Rose Byrne), the nubile daughter of the

Burgomaister of Saint Valencia, is forced through straitened family circumstances to take a job as a servant in the house. She recognises something special in Casanova and, when she discovers his identity, becomes intrigued about his life. On this pretext, escapades are related of the young Casanova and the three-part series cuts to a past depicted in the present with the young, impoverished Casanova trying to make his way in the wealthy and highly stratified culture of Venice. Though in a different way from *Blackpool*, *Casanova* is also concerned with surface pretence and tensions between pleasure and morality in a culture of indulgence. Edith's prim but curious nature is by turns repelled and drawn into the tales of Casanova's sexual pursuits. Old Casanova shocks her by suggesting that, knowing his reputation, she could only have visited him alone in the hope of sexual experience. Thus a frisson is established in the library between old roué and young virgin. To Edith, old Casanova's lack of repentance and refusal to believe in an afterlife is blasphemous and thus the pleasure of sexual licence is pitted against bourgeois morality.

As *Casanova* tells it, the juvenile Casanova is the neglected son of an actress who flees to the court at St Petersburg in search of a better life. He is only awakened from a mute frailty by a sexual encounter whilst in care. Following an education as a scholar-priest, he leaves Padua in disgrace to seek his fortune in Venice, 'a city that devours the weak' (Episode 1). The story, part-narrated by the old Casanova and part- enacted by the young, proceeds apace and is even literally animated by special effects to dress Tennant in fine clothes. Finding himself in Venice penniless, apart from his fine clothes, and spurned by high society as a commoner not worth consideration, Casanova is forced to resort to stratagem. Advised by a young noblewoman Henriette (Laura Fraser), to whom he is attracted on a chance meeting, that 'they're all pretending ... just lie with conviction' (Episode 1), Casanova realises that success in Venice is all about the conviction of confidence, of style over substance.

Setting up on Quattrigatti Street (at the back, on the corner, five floors up) with his black manservant Rocco, he holds his chin up as instructed and pretends. He pretends first to be a lawyer, then a doctor, and finally an astrologer. Not only are the wealthy to whom he offers his services taken in, the ploy actually works and he wins the legal case, cures an old woman of a bad foot, and correctly predicts the fortune of another, who, with a young man on her arm, thanks him for 'predicting that a lion would rise up in the Winter solstice and capture [her] heart' (Episode 1). But though he cons his way into society, makes money and even becomes something of a celebrity, Casanova's existence is precarious, partly because he has been drawn into conflict with Duke Grimani (Rupert Penry-Jones) who is engaged to Henriette Marie-Anne d'Albertas. A rivalry, centred in class, wealth and love, is set up and outdoes that between Holden and Carlisle in *Blackpool*.

Cutting back to the library, old Casanova titillates and offends Edith by cataloguing his sexual exploits in graphic detail which is conveyed televisually in a fast-cut collage of encounters in a range of sexual positions. The story of Bellino (Nina Sosanya), a castrato singer, is recounted more fully and affords visually colourful scenes appropriate to a period drama. In some indulgent scenes in Episode 1 (involving Matt Lucas of *Little Britain* fame as the outrageously gay 'kitten'. Villar), Bellino's true gender is called in question. For a wager, Casanova seeks to establish the truth and attests Bellino to be male, in spite of his strong attraction to him. Told by Henriette that he is a coward if he loves Bellino and will not follow his instincts, Casanova beds Bellino only to discover 'he' is actually female. The lovers agree to marry and throw a lavish party which affords the opportunity for a ballroom scene with fine costumes and period dancing. But this is undercut when, feeling uncomfortable if not fraudulent in this company, Bellina and Casanova tear their clothes and re-present themselves to the party dishevelled. After a moment's awkward pause, the company applauds their audacity and the celebrations continue. But observing Casanova in mimed conversation across the room with Henriette, Bellina realises that Henriette is Casanova's real love. In recompense for all the kindnesses he has done her, Bellina sets Casanova up to dance with Henriette. The sequence cuts back to the library where old Casanova in close-up stares with watery eyes into the middle distance. Amidst all the pretence, show and sexual romps, love apparently has a greater worth.

In Episode 2, it emerges, after they escape the party and dance together in a Venetian piazza to a musical box soundtrack, that Giacomo's love for Henriette is reciprocated. But Henriette will not leave Grimani because his wealth and position affords security. As she says to Giacomo, 'You're making it up as you go along … Grimani knows what he's doing every day of his life' (Episode 2). When Giacomo questions, 'Is it all about money?', Henriette replies, 'Yes, it is' (Episode 2). Though she acknowledges that she loves Giacomo completely, she leads him through the slum backstreets of Venice from whence she emerged by way of explaining to him why she needs Grimani.

As a cold wind blows across Venice, Casanova attends confession prior to setting about getting rich. The confession comically piles sin upon peccadillo upon sin until the priest finally collapses in shock. This event ironically transpires to be Casanova's salvation, since he gets the priest home, saves him from his doctors and, by loving care, restores him to health. So grateful is the priest that he bestows the heritage of the Bragadin family on Giacomo, observing, because he has no successors, 'I have found a son in you. None more deserving' (Episode 2). With inherited wealth and a title, Casanova is in a position to propose to Henrietta, who accepts and breaks off with Grimani. A celebration is arranged and a happy ending anticipated. Cutting back to the library, however, old Casanova cautions Edith about the formulaic codes and conventions of romance. 'Girls your age with no experience like to think all ends well' (Episode 2). And, indeed, in another violent reversal of fortunes, Grimani has Casanova arrested on a series of trumped-up allegations of treason against the state, and he is summarily found guilty and imprisoned.

Escaping from prison when he learns that the marriage of Henriette and Grimani is to go ahead, Casanova flees the city and sets off on another set of picaresque adventures to seek pardon from one of the European ambassadors to

Venice. This time, he is accompanied not only by his sidekick Rocco Scappino but also by young Jack, his son by one of the nuns he seduced. The young boy is sullenly mute like his father before him on the journey to Paris. The court of France affords another occasion of display as Casanova arrives to a colourful whirl of corals and mauves, silver–greys and pale blues at a court ball where he once again encounters Bellina, who herself has a small daughter. Casanova introduces the lottery to the court with many anachronistic references to the contemporary English lottery such as 'You've got to be in it to win it'. For a brief time Casanova is a success, but when young Jack is finally moved to smile on witnessing a gruesome execution at the start of the French Revolution, things begin to fall apart. Casanova loses a fortune at cards and they are soon on the move again to the English court of George II.

At the port of Dover, Casanova glimpses Henrietta, only to see her sail off to France with her two children. The journey to the English court affords the opportunity for more contemporary jokes: 'all the carriages are clean and punctual and fast and safe' but 'the schools aren't up to scratch' (Episode 3). Reaching the English court, Casanova is alerted by a flunkey that the court is a bit racey, and he opens the doors on a sedate tea party. He remarks that some men are 'wearing breeches cut just above the knee' and that some of the ladies have the audacity to 'drink tea with lemon'. But the real shock for Casanova is that Grimani has become Venice's English ambassador. Warning him that his old tricks will not wash in England, Grimani throws Casanova out. But, the old rivalry rekindled, Giacomo is determined to prove Grimani wrong. Needing money and reflecting on what he is good at, he realises that he's 'become famous simply for being outrageous' (Episode 3), so he sets up house outrageously and is soon the talk of London and on close terms with King George. Angered at his rival's nerve, Grimani contrives a duel which turns into a conversation about the love they both have for Henriette. Casanova realises that Henriette has left Grimani because she does not love him but the new insight is that Grimani, despite appearances, does actually love her. Thus the doppelganger rivalry is played out and Giacomo refuses to fight the duel. Grimani, in tears, shoots at Casanova, wounding him in the hand but, worse, pointing out that he is now a fugitive since he has fought an illegal duel on City of London territory, an offence punishable by death.

Fleeing again, Casanova finds himself seriously ill from the wound and dumped penniless in Saxony with Rocco and young Jack. All seems lost but, in another picaresque reversal, rescue arrives in the form of a matronly nurse who takes them to a large mansion and restores Giacomo's health. As she leaves, the hand of Henrietta is glimpsed in the departing carriage and Giacomo realises that, though she will not leave her children, she still loves him and is looking out for him. Rocco is not so lucky. As they travel on towards Naples, he dies of a common cold. The court of Naples is depicted as a cocaine-snorting cross between punk and gothic, presided over, as chance would have it, by Bellina and her now-grown-up daughter, Leonilda, who takes a shine to the-now grown-up Jack. When Leonilda leads Jack away to entertain him, Bellina reveals that she is Giacomo's daughter.

The prospective incest between his son and daughter proves a sexual encounter too far for 'the man who would try anything' (Episode 3) and Giacomo tries unsuccessfully to intervene. At this point *Casanova* cuts back to the library and a sentimental denouement.

At the end of Episode 2, Edith astounds old Casanova by revealing her knowledge that Henriette was still alive the previous year at the end of 'the dissolution of Venice on 12 May'. Excited at the prospect that they might meet again before he dies, old Casanova has written to her and is anxiously awaiting a response. He engages in the last of a series of seductive conversations with Edith in which he remains aware of her sexuality and her interest in him. Momentarily she appears at last to succumb to his charms, as if doubling for the youthful Henriette many years ago. Though she is offended by old Casanova's presumptions, Edith nevertheless tries to prevent him from burning his diaries as they are, in her view, 'the one thing that tells the truth' (Episode 3). Now very weak and near to death, old Casanova takes to his bed and, when a letter arrives for him, it is not immediately delivered as he had instructed. Eventually, Edith finds it and brings it, though, having read it, she is in a quandary as to whether to reveal its contents which relate that Henriette died just six months previously. Edith burns the letter but, as old Casanova fades, she relates to him the letter's report that Henriette 'never stopped loving [him]' and, in an act of kindness, she also lies to him, saying that Henriette sent her, Edith, to the castle to look after him. Thus the old roué dies with a smile on his lips, remembering not sexual conquest but enduring, unrequited love.

As is evident in the above account, the picaresque narrative of *Casanova* is somewhat protracted as if filling in sufficient historic time to cover Casanova's lifespan and sufficient episode time to lead into old Casanova's death. Thus some sequences seem a bit contrived and there is insufficient variation with regard to the experiences of the roué and social outcast to afford development. Furthermore, the picaresque turns in fortune, though they may be motivated behind the scenes by Henriette, appear somewhat gratuitous when they happen. Thus, although Russell T. Davies's reworking shows more of Casanova's character than the mere stereotype of a rampant ram and reveals him, beyond his addiction to pleasures of the flesh, genuinely to have loved Henriette, it does not afford the insights into psyche of, for example, Dennis Potter's (1971) TV drama treatment.

In Tennant's energetic performance, however, Casanova is an engaging character and the modern language and use of popular music references in the soundtrack consciously invite a perspective through twenty-first-century eyes. For *Casanova*, the BBC unusually targeted a youth demographic for what appeared otherwise to be a period or costume drama, usually associated with an ageing middle-class taste formation. As Steve Brie points out:

> One of the ways in which this audience was courted was via the use of music both within the dramatic narrative and as an aural accompaniment to the promotional teasers which the BBC ran both in the weeks leading up to the transmission of the first episode, and in the intervening weeks between episodes. These promotional teasers featured a selection of rapidly cut sequences of the most provocative and

exciting moments from the three-hour serial. Perhaps the most interesting aspect of these montage sequences was the way in which they were cut to the Sid Vicious punk version of *My Way*.[7]

Davies and the BBC were clearly signalling a treatment defying expectations. As an experiment in costume drama, *Casanova*, besides its eclectically sampled soundtrack, is also visually colourful and inventive, particularly in the Naples court scene which brings the series into the modern age in its sexual licence as much as in its punk visual references. The treatment overall – which perhaps most echoes in the period drama genre Andrew Davies's television adaptation of *Moll Flanders* – points to the potential of new, dynamic, multilayered approaches for a younger audience than is typical for period drama. But, in my judgement, it does not ultimately exploit them to full effect.

State of Play

If *Casanova* is ultimately an interesting but flawed experiment in an established form, *State of Play* is a consummate political thriller, sustaining something of the political critique associated with the British social realist tradition but produced with a multi-layered narrative complexity and contemporary visual stylishness. As indicated in its title, *State of Play* offers a snapshot of contemporary British life, not quite in the nineteenth-century sociological novel tradition attempting to adumbrate an entire society in all its complex relations, but certainly suggesting interconnections and parallels between worlds which are superficially disparate. It moves between the domains of marginalised urban black communities, big business (multinational oil companies), the middle-class environs of the London editorial office of a newspaper (something like *The Guardian*), leafy Manchester suburbs where the drama of a family break-up is played out, and the inner sanctums of the Houses of Parliament. Where the controlling discourse of a classic realist narrative tends towards moral closure by drawing together the strands, the variety of perspectives brought from the different viewpoints of these locations in *State of Play* are left open. The thriller plot is finally unravelled and tied up, but the murkiness of the worlds revealed in the process is not dispelled and thus its oblique commentary on the politics and ethics of the New Labour government and the Britain it has fostered continues to resonate.

Generically, *State of Play* is primarily a whodunnnit?, a political thriller addressing the mysterious death of a young woman, Sonia Baker, under a tube train in London's morning rush hour. But the exploration of the initial enigma, 'Did she jump or was she pushed?', leads into a web of deceit and double-bluff on several fronts. The mystery aspect drives the narrative and, very skilfully handled by writer Paul Abbott and director David Yates, is compelling. But, like so many examples of contemporary TV drama in this book, *State of Play* blurs generic boundaries and offers viewers a range of ways into a complex drama with elements of soap in romance and love affairs, aspects of exposé and critique of both transnational business and domestic politics. Above all, it blurs fact and fiction, taking the temperature of the times in terms of its dominant metaphor of the seat of government depicted as a world dominated by spin and a lack of sincerity, by a dislocation of sign from referent, of rhetoric from reality. A central irony of *State of Play*, however, is that the young investigative journalists, contrary to a dominant discourse of media bias and the somewhat arbitrary construction of news, doggedly pursue the truth. Their methods may be unorthodox, even deceitful at times, but they tenaciously follow the trails of the evidence to get to the heart of the matter, even to their own detriment.

The plot is complex and, to summarise just Episode 1 cannot convey the dramatic and emotional rollercoaster ride experienced in viewing, as the plot revelations and reversals twist and turn in surprising ways. Sonia, the young woman who has died, was the research assistant of the bright, young New Labour MP for Oldham, Stephen Collins (David Morrissey). It emerges, however, that Stephen and Sonia had been lovers for some time and that he had even indicated that he would leave his wife and children living in the Manchester family home for her. Stephen had been with Sonia the night before her death and, by his report, she showed no signs of distress such as might indicate suicide; indeed, she appeared happy. Although Stephen is shocked and upset by the news of her death, he has to assume that it was an accident since he has no apparent reason to suspect any foul play.

Cal McCaffrey (John Simm) has been a friend to Stephen Collins since he worked as his campaign manager at the time of the parliamentary election (assumed to be 1997 when a tide of young New Labour MPs was elected to the House of Commons). Now working as an investigative journalist for a London newspaper, Cal is initially not interested in the Sonia Baker story and even tries to protect Stephen. In response to front-page photographs of Collins in distress, Cal's wonderfully ironic editor, Cameron Foster (Bill Nighy), adopts an East London demotic to suggest, 'Eever he's fakin' it or he was nobbin' her',[8] and proposes to pursue the story. Unconvinced and resistant, Cal even asks, 'Did we shrink the format of the paper while I was away?' It is in such apparently innocuous bits of dialogue that Abbott mobilises the socio-political themes which resonate throughout *State of Play*, this one concerning the relative merits of the serious and tabloid press.[9] Cal is assigned to the 'drugs thing' which appears to be a standard London news story, though it turns out otherwise.

In another layer of the palimpsest that is *State of Play* a young black man, Kelvin Stagg, is professionally shot dead at close range in a backstreet of London. A motor-cycle courier is also found shot nearby. The police and press assume that the killings are drugs-related but, when Cal investigates, the Stagg family members, though acknowledging that Kelvin is a bag snatcher, are adamant that he did not deal in drugs. They mention a metal case, like a camera case, about which Kelvin seemed anxious. Information from a forensic laboratory contact known to Cal confirms that no traces of illegal drugs were found in Kelvin's body. But, by chance when checking out Sonia Baker's phone calls, Della Smith (Kelly

Macdonald) discovers that Kelvin Stagg phoned Sonia Baker at 7.10 on the morning of her death and talked to her for two minutes. Thus two narrative strands, apparently unrelated, appear to have a connection. Soon afterwards, Cal receives a call from Kelvin's brother to arrange a meeting with a young woman who is prepared to sell a metal case in her possession but on condition of absolute anonymity. Cal meets the young woman, who turns out to be Kelvin Stagg's girlfriend, and she explains how they nicked the bag at a station but were chased by the owner. They escaped but 'the bag's not what [they] thought it was'. It turns out to contain a gun and photographs of Stephen Collins and Sonia Baker. Kelvin had tried to sell it back to the owner, had arranged to meet him and had ended up dead.

In a parallel but more domestic narrative strand also apparently spinning out of control, Collins has bungled an attempt to tell his wife and family properly about his affair with Sonia. He has hurt and alienated his children, and his wife throws him out of the Manchester home. In the background, the New Labour spin doctors, in the form of chief whip Andrew Wilson (Michael Feast), are trying to keep the lid on press accounts. Wilson phones Anne Collins (Polly Walker) in apparent concern for her welfare but she retorts, 'Everyone knows the Energy Report's imminent', alluding to her husband's prestigious role as Chair of the Energy Committee and, in her view, Wilson's prime concern. To Wilson's discomfort, however, Collins visit Sonia's parents to express his condolences only to have the conversation taped by them and released to journalists. He is now on record acknowledging that he does not think that Sonia's death was an accident, contrary to his initial overt statements.

Having revived his friendship with Cal, Stephen accepts his invitation to use his spare room in order to avoid the paparazzi at his London home. Though on one level Cal is patently being kind, Stephen suspects that he also has a professional interest in him. Tensions rise and the two men have a blazing row centred on their respective professions. Stephen alleges that journalism is 'not a job it's a waste product', to which Cal sneers, 'Yeah, when you're pioneering the dawn of democracy!' He says to Stephen, 'You've been busy greasing your own arse since they gave you that shining badge' (the Chair of the Energy Committee), and asks, 'What have you done for your constituents in the last two years?' (Episode 1). Though the two ultimately apologise to each other, this tiff encapsulates how *State of Play*'s themes are obliquely mobilised: the trustworthiness of the media now being overtly compared with the integrity of New Labour in an age of spin in which sustaining surface appearances is all.

Back at the office, Cal brings the metal case and its contents to his editor. He realises that it is crucial in some, as yet unknown, way to both the Collins affair and the London street shootings but he wants to buy time to investigate further. Cal meets with editor Cameron, his colleague, Della, and the company lawyer to discuss the matter and, though Della particularly argues that the metal case constitutes evidence in a criminal matter and should accordingly be handed over to the police, the lawyer, under professional journalistic pressure from Cameron and

Cal, allows them five working days' grace. Della, who has made undercover contact with one DI Brown, proceeds to meet him again at the hospital where the motor-cycle courier is recovering consciousness under police guard. Knowing how keen the owner of the metal case is to cover all his traces, she feels conscience-bound to indicate to Brown that a stronger protection for the courier might be needed. What the alert viewer knows and she does not is that she has brushed against the hit-man as she entered the hospital. A fire is discovered and the hospital must be evacuated. Brown is forced to have the courier moved, and the support team with Della and DI Brown find refuge on the service stairs below the fire. The scene is tense and, through the window, Brown spies something in the distance above him. A bullet hits him in the chest, and blood is sprayed over the courier, Della and the hospital staff. Questioned by DCI William Bell (Philip Glenister) about what she knows, Della keeps her cool, even when he puts on additional pressure by angrily declaring, 'If one of my officers dies because you've got information that belongs with us, you'll be more than sorry.' Met outside by Cal in the rain, Della punches him weakly, and through tears, cries accusingly, 'You wouldn't bloody listen, would you?' (Episode 1).

This outline account of the plot of Episode 1 conveys some sense of the narrative strands and how they emerge to be interrelated and I have indicated how the thematic concerns of *State of Play* are introduced. But the account cannot convey the dexterity of Abbot's screenplay and the technique of the director, Yates, in creating both the dynamic energy of a thriller and the textual feel of a piece of political intrigue, comprised as it is of many moods. In aiming simply to recount the plot after several viewings of the series, I find that there are connections which remain murky. Returning to the DVD, it invariably transpires that moments which are indistinct in the memory are quite clear in the text but only in the form of deftly dropped hints which demand an alertness from viewers and highly active reading. For example, a dark-haired teenage girl in possession of the metal case is featured four times in the two-minute opening sequence which comprises some forty shots. The sequence mainly covers the foot chase through London back streets of a black man (later revealed to be Kelvin Stagg) by another man who finally corners Stagg behind a waste skip and shoots him.

The dark-haired girl is seen sitting at a café table opposite an empty chair against which the metal briefcase, loosely covered, stands on the floor. The first glimpse of her in a mid-shot (shot 6) establishes her face, and the reverse angle which immediately follows reveals that she is staring at the café door, giving the impression that she is waiting for someone who has recently left her and not returned. A mid-shot, similar to shot 6 but from a slightly higher angle, tilts down to foreground the metal briefcase loosely covered in plastic (shot 10). A big-close-up from her right side sees her looking anxious (shot 14) and, in the final shot before the main title appears, the girl is seen leaving the café with the metal case (shot 38). The overt link which relates her to Kelvin Stagg might just about be made when his mother and brother mention a metal case in a later conversation with Cal, but it is only fully discernible when Cal meets the girl in a parking lot and even then her face is hidden throughout. The significance of the contents of the metal case to the Collins affair can in any event only be apparent to Cal, who recognises Stephen in the photographs. The blonde young woman featured with Collins is only surmised, by Cal and viewers alike, to be Sonia (whose image we have not yet otherwise seen), and the implications of the link with the hit-man who owned the case remain to be unravelled. Viewers are required to work hard simply to keep up with the plot.

The challenge of the task is amplified by the intercutting in editing of the various strands of the plot related above. The episode opens with shots of feet in close-up running across cobbles. To the sound of a strong, fast drumbeat, a long two-shot from behind shows the legs in the left foreground of a figure in the right background being chased. A passing London bus wipes to a mid-shot of Collins walking towards camera amidst a crowd of commuters and cuts to a mid-shot of a young black man running to camera pushing past commuters and cuts back to Collins in close-up on an underground escalator before figuring the girl in the café. The juxtaposition, in similarly framed shots, of Collins and the black man might be read as bearing significance, namely two men under pressure, trying to move anonymously through the London crowd but, taking the full opening sequence into account, destined to be cornered. The fact that, as yet, any connection between the two narrative strands is not apparent invites a way other than plot logic of making sense of the images. The rapid inter-cutting of multiple strands of complex serial narratives in today's television drama invites sophisticated media-literate viewers to find resonances between images. These may not be as precise as the "third term" implicit in some montage editing, but the process of readers' production of significance is similar.[10] Whilst the connections arising from the juxtaposition of images and sounds produced by the intercutting of narrative segments in a multinarrative TV drama may be less explicit than modernist montage, the principles of composition of sophisticated texts such as *State of Play* suggest a conscious construction.

The soundtrack, for example, in the opening sequence under consideration sustains the rhythmic pulse of the drumbeat to lend it an energy and, indeed, a muffled echo of the drumbeat is used intermittently throughout *State of Play* to carry this energy forward. But in the opening two minutes, subtle variations are brought into play. When the girl in the café first appears, ambient sound comes into the mix. When she is seen looking anxious (shot 14) staccato strings are introduced. From here on, the drumbeat fades to background though remains audible as ambient sound is foregrounded. As the assailant shoots Stagg at close range with a silenced gun, only the ambient sound is heard but the drumbeat fades back into the mix for the final part of the sequence and the main title. Part of the upgrading of television towards cinematic production values in TV3 has afforded, where appropriately funded, more time to practitioners to take care in writing, shooting, editing and sounding a more sophisticated product. Because, however, the multilayered narratives of today's television series and serial texts yields a multilayered textuality, texts typically retain a dimension of openness requiring the reader to work hard actively to produce significance, even though the fabric of the text is carefully woven.

Following the energetic foot chase in the opening sequence, the young black man takes refuge behind the refuse skip, trying to contain his heavy breathing. The editing rhythm now slows as the endgame is approached. A close-up of the black man from the side (shot 16) zooms in on him as he waits, and cuts to a close-up of running legs in blue jeans foregrounded against a cobbled street as they slow to reveal black shoes. A big close-up (shot 18) shows the black man in a sweat. A pov. shot looking under the skip sees the black shoes pace and pause. A big close-up of the black man sees him stoop right, his shoulder disappearing from shot. A reverse pov. shot from the assailant's side of the skip, looks across to see the black man kneeling to look under it (shot 21). Thus the sequence slowly builds up to the climax of the moment of shooting when another apparently random incident which subsequently proves to be significant to the plot is featured.

Just as the black man has been shot, spattering crimson blood against the bright blue wall behind him, a motor-cycle engine is heard against a medium close-up of the assailant's expressionless face. A big close-up of a quarter of the assailant's head is foregrounded left frame as the motor-cycle comes into shot, the camera picking up in sharp focus centre-frame the man's eyes clearly clocking both the dead black man and the assailant (shot 33). The motor-cyclist accelerates out of shot, cutting to the hit-man facing the camera in mid-shot, gun arm raised (shot 34). A reverse angle shot then shows the hit-man from behind taking a few paces in the direction of the disappearing motor-cyclist and shooting him twice in the back until he falls over. The slower, more deliberate pace contrasts with the high energy of the initial chase and builds up again to a second climax with the second shooting. In one sense, of course, this is well-crafted composition but it is a mark of production quality which facilitates the textual richness noted above.

It would be impossible in the space available to recount here all six episodes of *State of Play* in shot-by-shot detail but the illustration of the opening sequence serves to suggest the compositional density of the serial. It would be equally redundant to follow the narrative twists blow by blow, so I propose now to consider the denouement in the final episode, referring back to key informing moments where necessary. Episode 6 continues with the press room narrative in which Cal McCaffrey and his colleagues are getting closer to the truth of the Sonia Baker murder mystery. This primary narrative is intercut with a drama of political intrigue involving the government and the oil industry and centring on Stephen Collins in his role as Chair of the Energy Committee whose report is now imminent. These stories are also inter-cut with a domestic narrative and further conflict between Stephen and Cal since Cal has been having an affair with Anne Collins, Stephen's estranged wife. Both men are in Cal's flat when Anne unexpectedly visits. At this point she is feeling a bit sorry for Stephen who is looking increasingly haunted, a man under extreme pressure. Cal is annoyed and, in the midst of a row in which Anne expresses a wish not entirely to destroy her family, Cal reveals that 'a week before she died, Sonia Baker discovered she was pregnant'.[11] Anne feels the force of this telling blow and retorts that Cal is as selfish as Stephen himself. Indeed, she explicitly draws out a doppelganger quality between them in her parting shot to Stephen as she leaves after a later row with him, declaring, 'No wonder that you and Cal ended up being glued to each other: you're like peas in a fucking pod.' All the narrative strands are logically connected since characters cross over from one to another but some character comparisons, like that between Cal and Stephen, are pointed up in the dialogue or the construction of images. They are also analogically connected in that they are all concerned with deceit, betrayal and double-dealing and this is brought out visually and aurally by the sustained, though modulated, soundtrack with its underlying drumbeat and in visual echoes of confinement in the *mise-en-scène*. It is the analogical parallels that create *State of Play's* dominant sense of a slippery culture of duplicity and possibly outright corruption.

Indeed, as the plot begins to unravel, complicity between the government and a major oil company, U-Ex Oil, seems certain. Sonia Baker, it transpires, is a place-woman in Stephen Collins's office, feeding information back to U-Ex Oil. As this connection is made, it at first seems that the oil company has manoeuvred Sonia into position, but checks with Collins's secretary, Greer Thornton (Deborah Findlay), reveal a competitive interview process. When further investigation reveals that Sonia's CV was less good than the other candidates, however, Greer reveals that she was guided in making the appointment against the paper evidence by George Fergus (James Laurenson), a cabinet insider, mentor to Collins and an old friend of Greer's whose judgement she felt she could trust. But, as Collins subsequently remarks with heavy irony, George uses that word [trust] a lot.' In sum, the higher echelons of the government had been aware all along of Sonia's role as a mole inside the Energy Committee. They knew that she was feeding information via Paul Channing, U-Ex Oil's main lobbyist, in order that the company might modify its behaviour in anticipation of criticisms that the Energy Committee report might make of the industry. As Collins puts it, U-Ex Oil was 'directly responding to hostile perceptions of their working practices'. U-Ex Oil could then appear favourably and gain business advantage over its competitors. Until very recently Stephen Collins was unaware both of Sonia's double agency and George Fergus's complicity with it.

Furious when he does find out, Collins is prepared to risk his career to expose the deceit. He resigns as Chair of the Energy Committee and reveals all that he knows, with affidavits to underwrite those points on which there is no corroborative evidence. Cal's home briefly becomes an annexe to the newspaper office in part because, getting wind of a massive scandal involving the government, the Media Group, who owns the paper, has sidelined Cameron Foster and installed Yvonne Shapps (Geraldine McEwan) with power over the budget for this one story. To clinch the final piece of evidence implicating U-Ex Oil top executives, Cal needs authority from Yvonne to spend £10,000 to buy an e-mail from Dominic Foy, a pawn in the game. Suspecting that she will not approve it, Cameron and Cal go to see her, having hatched a plot to get her sanction. When Yvonne demurs about the money, Cal claims copyright and threatens to take his story elsewhere.

Cameron bends the truth a little to confirm that Cal was indeed sacked some weeks previously and rehired on a freelance basis for this story alone. In an apparent double-cross action, however, he phones the company lawyer to see how much it would cost to breach Cal's contract. This sets Cal up to charge his heavier weapons. As he puts it to Yvonne:

> If the Media Group Board want to look like they've bottled it because they need a favour from the government …
>
> Well, I know that they want to buy the radio licences, which will not happen if they've pissed the government off.
>
> If this [story] gets out, and it will, you're going to look like mugs … Yvonne, grow up. Why have they given you power over the budget of this story alone.

The Cameron–Cal ploy works and they get authority. But this scene evidences again *State of Play*'s strategy of oblique critique of the collaboration between governments and media conglomerates.

It also contributes, in the underhand means which Cal and Cameron use to achieve their ends, a general murkiness in the press world, even though the team of young reporters ultimately show a deep professional integrity.[12] But, to clinch their story, they manipulate the police to have Dominic Foy arrested before he leaves the country, They bribe Foy, as noted, to give up a crucial e-mail. They use this to blackmail Mr Ziegler, a U-Ex Oil top executive himself, to give up an e-mail which incriminates the people above him in recording his conversation with Della under dubious legality. Ziegler in consequence commits suicide, placing his BMW head-on to a U-Ex Oil delivery truck on a dual carriageway. So, whilst the team members do what they do in pursuit of the truth, they do not escape the taint of the murky world they ultimately expose. And whilst their conviction that they have finally arrived at the truth proves to be partially upheld, it also proves to be fundamentally mistaken in a crucial aspect. They think correctly that they have proved that top executives in U-Ex Oil are implicated in the planting of Sonia Baker. They assume, and Mr Ziegler fearfully shares their assumption, that the same executives are behind the murder of Sonia Baker since she had very recently announced that she was withdrawing from her role as Collins's researcher and was in a position to expose and compromise them. But, in a final twist, Cal spots something in the wording of a Collins rant.

By this stage in the proceedings, Collins, if not quite a broken man, appears deeply disturbed, by turns angry and tearfully emotional. He feels in part betrayed by his wife and his supposedly best friend Cal, who, as noted, have been sleeping together. But he feels much more deeply betrayed by George Fergus and the New Labour party. His work with the Energy Committee which he thought was the ladder up to the cabinet office seems wasted. As he says to Cal, 'Sixteen people working their arses off all year round in their country's best interests – and for what?' He has discovered that senior government ministers knew about his relationship with Sonia before he was forced to disclose it at a press conference 'orchestrated by Andrew Wilson but suggested by George Fergus – a born liar'. To

Collins, Fergus had been a symbol of sincerity, 'the one person you could go to for a straight answer'. But, since he proves to be, at best, duplicitous and, at worst, corrupt, there would appear to be little positive to be said about other politicians.

Amidst Collins's railing against the world, Cal picks up on his remark that, 'Sonia met with Paul Channing on a daily basis down at the Trocadero.' This remark troubles him and he returns to the office to check with Della that the only place such meetings are mentioned is in 'the surveillance log in the hit-man's briefcase' to which Collins has not had access. Sharp and attentive viewers would at this point be able to connect the hit-man in Episode 1 with Collins, and Cal confirms his own worst fears through further investigations assisted by Della. These prove that periods of military service by Collins and one Richard Bingham in the army overlapped and that they would have come into contact with each other. Furthermore, Bingham owns a small security company in London used by Collins. Cal finally confronts Collins with the implication that he was involved in Sonia's death since this was the betrayal he fundamentally could not accept.

In a powerful exchange between the doppelganger rivals on the steps of Alexandra Palace overlooking the lights of London at night, Collins is forced by Cal to face up to the fact that, although Bingham shoved Sonia under the tube train, he is responsible for her death. Having been employed by Collins to follow up his suspicions of Sonia and discovered them to be founded, Bingham had proposed to stage an accident. Collins claims he 'told him no', but Cal points out that Collins carried on paying Bingham, saw Sonia more frequently than usual in the week leading up to her death and even slept with her the night before the 'accident'. Trying to understand Collins's motives, Cal finally asks, 'What could you have achieved, however high you went, that was worth demolishing all those families?' Again the sharp viewer at this moment of high emotional drama finally playing out the rivalry between the two reluctant antagonists will realise that Bingham is the hit-man who shot Kelvin Stagg and the motor-cycle courier as well as pushing Sonia under the train. The mind is called into play alongside any emotional response. As Cal points out to Stephen, Sonia Baker had recently resigned her post because she was carrying Collins's child, and had ultimately been prepared to testify against U-Ex Oil, 'because she loved you enough to take the flack'. The company had motive and was indeed unscrupulous enough to have carried out the killing. In this sense, the original newspaper scoop was not wholly unfounded. But the private ambition of Collins, not the public greed of multinational oil companies conspiring with a less than open government, is ultimately shown to be the cause of Sonia's death.

Cal is almost as distraught as Stephen at the end of this exchange. Returning to the office, he hears everything as if he is underwater and cannot speak, merely nodding to Della to affirm that his worst fears are confirmed. The press office, however, goes into overdrive, the tape of Collins's confession which Cal has made amidst all the emotional exchange being replayed in the process of transcription against the uproar. Editor Cameron Foster, now firmly back in control of the paper, presides over the proceedings with a benign but ironic smile. In the penultimate shot, the police come to arrest Collins and, in the final sequence, Cal – his rival, not for Anne, but ultimately for integrity in a murky world – visits the print room to see the edition which carries the truth being run off. As he lifts his protective earmuffs, the noise of the print machines rises and the end credits fade in.

In using a murder mystery as the generic basis of a prime-time serial, Abbott deploys a set of built-in devices to sustain viewers' attention through narrative hooks and plot reversals, but he does it over six one-hour episodes with consummate skill, as illustrated. The look of the series marks it immediately as a departure from the British murder mystery genre of *Miss Marple* and *Inspector Morse*. Indeed, *State of Play* looks more like *This Life* (BBC1, 1996–97) since the team of twentysomething investigators is set in a range of urban locations to a rhythmic drumbeat rather than the classical environs of Oxford or the mythical English village of St Mary Mead. The visual style of *State of Play*, as indicated, is sharp, the aural and visual editing rhythm is dynamic and the serial has a contemporary British feel. It is not, however, a feel-good piece. Though it entertains, it ultimately disturbs since Abbott has mixed political commentary in the British tradition of social realism with the murder mystery genre. Where *Miss Marple* is sedate and exemplifies "heritage television" to celebrate a myth of English culture drawing on an outmoded Victorian morality, *State of Play* addresses the murky world of contemporary business and politics As Alan McKee summarises the world of *Miss Marple*, 'although Miss Marple herself claims that "In English villages … You turn a stone and you have no idea what will crawl out", there is in fact very little of a sordid underside in these narratives'.[13] In *State of Play*, in marked contrast, all of the interrelated domains, when unmasked, reveal shadows ranging from a murky ethical ambiguity to outright double-dealing and corruption. Ultimately the standards of investigative journalism, much questioned at the time of the transmission of *State of Play*, stand up well.[14] But even the tenacious intelligence of the inquiring minds of the young team cannot keep them from underhand means to a virtuous end. Moreover, the doppelganger structure setting Stephen Collins in parallel with Cal McCaffrey denies an ultimate binary difference between the hunter and the hunted.

The density of the weft of the world depicted in *State of Play* lends it credibility. Even minor characters have a vitality conveyed partly through context and partly through the quality of the performances. These include such minor roles as the young woman junior in the press office whose insecurity leads her to assume an importance she does not have, and the under-manager in Anne Collins's music store in a Manchester mall who, with very few lines, conveys an understanding of the Collins family's difficulties and a willing sympathy for Anne tempered by an awareness of her fierce independence. The quality of the performances in the main roles of David Morrissey, John Simm, Kelly Macdonald and Bill Nighy and others is a testament to the strength in depth of the informal British acting collective noted above. The conviction of the performances of Morrissey and Sim locates them in a tradition of British realist acting able to convey depth of thought and emotional complexity through the ordinariness of everyday life. They are both outstanding in *State of Play*. Kelly Macdonald lends Della a strength of purpose tempered by an ethical sensibility beyond her male colleagues' cynicism. Nighy is able through the smallest of physical gestures, the arch of an eyebrow, a twitch of the shoulder, to add a level of irony to an otherwise convincing portrayal of the apparently cynical, but in fact deeply committed, newspaper editor. His satisfaction at the success of his young team in getting to the heart of the story, and his pride in his own capacity to win behind-the-scenes battles to facilitate them is conveyed in the smallest twist of the lips ('smile' is too strong a word) as he is framed in his office doorway looking over the young team putting their scoop to bed.

The political thrust of *State of Play* is not carried directly through a message but, as noted, indirectly conveyed (as it is in *Shameless*) through oblique commentary, particularly about the relative integrity of politicians and journalists. Snippets of dialogue, such as those cited above, momentarily bring into focus the commentary on contemporary society broadly carried in the *mise-en-scène*. But the murder mystery plot, which allows the finger of suspicion to be pointed at multinational oil companies and the inner cabinet of the government as well as individuals, allows a sense of institutional, and ultimately social, malaise to be conveyed, inviting viewers to reflect on contemporary society. This is an effective political strategy in a TV drama since it avoids the preachiness of a message more likely to put people off than to encourage them to think about what is implicit in what they have seen. Rather than hang the death of Sonia Baker directly on U-Ex Oil, the complex unfolding of the plot seems to leave everybody implicated, and the guilt of Stephen Collins, whilst affording a satisfactory conclusion in terms of human drama, is firmly located in the society which has enculturated him. A mix of assertive individualism and an overemphasis on appearances at the expense of more grounded values is ultimately to blame in *State of Play*. In this respect it is a drama of social realist lineage in situating agency within structure.

Coda: state of play – British TV drama

The three examples above suggest that, despite the pull of global marketing in TV3, British TV drama sustains a distinct identity. None of the above would have been made in the USA and, although they are potentially exportable, their production has not been led primarily by transnational commercial imperatives. In the White Paper on the future of the BBC published in the month of writing this summary (March 2006), the Labour government, through its Secretary of State for Culture, Media and Sport, Tessa Jowell, has affirmed the renewal of the BBC charter for a decade from 2007 and asked the BBC to concentrate on quality programmes and not the kind of 'copy-cat' output in which it is alleged to emulate the commercial enterprises in chasing ratings. In the light of my last example, there is irony in the fact that the integrity of the Secretary of State was called in question at precisely the time that she was to speak to the White Paper in the House of Commons because of murky financial dealings and a possible conflict of interest in respect of her husband's business relationship to Italian media mogul and prime minister, Silvio Berlusconi.[15] However, there is a clear government intention to retain a public service ethos at the heart of British broadcasting culture as it develops into a fully digital service after analogue 'switch-off', scheduled for 2012.

With the worldwide industry tending towards quality programming, particularly at the "high end" of TV drama, as recounted in this book, and with the key restraints on the dissolution of British television identity in place, the prospect for the future of drama on television looks reasonably bright. There is a danger that the very high production values of "American Quality TV" will demand funding levels higher than the BBC and ITV, let alone Channels 4, Five and the independents, can afford. Co-production for high-budget drama will be more necessary than ever and there may be a transnational impact on product in consequence. But mid-range budget British quality productions from companies such as Red, Kudos and Worldwide should have their creativity stimulated by the general improvement in production values. With the safeguards in place to ensure that they can benefit fairly from secondary rights, the stronger independents should at least sustain critical mass to continue their distinctive output with its range of British identities. The independents have more channels to pitch to and, particularly if Channel 4 emerges as second public service provider, there will even be a measure of competition in this sector for innovation within a public service ethos.

There is strength in depth in British talent, as noted above. New generations of writer-producers, directors and actors have found ways to harness elements of now outmoded British TV drama traditions to popular genres in hybrid mixes. Such programmes appeal to contemporary viewers and avoid sacrificing to populism the forces of critique which television in Britain has historically managed to mobilise, but exceptionally rather than regularly. Particularly in the serial drama form distinctive of today's television, there is potential, through careful crafting in production, to achieve sophisticated, multilayered, open texts actively to engage readers' minds and emotions. Whether this potential is fulfilled is a matter not of capacities, nor even simply of budgets, but of redressing what Paul Abbott has recently diagnosed as 'the malaise in television drama … at the moment: too much is under-ambitious, predictable and needlessly boring.'[16]

There is encouragement in the recognition of writers like Abbott that the formerly dominant 'ratings discourse' sold people short. In pointing to an executives' doxa, Paul Abbot notes the claim that 'the audience can't assimilate complex story-telling'. He continues, 'That's just patronising. Audiences today can take as much as you can throw at them.' The niche marketing which has led to product of high quality has, indeed, illustrated that many viewers are not only capable of dealing with more challenging, innovative work but actively choose it when given the opportunity. Examples abound, as illustrated, of distinctive drama output in TV3 to encourage ambition and the raising of standards. To give Abbott the last word, it is a matter of 'the willingness to renew what counts as modern television drama – to raise all of our expectations'.

Notes

1 See http://www.bbc.co.uk/pressoffice/pressreleases/stories/2004/09_september/28/casanova.shtml.
2 Christopher Ecclecstone and Jimmy McGovern, actor and writer respectively, might be included in this loose collective. Ecclestone took the lead role in Russell T Davies's *The Second Coming* (2003) before assuming the next eponymous incarnation in Davies's revival of *Dr Who* (2005). Besides "quality popular dramas" such as *Cracker* (1993-95 and on-going), McGovern has scripted powerful drama-documentaries such as *Hillsborough* (1996) and *Sunday* (2002).
3 For a summary account of English Regions Drama, see Cooke, 2003: 130 ff.
4 See http://www.bbc.co.uk/drama/blackpool/writer_producer.shtml.
5 Amongst its attractions, Blackpool is noted today as centre of gay culture.
6 See http://www.bbc.co.uk/drama/blackpool/episode6_yourreviews.shtm.
7 Forthcoming in *Critical Studies in Television*, vol 1. Autumn 2007.
8 All unascribed quotations in the first half of this section are from Episode 1 of *State of Play*.
9 If the paper Cameron Foster edits is based on *The Guardian*, as suggested, it is ironic that this broadsheet did shrink in 2005 shortly after *State of Play* was transmitted. However, it adopted the Berliner format and arguably retained its investigative edge.
10 Eisenstein's use of montage, for example, made fairly explicit connections between images inter-cut to the point of political critique, whilst the connections arising from the juxtaposition of images and sounds produced by the inter-cutting of narrative segments in a multi-narrative TV drama may be less explicit.
11 All quotations in the second part of this section are from Episode 6 of *State of Play*.
12 The contemporary political doubts about the integrity of the "Weapons of Mass Destruction" case as motive to promote a war with Iraq encourages sceptical readings.
13 http://www.museum.tv/archives/etv/M/htmlM/missmarple/missmarple.htm accessed 21 March 06.: 02.
14 In 2004, BBC journalist, Andrew Gilligan, came under scrutiny for careless use of notes from his interviews with Dr David Kelley who subsequently committed suicide. The BBC initially defended Gilligan and came under severe political pressure from Downing Street in consequence. Thus *State of Play*'s exploration of tensions between politicians and the media was highly topical.
15 Ms Jowell summarily separated from her husband in an attempt to distance herself and disentangle her probity from any questionable dealings, either financial or media-related.
16 All quotations in this final paragraph are taken from the 2005 Huw Wheldon lecture delivered by Paul Abbott for the Royal Television Society.

References

Books and articles

Adorno, T. W. (1979) *Dialectic of Enlightenment* (trans. J. Cumming from 1944 *Dialektik der Aufklarung*). London: Verso.

Akass, K. & McCabe, J. (2002) 'Beyond the Bada Bing!: negotiating female narrative authority in *The Sopranos*', in Lavery, D. (ed.), 2002.

——(eds) (2004) *Reading Sex and the City*. London & New York: I. B. Tauris.

Ang, Ien (1985) *Watching Dallas: Soap Opera and the Melodramatic Imagination*. London: Routledge.

——(1991) *Desperately Seeking the Audience*. London & New York: Routledge.

——(1996) *Living Room Wars*. London: Routledge.

Auslander, Philip (1999) *Liveness*. London & New York: Routledge.

Barthes, Roland (1997) *Image, Music, Text*. London: Fontana Press.

Behrens, S. (1986) 'Technological convergence: towards a united state of media'. *Channels of Communication 1986 Field Guide*, 8–10.

Bianculli, David (1994) *Tele-Literacy*. New York: Touchstone.

Bignell, Jonathan (2004) 'Sex, confession and witness', in Akass, K. & McCabe, J. (eds) (2004), 161–176.

Bignell, J. & Lacey, S. (eds) (2005) *Popular Television Drama: Critical Perspectives*. Manchester & New York: Manchester University Press.

Billen, Andrew (2001) *Evening Standard*, 22 January.

——(2002) 'Why I love American TV', *Observer*, 28 July 2002, 5.

Bolter, Jay David & Grusin, Richard (2000) *Remediation: Understanding New Media*. Cambridge, MA: MIT Press.

Brandt, George (1981) *British Television Drama*. Cambridge: Cambridge University Press.

——(1993) *British Television Drama in the 1980s*. Cambridge: Cambridge University Press.

Brent Zook, Kristal (1999) *Color by FOX*. New York: Oxford University Press.

Brunsdon, Charlotte (1990) 'Problems with quality', *Screen*, 31:1 Spring, 67–91.

Buxton, David (1990) *From The Avengers to Miami Vice*. Manchester: Manchester University Press.

Caldwell, John T. (1995) *Televisuality: Style, Crisis and Authority in American Television*. New Brunswick, NJ: Rutgers University Press.

Cardwell, Sarah (2006) 'Patterns, layers and values: Poliakoff's *The Lost Prince*', *Journal of British Cinema and Television*, 3:1, 134–141.

Carroll, Noel (2003) *Engaging the Moving Image*. New Haven, CT & London: Yale University Press.

Caughie, Jonn (2000) *Television Drama: Realism, Modernism and British Culture*. Oxford: Oxford University Press.

Coleman, James & Rollett, Brigitte (eds) (1997) *Television and Europe (European Studies)*. Exeter: Intellect Books.

Cooke, Lez (2003) *British Television Drama*. London: British Film Institute.

——(2005) 'The new social realism of *Clocking Off*', in Bignell, J. & Lacey, S. (2005), 183–197.

Creeber, Glen (ed.) (2001) *The Television Genre Book*. London: British Film Institute.

——(2004a) *Serial Television: Big Drama on the Small Screen*. London: British Film Institute.

——(2004b) *Fifty Key Television Programmes*. London: Arnold.

Cunningham, S. & Jacka, E. (1996) *Australian Television and International Mediascapes*. Cambridge: Cambridge University Press.

DCMS (1999) *Building a Global Audience: British Television in Overseas Markets*, a report by David Graham & Associates. London: DCMS.

Derrida, Jacques (1978) *Writing and Difference* (trans. A. Bass). London: Routledge & Kegan Paul.

Dow, Bonnie, J. (1996) *Prime-Time Feminism: Television, Media and the Women's Movement since 1970*. Philadelphia: University of Pennsylvania Press.

Drummond, P. & Paterson, R. (eds) (1985) *Television in Transition*. London: British Film Institute.

DTI/DCMS (2002) *The Draft Communications Bill – The Policy*. London: TSO.

Eco, Umberto (1979) *The Role of the Reader*. Bloomington & London: Indiana University Press.

Ellis, John (1994, orig. 1982) *Visible Fictions*. London: Routledge.

——(2002) *Seeing Things: Television in the Age of Uncertainty*. London & New York: I. B. Tauris.

Feuer, Jane (1995) *Seeing Through the Eighties: Television and Reaganism*. Durham, N.C.: Duke University Press.

Feuer, Jane, Kerr, Paul & Vahimagi, Tise (1984) *MTM: Quality Television*. London: British Film Institute.

Fiske, John (1987) *Television Culture*. London: Methuen.

Foucault, Michel (1979) *The Archaeology of Knowledge*. London & New York: Routledge.

Galbraith, J. K. (1992) *The Culture of Contentment*. London: Sinclair-Stevenson.

Giddens, Anthony (1992) *The Transformation of Intimacy: Sexuality, Love and Eroticism in Modern Societies*. Stanford, CA: Stanford University Press.

Gitlin, Todd (1994, orig. 1983) *Inside Prime Time*. London & New York: Routledge.

Grant, P. & Wood, C. (2004) *Blockbusters and Trade Wars; Popular Culture in a Globalized World*. Vancouver/Toronto: Douglas & McIntyre.

Greven, David (2004) 'The museum of unnatural history', in Akass, K. & McCabe, J. (eds) (2004), 33–47.

Grochowski, Tom (2004) 'Neurotic in New York: the Woody Allen touches in Sex and the City', in Akass, K. & McCabe, J. (eds) (2004), 149–160.

Hartley, J. & McKee, A. (2000) *The Indigenous Public Sphere*. Oxford: Oxford University Press.

Harvey, David (1989) *The Condition of Postmodernity*. Oxford: Blackwell.

Henry, Astrid (2004) 'Orgasms and empowerment', in Akass, K. & McCabe, J. (eds) (2004), 65–82.

Hills, Matt (2002) *Fan Cultures*. London & New York: Routledge.

Hilmes, Michelle (2003) *The Television History Book*. London: British Film Institute.

Hobson, Dorothy (1982) *Crossroads: The Drama of a Soap Opera*. London: Methuen.

Hoggart, Richard (1958) *The Uses of Literacy*. London: Chatto & Windus.

Holquist, Michael (2002) *Dialogism: Bakhtin and his World*. London: Routledge.

Holt, Jennifer (2003) 'Vertical vision: deregulation, industrial economy and prime-time design', in Jancovich, M. & Lyons, J. (eds) (2003), 11–31.

Hoskins, C. & Mirus, R. (1988) 'Reasons for the US dominance of the international trade in television programs'. *Media, Culture & Society* 10.

Hutcheon, Linda (1989) *The Politics of Postmodernism*. London & New York: Routledge.

ITC (2002) *A Review of the UK Programme Supply Market*. London: Independent Television Commission. Available at www.itc.org.uk.

Jameson, Fredric (1993) *Postmodernism or the Cultural Logic of Late Capitalism*. London: Verso.

Jancovich, M. & Lyons, J. (eds) (2003) *Quality Popular Television*. London: British Film Institute.

Jermyn, Deborah (2004) 'In love with Sarah Jessica Parker: celebrating female fandom and friendship in *Sex and the City*', in Akass, K. & McCabe, J. (eds) (2004), 201–218.

Johnson, Catherine (2005) *Telefantasy*. London: British Film Institute.

Kaplan, E. Anne (1987) *Rocking Around the Clock*. London & New York: Methuen.

Katz, E. & Liebes, T. (1985) 'Mutual aid in the decoding of *Dallas*: preliminary notes from a cross-cultural study', in Drummond, P. and Paterson, R. (eds) (1985).

Kemal, Salim (1992) *Kant's Aesthetic Theory*, Basingstoke: Macmillan.

Kimmel, Daniel, M. (2004) *The Fourth Network*. Chicago: Ivan R. Dee.

König, Anna (2004) '*Sex and the City*: a fashion editor's dream?', in Akass, K. & McCabe, J. (eds) 2004, 130–142.

Lavery, David (ed.) (2002) *This Thing of Ours: Investigating the Sopranos*. London and New York: Wallflower/Columbia University Press.

Lavery, David & Thompson, Robert J. (2002) 'David Chase, *The Sopranos*, and Television Creativity', in Lavery, D. (ed.) (2002), 18–25.

Levin, Gary (2003) 'The inside story on HBO's *Oz*. True to form, it's final season won't be pretty either', *USA Today*, 1 February 2003.

Lury, Karen (2005) *Interpreting Television*. London: Hodder Education.

Lyotard, Jean-François (1984) *The Postmodern Condition: A Report on Knowledge* (trans. G. Bennington and B. Massumi) Manchester: University of Minnesota/Manchester University Press.

McCabe, Colin (1976) 'Realism and the cinema: notes on some Brechtian theses', *Screen*, 15:2, 7–27

McCarthy, Anna (2003) '"Must See" Queer TV: History and Serial Form in *Ellen*', in Jancovich, M. & Lyons, J. (eds) (2003), 88–102.

McMurria, John (2003) 'Long-format TV: globalisation and network branding in a multichannel Era', in Jancovich, M. & Lyons, J. (eds) (2003), 65–87.

McRobbie, Angela (1998) *British Fashion Design: Rag Trade or Image Industry*. London and New York: Routledge.

Merck, Mandy (2004) 'Sexuality in the City', in Akass, K. & McCabe, J. (eds) (2004), 48–64.

Miller, Jeffrey, S. (2000) *Something Completely Different: British Television and American Culture*. Minneapolis: University of Minnesota Press.

Millington, R. & Nelson, R. (1986) *Boys from the Blackstuff: The Making of TV Drama*. London: Comedia.

Morley, David (1980) *The Nationwide Audience: Structure and Decoding*. London: British Film Institute.

——(1992) *Television Audiences & Cultural Studies*. London & New York: Routledge.

Mulvey, Laura (1975) 'Visual pleasure and narrative cinema', *Screen*, 15:3, Autumn, 6–18.

Murdoch, Rupert (1989) James MacTaggart Memorial Lecture, Edinburgh.

Negus, Keith & Street, John (2002) 'Introduction to "Music and Television" special issue', *Popular Music*, 21:3, 245–248.

Nelson, Ashley (2004) 'Sister Carrie meets Carrie Bradshaw' in Akass, K. & McCabe, J. (eds) (2004), 83–95.

Nelson, Robin (1996) 'From *Twin Peaks*, USA to lesser peaks, UK: building the postmodern TV audience', *Media, Culture & Society*, October, 18:4, 677–682.

——(1997) *TV Drama in Transition*. Basingstoke: Macmillan.

——(2000) 'Flexi-narrative Form', and 'A New Affective Order', in Eckart Voigts-Virchow (ed.), *Mediatized Drama/Dramatized Media*, Contemporary Drama in English, Vol. 7, 111–118. Frankfurt am Main: Wissenschafstlicher Verlag, Trier.

——(2002) 'Ally McBeal', in Creeber, G. (ed.) (2001), 45.

——(2005) Conference Review: 'American Quality Television', *European Journal of Cultural Studies*, 8: 1, 113–124.

Nublock, Sarah (2004) '"My Manolos, My Self": Manolo Blahnik, Shoes and Desire', in Akass, J. & McCabe, J. (eds) 2004, 144–148.

Pattie, David (2002) 'Mobbed up: *The Sopranos* and the modern gangster film', in Lavery, D. (ed.), 2002, 135–145.

Portman, Neil (1987) *Amusing Ourselves to Death*. London: Methuen.

Rixon, Paul (2006) *American Television on British Screens: A Story of Cultural Interaction*. Basingstoke: Palgrave Macmillan.

Rogers, M. C., Epstein, M. & Reeves, J. L. (2002) '*The Sopranos* as HBO brand equity: the art of commerce in the age of digital reproduction', in Lavery, D. (ed.) (2002), 42–59.

Rorty, Richard (1989) *Contingency, Irony, Solidarity*. Cambridge: Cambridge University Press.

Schiller, Henry (1969) *Mass Communications and American Empire*. New York: Augustus M. Kelly.

——(1991) 'The international flow of television programmes', *Critical Studies in Mass Communication*, 8, 13–28.

Schroder, Kim Christian (1992) 'Cultural quality: search for a phantom?', in Skovmand, M. & Schroder, K. C. (eds) (1992), 199–219.

Searle, John R. (1969) *Speech Acts: An Essay in the Philosophy of Language*. London: Cambridge University Press.

Sikes, Gini (1998) 'Sex and the cynical girl: a gentler approach?', *New York Times*, Section 2, 5 April 1998, 37.

Silverstone, Roger (1994) *Television and Everyday Life*. London: Routledge.

Steemers, Jeanette (2004) *Selling Television*. London: British Film Institute.

Strinati, Dominic (1995) *An Introduction to Theories of Popular Culture*. London: Routledge.

Styan, J. L. (1981) *Modern Drama in Theory and Practice 1: Realism and Naturalism*. Cambridge: Cambridge University Press.

Thompson, Robert, J. (1996) *Television's Second Golden Age*. New York: Continuum.

Thussu, Daya Kishan (ed.) (1998) *Electronic Empires*. London: Arnold.

Todreas, Timothy M. (1999) *Value Creation and Branding in television's Digital Age*. London & Westport, CT: Quorum Books.

Tracey, Michael (1985) cited in Cunningham, S. and Jacka, D. (eds) (1996).

Tropiano, Stephen (2002) *The Prime Time Closet: A History of Gays and Lesbians on TV*. New York: Applause Theatre and Cinema Books.

Vliet, Harry van (2002) 'Where television and internet meet … new experience for rich media', *E-view*, 02 1 (online journal: http://comcom.uvt.ni/e-view–02–1/vliet.htm, accessed 29 March 2005).

White, Rob (2002) 'Against the clock', *Sight & Sound*, 12:7, July 2002.

Williams, Michael (2001) *Problems of Knowledge*. Oxford: Oxford University Press.

Williams, Raymond (1974) *Television, Technology and Cultural Form*. London: Fontana.

——(1981, orig. 1976) *Keywords*. London: Fontana.

——(1997) 'Social environment and theatrical environment', in *English Drama: Forms and Development*. Cambridge: Cambridge University Press, 203–223.

Wittgenstein, Ludwig (1994, orig. 1953) *Philosophical Investigations*. Oxford: Blackwell.

Wright, Elizabeth (1989) *Postmodern Brecht : A Re-presentation*. London: Routledge.

Websites

http://abc.go.com/primetime/desperate/about.html
http://comcom.uvt.ni/e-view–02–1/vliet.htm
http://en.wikipedia.org/wiki/Carniv%C3%A0le
http://news.bbc.co.uk/1/hi/entertainment/4534126.stm
http://www.bbc.co.uk/commissioning/tv/network/wocc.shtml
www.bbc.co.uk/drama/blackpool/episode6_yourreviews.shtml
www.bbc.co.uk/drama/blackpool/writer_producer.shtml
http://www.bbc.co.uk/drama/lifeonmars/series2.shtml
www/bbc.co.uk/pressoffice/pressreleases/stories/2004/09_september/28/casanova.shtml
http://www,channel4.com/entertainment/tv/microsites/S/shameless/interviews_2.html
http://www.hbo.com/carnivale/behind/danile_kauf2.shtml
http://www.hbo.com/carnivale/behind/index.shtml
http://www.hbo.com/carnivale/behind/mary_corey.sthml
http://www.hbo.com/carnivale/behind/music_supervisors.shtml
http://www.hbo.com/carnivale/behind/rodrigo_garcia.shtml
www.methuen.co.uk/shootingthepast.html
www.museum.tv/archives/etv/M/htmlM/missmarple/missmarple.htm
http://www.radio.cz/en/issue/58027
http://www.ruralmedia.co.uk
http://www.salon.com/ent/tv/feature/2002/05/14/24_split/print.html
http://www.thefreedictionary.com/high-density
http://www.timewarner.com/corp/businesses/detail/global_marketing/index.html
http://www.uce.ac.uk/web2/newsline/archive/people05.html

Index

Note: 'n.' after a page reference indicates the number of a note on that page